First Thought

Also by Michael Schumacher
Published by the University of Minnesota Press

Dharma Lion: A Biography of Allen Ginsberg

First Thought

Conversations with Allen Ginsberg

Michael Schumacher EDITOR

University of Minnesota Press

MINNEAPOLIS

LONDON

Published by the University of Minnesota Press
111 Third Avenue South, Suite 290
Minneapolis, MN 55401-2520
http://www.upress.umn.edu

ISBN 978-0-8166-9917-9
A Cataloging-in-Publication record for this book is available from the Library of Congress.

Printed in the United States of America on acid-free paper

The University of Minnesota is an equal-opportunity educator and employer.

23 22 21 20 19 18 17   10 9 8 7 6 5 4 3 2 1

Contents

Introduction
Ginsberg's Visions of Ordinary Mind

MICHAEL SCHUMACHER

ALLEN GINSBERG ALWAYS SEEMED TO BE AT WORK. The volume of his published poetry and prose, recorded music, and photographs—substantial by any artist's measure—along with his participation in poetry readings, classroom lectures, conferences, political gatherings, concerts, gallery openings, and television and radio talk shows, attests to a life dedicated to the constant use and expansion of the creative mind. And this doesn't even include the time he devoted to recording his journals, scribbling letters and postcards, and engaging in other writing-related tasks.

Ginsberg considered interviews to be a vital part of his work, as one might surmise from the titles of two previously published anthologies of interviews: *Composed on the Tongue*, a relatively slender collection edited by Don Allen and issued by Grey Fox Press in 1980; and *Spontaneous Mind*, a hefty volume edited by David Carter and published by HarperCollins three years after Ginsberg's death in 1997.

Ginsberg carefully filed his interviews and, in many cases, scribbled comments or corrections directly onto photocopies of the published pieces. He bristled at the mistakes or misquotations; he worried about how they might detract, first, from his message, and, ultimately, his place in literary history. The Carter volume was delayed endlessly while Ginsberg pored over every line of every interview, checking out the editing and, in some cases, insisting on corrections.

One day in 1986, while I was interviewing him for *Dharma Lion*, my biography of Ginsberg, I brought his busy schedule and prolific writing to his attention. After all, he wasn't getting any younger, and he had an imposing body of unpublished work, including interviews, that he wanted to usher into print.

"Don't you ever give your mind a rest?" I wanted to know. "Don't you ever feel like just shutting it all down and taking a break?"

"Why?" he responded, his tone suggesting that I might have just posed the most absurd question in human history.

Why, indeed.

Ginsberg not only flourished because of all the work; he *survived* because of it. When he first arrived in New York, a seventeen-year-old New Jersey–born and –raised son of a lyric poet father and an institutionalized paranoid schizophrenic mother, his eyes trained not on becoming a poet but, rather, a labor lawyer in the tradition of Eugene Debs, Ginsberg's mental landscape was flat and only moderately interesting; it lacked the dizzyingly fascinating topography we'd come to recognize in his later years, when he'd become an iconic countercultural figure and, as the mind behind "Howl" and "Kaddish," one of the most influential poets of the twentieth century. By nature, Ginsberg possessed a curiosity without boundaries, some of which served him well, some of which did not. While he learned his formal intellectual scales from such renowned Columbia University professors as Lionel Trilling, Mark Van Doren, and Raymond Weaver, he picked up his jazz chops from the likes of Jack Kerouac, William S. Burroughs, Neal Cassady, Herbert Huncke, and a host of others. By the time he sat down to write "Howl" in the summer of 1955, he had witnessed and experienced a lifetime of poetry-in-waiting: he'd received an Ivy League education but only after a series of misadventures leading to his being kicked off the campus and being readmitted; he'd seen the violent deaths of several friends and the suicides of others; he had been arrested for his minor role in a small-time burglary ring and placed in a psychiatric institute, where he was programmed to reform; he'd experimented in heterosexuality long enough to know he wanted to live as an open homosexual; he'd hobnobbed with some of the most important poets and writers of his time; he'd had a series of "visions" in which he heard the voice of William Blake reciting his poems and speaking to him through the ages, directing him to devote his life to poetry; he'd moved to the West Coast, met his life partner, and begun composing the poetry eventually published in *Howl and Other Poems*. In his introduction to that volume, William Carlos Williams, Ginsberg's mentor during some of the darkest times of his early adulthood, confessed that he had wondered if the young poet would survive to complete his full realization as a poet.

"I never thought he'd live to grow up and write a book of poems," Williams wrote. "His ability to survive, travel, and go on writing astonishes me. That he has gone on developing and perfecting his art is no less amazing to me."

It's important, I think, to remember that this Allen Ginsberg is also a part of this book. We don't hear directly from this confused, still evolving poet in these pages—he's already an established literary figure, a major voice in the Beat Generation, when he appears in the earliest interview in this collection—but to understand and appreciate the Allen Ginsberg herein, it's crucial to understand that, to his dying day, Ginsberg was a work in progress. He remained remarkably consistent in his attitudes about poetry and social issues, but he also grew enormously—artistically and intellectually—from the early days of his youth, when he was, in the words of Jack Kerouac, "a spindly Jewish kid with big ears," to his eventual stature as elder statesman in the poetry world.

And one doesn't attain that status by shutting it all down and giving the mind a rest. His life, as any casual reader can determine by reading a selection of his poetry, *was* his work. In this volume's first entry, we meet the familiar, public Allen Ginsberg, even if he is still cultivating his national presence. Expanded from Al Aronowitz's Ginsberg entry in the groundbreaking, multipart "The Beat Generation" series of articles published in the *New York Post*, "Portrait of a Beat" depicts Ginsberg as intelligent, outspoken, thoughtful, and provocative, eager in almost equal measures to explain and outrage, seemingly fearless of the consequences of exposing his mind. He had already written what would prove to be one of the most influential poems in the history of American poetry, and seen it successfully defended in a highly publicized obscenity trial. He'd been at the core of a major cultural movement and he had traveled extensively, living for a while as an expatriate in Paris. He had morphed from the self-conscious, derivative, sexually insecure, almost misanthropic youth into a confident, self-aware, important young artist. His voice is strong and clear.

Other entries in this book offer further evidence of the evolution. The often contentious exchange between Allen Ginsberg and his father, Louis (Stephen M. H. Breitman's "Slice of Reality Life"), illustrates the striking similarities and differences between the two poets, and acts as a strong contrast to John Tytell's "A Conversation with Allen Ginsberg," Ginsberg's generous (although occasionally patronizing) discussion of William S. Burroughs and his influence on Ginsberg, Kerouac, and others. The two interviews hint at the polarizing influences tugging at Ginsberg in his early work. "Visions of Ordinary Mind" by Paul Portuges meticulously traces the timeline and development of Ginsberg's early poetry, from the derivative, Blake-influenced works of 1948–49 (eventually published in *The Gates of Wrath*), through the William Carlos Williams–inspired works of the later 1940s and early 1950s (contained in *Empty Mirror*), through the writing of "Howl."

When I wrote *Dharma Lion*, I separated Ginsberg's life into three essential roles; poet, prophet, and teacher. (He was more than this, of course, but these three appeared, to me at least, to be the most important of Ginsberg's contributions as a man and artist.) In the 1950s and early 1960s, his main interests and pursuits were clearly in poetry, in finding the optimum way to make art out of life. He pursued this throughout his life, but by the mid-1960s, when he was writing the poems gathered in two of his most important volumes, *Planet News* and *The Fall of America*, he had expanded his vision from personal to worldview. Richard Kostelenetz's "Ginsberg Makes the World Scene," written shortly after Ginsberg's 1965 expulsion from Czechoslovakia, is not only a highly detailed account of one of the most controversial periods of Ginsberg's life; it examines the origins of Ginsberg as an international icon.

Ginsberg's prophetic voice, strong and resounding in such works as his antiwar anthem "Wichita Vortex Sutra," and in his antinuclear-power diatribe, "Plutonium Ode," along with the best of his work in his National Book Award–winning *The Fall of America*, can be heard throughout this book. Depending on his mood and circumstances, he can be patient or wrathful when expressing his feelings about war, drugs, censorship, sexuality, and international politics; the respectful explanations given during his appearance before a Senate subcommittee in Washington, D.C. ("Ginsberg in Washington: Lobbying for Tenderness" by Don McNeill) seem utterly tame when measured against his commentary about drugs in Tom McIntyre's "A Conversation with Allen Ginsberg," recorded nearly three decades later, when Ginsberg was confronting his own mortality and addressing career-retrospective questions.

Ginsberg enjoyed teaching, and I've included three classroom environment lectures/conversations—the already cited "Visions of Ordinary Mind," conducted at the Jack Kerouac School of Disembodied Poetics at Naropa Institute, an informal "rap session" with students at Davis College (Gordon Ball's "Identity Gossip"), and a round-robin discussion about writing with William S. Burroughs and Norman Mailer. The last of these three, like Ginsberg's conversation with Ezra Pound (Michael Reck's "A Conversation between Ezra Pound and Allen Ginsberg"), finds Ginsberg assuming the role of the interviewer, deferring to other literary giants, inquiring about work that influenced his own, acting as a conduit between the masters and artists of the future. The calm voice in these conversations, a far cry from the angry or outrageous voices in other entries, offers a glimpse of another aspect of one of the most complex literary figures American has ever produced.

In choosing the interviews for this book, I read through a wealth of material and tried to select entries that cast some light on all of Ginsberg's different interests. I wanted to avoid repetition, so I picked interviews not included in the previous collections. Finding worthy entries presented no problems: there were enough for several large anthologies. The challenge was to include entries that addressed the biographical and artistic highlights of a career spanning five decades.

Because I wanted to get as much Ginsberg as possible in this book, I heavily favored the Q/A format, where the reader gets more Ginsberg (and less interviewer) than in the profile/article format. I looked for rarities, often originally published in small presses no longer in existence. One interview ("Dreams, Reconciliations, and 'Spots of Time'") was previously unpublished. Two others, Tom McIntyre's "A Conversation with Allen Ginsberg" and Gary Pacernick's "Allen Ginsberg: An Interview," are herein expanded to included previously unpublished material.

I owe all the interviewers and publishers an enormous debt of gratitude for permission to reprint these pieces. I'd also like to acknowledge the long-standing contributions of Bob Rosenthal, Peter Hale, and Bill Morgan, all of whom worked for Ginsberg while he was alive, and all of whom continue to see that the man and his work stay in front of new and older readers alike. David Carter and Gordon Ball, two Ginsberg friends, editors, and scholars, deserve extra recognition for the advice and encouragement they offered when I was putting this book together. Thanks to Erik Anderson, Kristian Tvedten, and all the others at the University of Minnesota Press, for their patience and assistance in seeing this book into print.

Thanks, finally, to Allen Ginsberg. I feel blessed to have known him, at least for a little bit, in the final sixteen years of his life, and I feel fortunate to still hear his voice, in these interviews and in his work, all these years later. His work—a constant while he was alive—endures.

First Thought

Portrait of a Beat

AL ARONOWITZ, 1960

JOURNALIST AL ARONOWITZ had the distinction of writing the first in-depth, serious assessment of the Beat Generation writers when, in 1959, the *New York Post* published his series of articles titled, simply enough, "The Beat Generation." When the series made its appearance, the Beat Generation had become a cultural and, to a lesser extent, literary phenomenon. Jack Kerouac's novel *On the Road,* published in 1957, and Allen Ginsberg's epic poem "Howl," published a year earlier, had provided a template for a new, energetic, deeply personal style of writing—"a new vision," as they called it back in the late 1940s, when they boldly rejected the highly structured fiction and poetry popular with critics and university professors. The Beat Generation writers favored the outsiders, the margins, jazz and blues musicians, the new bohemians, the survivors and existentialists.

They met, as they expected, with great resistance. It took Kerouac the better part of a decade to see *On the Road* to publication. "Howl" was the subject of a highly publicized obscenity trial in San Francisco—a trial that ultimately decided in the poem's favor in a landmark decision. The Beats were largely denied their literary status; instead, they were viewed as "Know Nothing Bohemians" (as Norman Podhoretz called then in a *Partisan Review* essay), social misfits, misanthropes. FBI Director J. Edgar Hoover demonized them as dangerous.

Kerouac tried to escape the publicity; Ginsberg used it to bolster attention on his and his friends' work. Through Ginsberg, Al Aronowitz met many of the principal figures of the Beat Generation. He shrewdly separated the cultural and literary aspects of the Beats, even as he examined their connections.

The following portrait is an expanded version of Aronowitz's *Post* article on Ginsberg.

IN CHICAGO ONCE, a woman asked Allen Ginsberg: "Why is it that you have so much homosexuality in your poetry?"

"I sleep," he has since said, "with men and with women. I am neither queer, nor am I bisexual. My name is Allen Ginsberg and I sleep with whoever I want."

Obviously, Mr. Ginsberg also says what he wants. But then it is as the most outspoken of the Beat Generation poets that he has become the most spoken about. In the salons of literary respectability the name Ginsberg today is on more lips than care to pronounce it, even with a sneer. Nevertheless, Ginsberg, although he may believe, as do so many of his Beat colleagues, that life is an illusion, has no illusions about life, and especially about sex life. He lives it, as he presumes to do everything else, in the best of poetic traditions, if not the best of social ones.

"I don't know whether it's a great sociological problem or not," he says, "but I think that it's pretty shameful that in this culture people have to be so frightened of their own normal sex lives and frightened of other people knowing about it to the point where they have to go slinking around making ridiculous tragedies of their lives. So it seems, for one thing, at this point, that it's necessary for the poets to speak out directly about intimate matters, if they come into the poetry, which they do in mine, and not attempt to hide them or evade the issues. Life is full of strange experiences."

Certainly Ginsberg's has been.

He has handled luggage in the baggage room at Greyhound, carrying suitcases as heavy as his thoughts. He has written speeches for a candidate for Congress. He has taken off his clothes at somewhat genteel parties, proclaiming that those who objected to his body were really ashamed of their own. He has run copy for the Associated Press. He has shipped out as a seaman on tramp steamers, sailing to places as remote as some people find his verse. He has been a Young Liberal, running a mimeograph machine in a labor union organizing office but now he considers labor unions cut from the same stencil as managements. He has washed dishes in greasy spoon restaurants, which, by the way, are his usual eating places. He has harbored thieves and helped them store their loot, justifying himself with the thought that Dostoevsky would have smiled upon him. He has hitchhiked over most of the country. He has undergone eight months of treatment in an insane asylum, suspecting all the while that it was everyone else who was insane. He has taken heroin, cocaine, and what has been called "the true morphine," and he says he's never had a Habit. And, between New York and San Francisco, among young American poets who once didn't know that one another existed, he has organized what the literary crust seems to think is a literary underground.

If Jack Kerouac is, as he has been called, the St. Jack of the Beat Generation, then Allen Ginsberg is its Prophet.

His first published contribution to the growing library of Beat books was a poem which he calls *Howl* and which others with what may be less foresight call blasphemous.

"*Howl* was written," says Ginsberg, peering as he does through his glasses with a friendly intermingling of smile and solemnity, "in some of the rhythm of Hebraic liturgy—chants as they were set down by the Old Testament prophets. That's what they were supposed to represent— prophets howling in the Wilderness. That, in fact, is what the whole Beat Generation is, if it's anything—prophets howling in the Wilderness against a crazy civilization. It was Jack Kerouac, you know, who gave the poem its name. I mailed him a copy just after I wrote it—it was still untitled—and he wrote back, 'I got your howl. . . .'"

The critics got *Howl,* too, or at least they received it. "Nothing goes to show how square the squares are so much as the *favorable* reviews they've given it," groaned poetic colleague Kenneth Rexroth, who himself called *Howl* "much more than the most sensational book of poetry of 1957." Almost overnight, *Howl* became the Manifesto of the Beat Generation. And if that wasn't enough to insure Ginsberg's rise, or plummet, to fame, depending upon whether one looks up toward him or down, the San Francisco Department of Police gave him the final shove. It tried to ban the book.

"Allen seems to think he is a latter-day Ezra Pound," says Norman Podhoretz, who has been the most critical of the critics, although he wasn't quite square enough to give *Howl* a favorable review. "In Ginsberg's letters I see the epistolary style of Pound, who, you know, was always writing letters to editors, letters full of profanity, encouraging them to publish his boys. Pound was the great literary talent scout of his day—he discovered T. S. Eliot and helped Yeats become a great poet. He acted not only as leading poet and leading brain but also pushed all the other poets ... Now Allen is doing the same thing. ..."

Ginsberg, of course, takes Pound with a grain of salt and Podhoretz with a pound. Although Ginsberg considers the Beat movement to be heir poetic to the movement which Pound once led, Ginsberg rejects Pound much the same as Pound eventually rejected his former colleagues. As for Podhoretz, Ginsberg has commented: "He is totally and technically incompetent." For his part, Podhoretz is not so sweeping in his opinion of Ginsberg. A freshman at Columbia College when Ginsberg was an upper classman there, Podhoretz, writing in a constant complaint that his is a generation without a literary voice, refuses to accept the Beat Generation even as a falsetto. Insisting that there isn't enough vitality in other American writing and that there is too much violence in the Beat, he has, consequently, become as much a villain to the Beats as he considers them to literature. There have, however, been attempts at reconciliation.

"I was working at home one Saturday night," Podhoretz recalls, "when I got a telephone call from some kid—it must have been Ginsberg's friend, Peter Orlovsky. He said, 'Allen and Jack are here having a ball. Why don't you come down and have some kicks?' I told him no, I was busy, and he said, 'Wait, Allen'll talk to you.' So Ginsberg came to the phone—I knew him at Columbia but I hadn't talked to him in years—and he started talking in bop language. So I told him to come off it and he said, 'Come on down we're having a party. We'll teach you the Dharma.' Well, I guess I was crazy. I went. But it turned out not to be a party at all. There was just Ginsberg, Orlovsky and Kerouac at the apartment of one of Kerouac's girl friends. Kerouac asked me, 'Why is it that all the biggest young critics . . . Why are you against us? Why aren't you for the best talent in your generation?' I said I didn't think he was the best talent of my generation . . . Kerouac was indignant and said that I said he wasn't intelligent. He really didn't argue, he kept making cracks and being charming, and he *is* charming. But I think much more highly of Ginsberg's literary abilities than Kerouac's. I've always thought highly of Ginsberg as a poet, you know. This Beat stuff is a fairly recent kick of his. He may still become a great poet. He may write important poetry some day. Ginsberg has a superb ear—he can do most anything he wants to do with verse. As an undergraduate in college he was writing fantastic things."

Although the meeting was not quite a meeting of the minds, there is evidence that some of their opinions have since mellowed. In any event, the parallel Podhoretz has drawn between Ginsberg and Pound is almost letter-perfect. From his soap-box-furnished tenement flat in the cheap-rent district of New York's Lower East Side, Ginsberg's outgoing mail is exceeded only by his incoming mail, which, daily, brings him new correspondents to answer. Among the regular correspondents, there is, for example, William Seward Burroughs, author of *Naked Lunch*, writing from a flea hotel in Paris or from Tangiers, telling about the shortcomings of French mysticism, reporting on incidents and sights that could be seen only by an eye as naked as his own, letters that will make another novel, "endless," as Ginsberg says of *Naked Lunch*, and "that will drive everybody mad." Another is Gregory Corso, sending letters from France or Italy or Crete or Greece, where "I shall surely sleep a night in the Parthenon," telling of a vision of skinless air, questioning death and denouncing its fear, writing a poem about it and enclosing the manuscript. Another is Robert Creeley, a modern jazz poet, editor of *The Black Mountain Review*, not Beat himself, perhaps, but with a beat, writing from Majorca or the Grand Canyon, enclosing poems, too, that fascinate and delight Ginsberg and he sends his own in answer. Another is poet Gary Snyder, his missives inked with a calligraphy that once marked other illuminated manuscripts, a penmanship borrowed from the monks of Middle Ages monasteries, writing now from San Francisco, now from Japan, with an ancient alphabet that speaks a whole new hip language. And there is Lawrence Ferlinghetti, owner of the San Francisco bookstore called City Lights, a beacon for the Beats and other poets, publisher of *Howl,* a poet like the rest, exchanging manuscripts and compliments, sometimes urgently, by telegram: ALLEN: I READ 'APOLLINAIRE'S TOMB' STRUCK DUM & POOR. YOU ARE HUGEST DARK GENIUS VOICE STILL UNRECOGNIZED.

"Allen is always sending me copies of poems written by his friends, and he's always scrawling notes on the margins," says Ferlinghetti. "He always writes, 'You must publish this—this is mad, this is wild!'"

In addition to his vast correspondence with the various agents of his Underground at their various outposts on The Road, Ginsberg receives a daily deluge of unsolicited letters, some from publications asking for articles or looking for arguments, some from publishers seeking publication rights for an aroused and enthusiastic overseas audience, and many from colleges and universities asking Ginsberg to give poetry readings, a task Ginsberg has been happy to perform for nothing, even happier to perform for money, but lately is just as happy not to perform at all—he doesn't do it anymore.

Ginsberg, of course, had become a literary figure even before he wrote *Howl.* Certainly his name, or at least suitable aliases thereof, had already been imprinted in a large, although largely unpublished, body of literature. By 1957, when *Howl* came off the presses, he was a major, if not heroic, character in most of Kerouac's books and also had put in an appearance as David Stofsky, the so-called mad poet, in John Clellon Holmes's *Go.* But all this, naturally, was of little satisfaction to Ginsberg, who had insisted on following his own angel and whose ambitions were written in his own manuscripts.

"I can be pretty persuasive," Ginsberg has said on occasion, and the fact of the matter is that he can. A deft and positive logician, even though he believes in intuition over rationality, Ginsberg is at his best in conversation, and he has changed many minds by the sheer power of his own, so much so that critics who started out doubting Ginsberg's idea of his destiny are now beginning to doubt their own ideas of it.

Culturally, he has charmed Chicago, captured San Francisco and corrupted Los Angeles. "In California," he recalls with a gentle glee, "in L.A., we went down for a poetry reading among what was a bunch of, basically, social Philistines. We came down, offered ourselves, free, to read poetry for them—we were going to Mexico to meet Jack. They were a rather unruly audience, but they were all right, there were some interesting people there. But there was one creepy red-haired guy who kept on saying, 'What are you guys trying to prove?' And I said, 'Nakedness'—he was interrupting the poetry. So he said, 'Nakedness? What do you mean by nakedness?' So I suddenly understood that I had to show him what I meant in some way that would really get across and a way that would move him. So I pulled my clothes off, which shut him up."

Ginsberg concedes that his poetry readings in Chicago were a bit more dignified. Sponsoring one reading was the Chicago Shaw Society, to whom Ginsberg announced, "... *this poetry is droppings of the mind ...*" and whose members, according to the Shaw Society bulletin, responded by dropping the preconceptions from *their* mind. In fact, the only real heckler at the Chicago readings apparently was *Time* magazine (February 9, 1959): "... In the richly appointed Lake Shore Drive apartment of Chicago Financier Albert Newman, the guests chatted animatedly, gazed at the original Picasso on the wall, and the Monet, the Jackson Pollock ... At length Poet Ginsberg arrived, wearing blue jeans and a checked black-and-red lumberjack shirt with black patches at the elbows. With him were two other shabbily dressed Beatniks. One was Ginsberg's intimate friend, a mental-hospital attendant named Peter Orlovsky, twenty-five, who writes poetry (*I talk to the fire hydrant, asking: 'Do you have bigger tears than I do?'*); the other was Gregory Corso, twenty-eight, a shabby, dark little man who boasts that he has never combed his hair—and never gets an argument."

According to Ginsberg, there is much that *Time* hasn't said, either about the Chicago readings or about all the other occasions when *Time* has turned on the Beats. "Knowing what I do about the way they've exaggerated and distorted actual events which concern me," he says, "I shudder to think of what they've done to international events, news that's really important. Think of how many people read *Time* every week and get their picture of the world from it." The result has been something of a feud. "*Are you going to let your emotional life be run by Time Magazine?*"

Ginsberg asks in a poem. "*I'm obsessed by Time Magazine. I read it every week. Its cover stares at me every time I slink past the corner candystore.*" Once a *LIFE* magazine reporter assaulted Ginsberg's flat seeking an interview, and Ginsberg threw him out, although not bodily.

"He tried to tell me why I should talk to him even though the article was going to be unfriendly," Ginsberg says. "Why should I talk to him?"

The flat in which Ginsberg is not at home to *Life* reporters is of the type that might be expected to house a poet who has taken a vow of poverty the better to be untrammeled by modern society, a vow which modern society—the economics of poetry publishing being what they are—has helped him keep. Two stories above a Puerto Rican storefront church, it lies behind a large, enchanted door that most of the time is locked and unresponding but sometimes answers with a "Who is it?" A few steps past the bathroom, with its eternal light, because someone has to climb on the rim of the tub to turn it off, and there is the kitchen, light green or light blue behind the wall soot on which someone has finger painted, with convincing expertness, a mystical Chinese or Japanese legend that has no explanation. Over the refrigerator, sketched on brown wrapping paper, is Kerouac's drawing of Dr. Sax, just as it appears on the title page of his book, *Dr. Sax.* On a ledge over the brown metal table, usually cluttered with slightly used dishes, glasses, cups, sugar, salt and an extensively used typewriter, a tiny souvenir bust of Napoleon faces the wall, his back toward everyone. A few inches away on the same ledge, another souvenir, a post card with a picture of the house in Rome where Shelley once lived. And on the wall in the corner is the photograph of another hero, William Carlos Williams, silhouetted atop Garrett Mountain overlooking his city, once Ginsberg's, Paterson.

Ginsberg and Orlovsky share the apartment with Corso, when he is New York, and with a continuum of visitors, many uninvited or announced. There is no telephone to announce their coming. At the kitchen table there may be novelist Paul Bowles for dinner, a friend from Tangiers, or Jack Kerouac, arrived for the weekend, or Philip Whalen and Michael McClure, San Francisco poets, houseguests, or Fernando Arrabal, French novelist, paying a social call, or friends and literati.

In the largest of the three bedrooms, with its balcony, a fire escape, there is a television, a second-hand set worth its weight in mahogany, of-fering treasures such as Popeye, The Three Stooges, and occasional Marx Brothers films, comedies of a life that is frightening to live, scripts whose writers of old Hollywood probably never even realized were copies from Kafka. In Ginsberg's flat on quiet evenings at home sometimes all the occupants are on separate typewriters in separate rooms listening to sep-arate voices, working late into the night, sleeping late into the day, with Ginsberg, his digestive tract as sensitive as all of him, awakening some-times ill, the after-effect of hostile audiences, perhaps, or of cough-syrup euphoria or perhaps of simple poetic brooding. Once a bum from the nearby Bowery knocked on the door, came in and told of hearing that Ginsberg was really a secret philanthropist, a benefactor of mankind. Ginsberg gave him his total assets, a dollar and change.

"People used to ask me if Allen wrote poetry, too," recalls Ginsberg's father, Louis Ginsberg, an English teacher in Paterson, and a poet as well. "And I would tell them, 'No—he's the only one in the family who's normal.' Then I found out he had all these poems hidden in his room at Columbia.

"As a father, I'm happy that Allen has made his success in poetry, and I certainly like some of his poems very much," the elder Ginsberg says. "My poetry is a little different but I guess each one has his inner nature that he has to satisfy."

Allen Ginsberg was born June 3, 1926. While he was a boy growing up in Paterson, his mother was in and out of mental hospitals. She died in Pilgrim State Hospital in 1955. Ginsberg has written several poems for his mother, including, curiously enough, *Howl*—curiously, because its full title is *Howl for Carl Solomon*.

"I realized after I wrote it that it was addressed to her," he says, sit-ting on the bed with two cats playing at his feet and a parakeet in a cage intruding an occasional raucous reminder of its existence. "I realized that *Howl* is actually to her rather than to Carl in a sense. Because the emotion that comes from it is built on my mother, not on anything as superficial as a later acquaintance, such as Carl."

Ginsberg was with Solomon at the New York State Psychiatric Insti-tute. Born in 1928, Solomon, according to other bits of biography, was proclaimed a child prodigy at the age of seven, when several New York newspapers commemorated with headlined awe his ability to memorize the batting averages of all the players in the National and American leagues. Educated in New York and at the Sorbonne, and later an editor with a New York publishing house, he, like Ginsberg, spent time in the Merchant Marine as well as in the asylum.

"Carl?" says Ginsberg, stroking a cat purring on his lap, as the clock ticks loudly on the makeshift night table. "I met him in the bug house. The New York State Psychiatric Institute. Our first meeting was funny. I mean, my mother had been in that hospital, and here *I* was in the hospital now. I walked down to the ward with my bags and sat down at the table at the end of the corridor in the afternoon sunlight and Carl was just coming up in a big bathrobe, just out of shock. And he walked up to me, you know, new meat in the ward, and said, 'Who are you?' So I said, 'I'm Alyosha'—you know, the saintly character in Dostoevsky's *Brothers Karamazov.* So Carl said, 'Well, I'm Kirilov—Wait'll you meet the other saints here.'"—and Ginsberg laughs. "We immediately had a rapport. Carl had a great project. He was going to publish my work, Kerouac's work, William S. Burroughs's work, John Holmes's work, Jean Genet's work, if he could, Louis Ferdinand Celine's work, if he could—all the new literature that's coming out now. He would have made a million dollars, I guess. But they thought he was crazy. Now he's back in Pilgrim State. But he's not crazy at all."

At Columbia, from which he received a degree, Ginsberg is remembered not with reverent silence, perhaps, but usually with silence, and mention of him brings a great shushing of lips from former professors and classmates alike. Part of the shushing, of course, covers his commitment to the New York State Psychiatric Institute, even though the doctors there finally conceded he was not a schizophrenic but merely a neurotic. Also covered by the shushing, however, is the year Ginsberg was suspended for tracing obscene odes on a dusty window in Columbia's Hartley Hall.

Professor Lionel Trilling played a major role in Ginsberg's undergraduate life and has continued to play bit parts in Ginsberg's life ever since. In retrospect, Trilling seems to look upon Ginsberg with a professorial and growing affection. Certainly Ginsberg courted this affection, although during his studenthood it wasn't apples which Ginsberg brought to his teacher but revelations of Kerouac and Burroughs and what Ginsberg had learned of the reality outside the Nineteenth Century coffin he considers his classes to have been. "In the early years, I tried to be open with him," Ginsberg says, "and laid on him my understanding of Burroughs and Jack—stories about them, hoping he would be interested or see some freshness or light, but all he or the others at Columbia could see was me searching for a father or pushing myself or bucking for an instructorship or whatever they have been conditioned to think in terms of." Ginsberg invaded Trilling's after-school privacy with samples of his own poetry, which at first pleased Trilling much as Ginsberg's present poetry displeases him. Because he is displeased. Unwilling, even as a literary critic, to be drawn into any public discussion of his former student's literature—or even of Beat literature—Trilling has, in more private company, said he is bored both with Ginsberg's manner and Ginsberg's doctrine and is not much interested in his poetry, either, but has, on occasion, defended it.

By his travels through the seamier side of life, Ginsberg has come to believe that civilization is coming apart at the seams. Ginsberg's guide, of course, was Jack Kerouac, whose friendship is at least one debt that Ginsberg owes Columbia. It was with Kerouac that Ginsberg found his way to the neon connections of Times Square, the switchblade dives of Eighth Avenue and the society that William S. Burroughs introduced them to, a society which can be found in the writings of all of them. Together, Ginsberg and Kerouac launched an investigation of the Underworld that might have pleased Dostoevsky but probably would have irked that other expert on crime, also a boyhood hero of Kerouac, The Shadow. But then it was souls they said they were seeking, not criminals.

Sometimes it was difficult to tell the guide from the guided. "Allen . . ." says Kerouac, "Allen's a great influence on me." But Neal Cassady, another great influence on Kerouac, adds, "Jack's always putting Allen down. We'll be riding along and we'll pass a beach and it'll be a big Jewish resort, see, and Jack'll say to Allen, 'How come there's no beach for French-Canadians, huh?'" In any event, the relationship between Kerouac and

Ginsberg has had its effect not only on the writing of each other but apparently on that of a whole new generation of poets, building on a writing style which Ginsberg and Kerouac call *spontaneous bop prosody*, based on the rhythms of hipster speech and drawn from jazz and everyday talk, words meant to be music and set down on paper in the same mystical pattern in which they appear in the mind.

Ginsberg's poetry has been translated into Japanese, German, Spanish and Bengali and he has read it to audiences in at least a dozen countries. The Chilean government has had him as its guest for an international literary conference, at which, by the way, other guests were Arnold Toynbee and Pierre Mendès-France. And if he has read in coffee houses and bars all over the United States he also has read, by invitation, at the Library of Congress, where, for the benefit of a tape recorder and the archives, he chose a special poem denouncing America: "*. . . Millions of tons of human wheat were burned in the halls of Congress while India starved and screamed and ate mad dots full of rain . . .*"

"If I were living in Russia," he said later, "I probably would have written a poem denouncing Russia."

In other more recent experiences, he has undergone electric shock treatment just to see what it would do to his mind, he has attended, with full beard, a Brooklyn convention of Hassidic rabbis, and he has taken lysergic acid, a new wonder drug that he thinks might undermine the price of heroin.

"It seems to have approximated and reaffirmed my memory of the Harlem 'sensation,'" he says.

Traveling in Europe, he has sought out Samuel Beckett in Paris, talked with Dame Edith Sitwell in London, and walked with W. H. Auden on Oxford campus.

He has visited the graves of Shelley, Apollinaire and Blake.

"They didn't say a word," Ginsberg reports. "Not a word."

Today, Ginsberg, dressed in eternal blue jeans and living on scattered royalties and honorariums which sometimes total as much as eighty dollars a month, continues seeking new experience, new Gnostic insight and a new poetry along with Corso, Orlovsky and weekend friend Kerouac, who, when asked why he has never used Ginsberg as the prototype for a central figure in any of his novels, answered:

"Oh, because he's not an interesting character, to me. He doesn't do anything but talk."

But he adds: "Let the world know that I love Allen Ginsberg."

"Kerouac," commented poet Ray Bremser, "is a genius. But Allen . . . Allen's more important!"

Sometimes saddened by the jeers of a daily press that knows little more than the word, "Beatnik," Ginsberg says quietly and with sureness: "Well, I guess it doesn't matter in the long run . . . I write for God's ear."

From *Nugget* 5, no. 5 (October 1960): 15–18, 24. Reprinted by permission of the estate of Alfred Aronowitz.

Ginsberg Makes the World Scene

RICHARD KOSTELANETZ, 1965

I N 1965, Ginsberg made international headlines when he was expelled from, first, Cuba and, weeks later, Czechoslovakia. Two of his more memorable poems are "Kral Majales" and "Who Be Kind To," the latter read at an international poetry festival in the Royal Albert Hall in London (which Ginsberg helped to organize after his Czech expulsion).

In this interview/profile, Ginsberg made his first extended statements about these experiences.

TO UNIVERSITY STUDENTS all over the world today, Allen Ginsberg is a kind of cultural hero and sometimes a true prophet. In America, as the critic Leslie Fiedler put it, "In less than a decade, [he] moved to the center of the national scene, capturing the newest anthologies and preempting the imaginations of the young." In England, the manager of a lively paperback bookstore reports, "More Ginsberg mysteriously disappears than anything else," and last month his barely publicized poetry readings in London drew capacity crowds.

What has been happening in the West has parallels behind the Iron Curtain. In Czechoslovakia this year, Ginsberg was chosen *Kral Majales* (King of the May) of all Prague universities as an estimated 100,000 students looked on. His popularity, one suspects, was the prime reason for his harassment by Czechoslovakian police and his subsequent expulsion from the country. For various reasons the entire story has never been fully reported in the West, until now.

After visiting Cuba as a reporter for *The Evergreen Review* and as a guest of a Cuban writers' organization, Ginsberg flew to Prague where, he discovered, his work had attracted a following. The leading night club for poetry, the Viola Cafe, had frequently presented readings of Ginsberg's poetry in translation, and the Union of Czech Writers was planning to publish a book of his verse.

With his accumulated Czech royalties, Ginsberg traveled to Russia, where he re-established contact with many of the young Russian poets he had met previously. Then he went on to Poland and returned to Prague on April 30 in time to see the May Day Festival, the *Majales*. This celebration, he told me, had been terminated since the Communist regime took over; but as students had, in recent years, marked the day by protest riots, the Government decided this year to reinstate the traditional festival.

"I walked in the May Day parade that morning," Ginsberg recalled, "and that afternoon some students asked me to be their king. I agreed; they put me on a truck, and I traveled in the procession of the Polytechnic School, with a Dixieland band on a nearby truck. The procession went through the city to a main square, where 10,000 to 15,000 people had gathered. I made a speech, dedicating the glory of my crown to Franz Kafka, who once lived on that square."

From there, the Polytechnic's procession traveled to the Park of Culture and Rest, to join the parades from the other colleges. After a grand competition, Ginsberg found himself elected King of the May, along with a May queen, a beautiful Czech girl.

When asked to address the audience, Ginsberg, being innocent of Czech, chanted the "Hymn to the Buddha of the Future" (*"Om Shri Maitreya"*) to the accompaniment of his own small cymbals. The instruments, he said, "were from Times Square," and the hymn likewise was learned in New York—"from an old girl friend of mine who learned it from Tibetan Buddhists." (These hymns, called *mantras*, Ginsberg also chanted during demonstrations in New York early in 1965 to legalize marijuana.)

Although the Czech government was disturbed by the coronation of a non-Czech—even worse, an American—there were no immediate repercussions. "The next few days I spent running around with groups of students, acting in a spontaneous, improvised manner—making love. I spent a lot of time with rock 'n' roll musicians. There it's called the 'big beat,' and the Czechs take this music with the same fervor as Liverpool." At one concert, however, he lost his notebook. "At least I assume it was lost. Suddenly it wasn't in my pocket any more.

"A few days after," Ginsberg went on, "late at night, someone suddenly attacked me on the street, screaming '*bouzerant,*' which means 'fairy' or 'queer'; and all of us, including the students with me, were arrested by the police and taken down to the station. I wasn't released until 5 A.M.; they took affidavits from the others. I suspect the attacker was a police *provocateur,* but I can't prove it."

On May 6, Ginsberg remembers, the police, who had been conspicuously following him, "picked me up at a restaurant, promising to give me back my notebook if I would come down to the police station. Down there, someone informed me that on surface examination the book seemed to contain illegal writings, and that the book would be held for further examination."

The Czechs said the notebook had been picked off the ground by a citizen who happened to be the father of a young man in Ginsberg's entourage. The authorities charged that, in addition to this father, numerous other parents had complained that Ginsberg was corrupting many of the local youth. Ginsberg was escorted to his hotel, forbidden to make any calls and four hours later put on a plane for London. "I tried to tell them I was leaving anyway, and that my expulsion might cause some embarrassment, but it wasn't any use," he said.

The lost notebook, Ginsberg declared, was not different from the others he carries with him. It contained "poems and drafts of poems, dreams—I've been writing down all my dreams for 20 years—stray thoughts, descriptions of sex orgies and ecstasies in intimate detail, private scribbles. There were probably some political remarks, too; I can't remember. If they publish the complete diaries, it will blow up in everybody's face—mine as well as theirs. I won't mind. But they'll never publish it."

Rather, Ginsberg fears repercussions against people whose names he mentioned in it; and this is why, when he first landed in London, he did not mention the expulsion to the newspapers or to United States authorities. Indeed, since Czech papers didn't announce the expulsion until some days later, when the newspaper *Mlada Fronta* launched an editorial attack against Ginsberg, the public was unaware of it for many days after the fact.

Ginsberg admitted that Czech authorities might have found his speeches subversive. "People asked me what I thought, so I told them. I talked about the greater values, the sense of new consciousness which seems to be going through the youth of all countries—the sexual revolution, the widening of the areas of consciousness, the abhorrence of ideology, direct contact (soul to soul, body to body), Dostoevskian tolerance, Blakean vision, Buddhist *mantras* (concerned basically with the expansion of consciousness, to complete consciousness). I have no formal ideology at all; these ideas I present to make them think about themselves."

When asked why he made such an impact on Prague, becoming, in his own words, "a surrealist folk-hero," Ginsberg surmised, "Probably because everyone is sick of the politicians there."

Ginsberg is about five feet eight inches tall, weighs one hundred fifty pounds, and looks considerably less than his age, thirty-nine, despite the fact that he is almost bald. A mass of luxuriant black curls hangs from a horseshoe-shaped ring of hair on the fringe of his head. His face is nearly covered by an untrimmed, thick, gray-streaked black beard that runs from just below his eyes to his button-down shirt. Behind horn-rimmed glasses are dark eyes which stare directly at whomever Ginsberg addresses, hardly blinking and rarely distracted. His voice is a resonant bass, able to carry an Oriental tune; his diction has the clarity of one accustomed to public speaking. In many ways he looks and sounds, one immediately thinks, like a Hasidic rabbi chanting, not *mantras*, but Hebrew prayers.

Ginsberg estimated he earns about fifteen hundred dollars a year from royalties from the publisher of his poetry, Lawrence Ferlinghetti's City Lights Bookshop, and picks up scraps here and there when his poetry appears in magazines. He once soaked *Playboy* for a five-hundred-dollar advance on an article—"the only time I ever took money from a slick"—but three years later he has still to complete the commissioned piece. As a matter of policy, he never takes money for poetry readings, and he especially likes to read at benefits for little magazines. As he is known to have very little income, people are continually offering rides, plane fares, meals, parties, lodging; when Ginsberg comes to town—whether to London, New Delhi, Moscow or Prague—it is an occasion. As word spreads quickly, events are organized, hospitality arranged.

Although he has been publicly cast in a number of unflattering images, ranging from a clown to an exhibitionist, the dominant impression he gives in conversation is that he is, and has always been, primarily a poet. Unlike any other American poet of note, Ginsberg is of a species more common in England and Europe: he is the son of a poet, Louis Ginsberg, a high-school teacher by trade whose work was more admired in the thirties than now. Though Ginsberg has as varied a collection of friends as any eminent, well-traveled man, those he calls his best friends are all writers—William Burroughs, Jack Kerouac, Gregory Corso, Peter Orlovsky, Herbert Huncke.

Born in Newark, New Jersey, in 1926, Ginsberg went to high school in Paterson, "where I thought of myself as a creep, a mystical creep. I had a good time, was lonesome; but I first read Whitman there." Although the poet William Carlos Williams lived near Paterson, Ginsberg never approached him until after he went to college, first to interview him for a local newspaper and then to make him a friend. Ginsberg acknowledges Williams as one of his early influences, and Williams in turn wrote the introduction to Ginsberg's *Howl* and even incorporated the younger poet's letters in his own "Paterson."

At seventeen, Ginsberg entered Columbia, attended classes taught by Meyer Schapiro, Mark Van Doren, Lionel Trilling; he became a member of the debating team, editor of *The Columbia Review*, president of the Philolexian Society (for word-lovers). He majored in English, attained an A-minus average, won several prizes for poems which Ginsberg remembers as stylistically "after Wyatt and the silver poets." He thinks of the late Raymond Weaver, the biographer of Melville and the discoverer of the manuscript of *Billy Budd* as "one of the few true teachers there. He was using Zen Koans [e.g., 'What is the sound of one hand clapping?'] as a method for awakening the student's mind in a course called 'Communications.'"

During the years at Columbia, he first met William Burroughs, who lived several blocks south of Columbia and was at that time addicted to junk. Burroughs, Ginsberg believes, "was my greatest teacher at that time. He put me on to Spengler, Yeats, Rimbaud, Korzybski, Proust and Celine. Burroughs educated me more than Columbia, really."

There and then, too, he first encountered Jack Kerouac, who came to Columbia as a football player, quit the sport, lost his football scholarship, and was subsequently dismissed from Columbia for not paying his bills. "Hanging around with Kerouac" was one of the reasons for Ginsberg's own subsequent dismissal in 1945. The other was two obscenities, atop a skull and crossbones, which Ginsberg drew in the dust of his dormitory window.

One scribble defamed the Jews and the other made an unflattering reference to the then-president of Columbia. Critic Diana Trilling, in a controversial essay, "The Other Night at Columbia," has since interpreted the first remark as a symbol of Ginsberg's rejection of the Jewish middle class. Ginsberg to this day insists he had no intention beyond trying to shock an anti-Semitic Irish cleaning woman who worked in the dormitories. The cleaning woman was, in fact, offended. She reported the scribble to the dean who, likewise offended, expelled Ginsberg. He was later readmitted to graduate with a B.A. in 1948.

That same year Ginsberg had another sort of experience which, like Burroughs, had a greater effect upon his life than academic matters: "a vision in which I heard Blake's voice, experienced a sense of lightness of my body and a spiritual illumination of the entire universe as the Great Live Self of the Creator."

(He has always been an avid admirer of Blake's work, and during his recent stay in London, he acquired a special pass to the Blake illuminate books in the British Museum.)

After graduating from Columbia, he took a variety of odd jobs— dishwasher at Bickford's, book reviewer for a summer at *Newsweek*, market research consultant, reporter for a labor newspaper in Newark. At this time, he started to publish his poems, many of them collected in *Empty Mirror: Early Poems* from 1946–51. Particularly in the early fifties, Ginsberg was, as he wrote, working under the influence of "W. C. Williams' Imagist preoccupations." But in 1955, "I suddenly turned aside in San Francisco, while enjoying unemployment compensation leisure, to follow my romantic inspiration—Hebraic-Melvillian bardic breath." Perhaps one mixture included a bit of Whitman too, for the result was "Howl," the poem that first established Ginsberg's poetic talent and popular impact.

Since then, City Lights issued in 1961 *Kaddish and Other Poems* of 1958–60; and *Reality Sandwiches,* in 1963. Here, as elsewhere, Ginsberg insists upon the precise dating of his poems, and the English edition, at his request, will run all his work in chronological order.

"Everything I write," he says, "is in one way or another autobiographical or present consciousness at the time of writing. Whatever travels or psychic progressions I've had are recorded there." His work has been translated into Italian, German, French, Spanish, Bengali, Russian, Czech, Japanese, Hindu [sic]. It is hard to prove, but not unfair to say, that although other poets have greater reputations at home, to the world at large Ginsberg is the most famous and admired of contemporary American poets.

Ginsberg's poetry has ranged in style from conventionally rhymed lyrics to the freest of forms, in purpose from meditation to polemics, in tone from Apollinairean surrealism to uncompromising negation to anarchic humor, and in stance from objective statement to the personal confession of "Kaddish" (by esthetic standards his best poem).

But Ginsberg's particular success has been to become the truly popular poet that Whitman only imagined himself to be—the author of lines that live in the heads of the literary young in America and, increasingly, in Europe:

> I saw the best minds of my generation destroyed by madness,
>   starving hysterical naked,

dragging themselves through negro streets at dawn looking for an
    angry fix ...
who talked continuously seventy hours from park to pad to bar to
    Bellevue to museum to the Brooklyn Bridge ...
and who were given instead the concrete void of insulin metasol
    electricity hydrotherapy psychotherapy occupational therapy
    pingpong & amnesia ...

These lines come from "Howl," Ginsberg's violent indictment of the
"Moloch," a materialistic American civilization. The poem does not attain the structural balance and economy characteristic of the best modern poetry; yet, like Whitman, Ginsberg is finally the poet of brilliant
lines and a consistent, or be it simplistic, frame of ideas and images.

Part of Ginsberg's popularity as an international poet stems from his
commanding personality: like many popular public figures, he possesses
that quality Max Weber once defined as "charisma"—the ability to establish confidence by sheer presence. He is naturally gregarious, particularly
inclined to speak frankly of his own experience and opinions. Yet precisely because he is so unself-conscious about his unconventionality and
endeavors to speak directly to people, his capacity to offend is minimal,
even among those who disagree with him.

He has the instincts of a seminar leader—he listens attentively, re-
plies quickly and directly, tries to coin aphorisms. Ideally, he would like
to teach in a university, but no one has asked him, nor does he think any
university is tolerant enough for him. "After all," he observes, "I teach all
the time right now."

His various experiences with psychoanalysis have left him skeptical
about its methodology and more confident about its value as a human
relationship. The first relationship, he says, was with Burroughs, "back in
the Columbia days"; the second, for three months, with "a Reichian who
is no longer a Reichian"; the third, for eight months with "dreary Freud-
ians" as an "inpatient" at the New York State Psychiatric Institute; the
fourth, for two-and-a-half years, with a doctor formerly attached to the
institute. Then, "in 1955, in San Francisco, I did a year with a good doctor

from the Washington School—you know, Harry Stack Sullivan's—he was the best."

"If an analyst is a good man," says Ginsberg, "then the analysis will be good. What's necessary is tender communication between two people—in analysis or life." So, his outlook remains more similar to that of Martin Buber and Hasidism than to the Jewish rationalistic tradition exemplified by Freud.

Ginsberg would like to think of himself as apolitical, but he has signed advertisements in support of the pro-Castro Fair Play for Cuba Committee and petitions against American activities in Vietnam. In all, he is less anti-American than against certain forces and ideas in both superpowers. "America," he explains, "is one of the main Judases of the contemporary world. As things are going now, it seems to me that dogmatic Cold-War types in the U.S. and the Socialist countries are mirror images of each other and are bent on world destruction. Everything we say about the Communists is right, too, give or take a little bit of inaccurate reporting here and there. Everybody's bankrupt except for the long-haired young and the peaceful old." So, when Czechoslovakia invited him to make statements critical of America, Ginsberg, the truest of anarchists, surprised them by making anti-Communist ones too.

Ginsberg will receive a Guggenheim Fellowship next year to travel and write poetry. He applied for a Guggenheim in 1960, when "Kaddish" was published, but didn't get it. Though not ungrateful, he still believes that "too much money goes to the wrong places, to the wrong poets in America. Many major poets haven't gotten much at all, for a long time."

As for the future beyond next year, Ginsberg conjectures that 10 years from now, "I'll be living in a little cottage in the country, with a wife and 12 children." He paused and added: "I'll be scribbling poems." Fame? "It's a Kafkian situation," he says, "like a repetition of consciousness. If one takes one's identity from a vague idea of oneself, fame can cause confusion of identity. If one takes one's identity from one's desire in the body, then one is stabilized." He stopped for a moment, fumbled for words. "If your soul is your belly, nobody can drive you out of your skull."

Second to John F. Kennedy, Ginsberg would seem to be the most widely acclaimed American cultural ambassador, hailed particularly by the young, which is to say, the future. To them, his presence symbolizes effectively the variousness and tolerance of America. He contradicts the pervasive image of an endless, vulgarly mindless suburbia that our movies present to Europe and which too many of our official representatives confirm.

Also, there is, all over the world, a younger generation with values and aspirations different from their elders? Ginsberg's impact, coupled with, and perhaps abetted by, the vehement disapproval of him by established authorities, is a conclusive sign of youth's rebellion. For he does and says publicly what many of the world's young do and say privately, and thus becomes their spokesman.

Fulfilling Whitman's dream, Ginsberg is, like his friend Yevgeny Yevtushenko, a public poet who has attained a cultural importance beyond the merit of his poetry. He is a prophet not only of youth and disappointment—but also perhaps an "unacknowledged legislator" or harbinger of a new kind of existence in an age of cybernation and increased leisure. It is an age when many more people will be able to devote a larger portion of their lives, as Ginsberg does, not only to poetry and the arts but also to the cultivation of an uninhibited variety of possible pleasures.

From *New York Times Magazine* (July 11, 1965): 22-23, 27-28, 30, 32-33. Reprinted by permission of Richard Kostelanetz.

Ginsberg in Washington
Lobbying for Tenderness

DON MCNEILL, 1966

ALLEN GINSBERG strongly advocated the use of psychedelic drugs, particularly LSD and psilocybin, as a means of self-discovery through the expansion of consciousness. He kept massive files of news clippings and magazine articles, general interest and scholarly, on drug use, legislation, law enforcement, and scientific and anecdotal studies; his knowledge on drug-related issues was encyclopedic, and, not surprisingly, he was very vocal in expressing his opinions on such topics as Timothy Leary and his Harvard LSD experiments, and on the legalization of marijuana, to name just two.

His knowledge and high media visibility made him an ideal witness when, in 1966, a Senate subcommittee conducted hearings about LSD and the drug's impact on society.

ALLEN GINSBERG, lobbying for tenderness, bared a large part of his soul last week before a Senate subcommittee investigating the use of LSD.

"I'm here to tell you about my personal experiences," he began softly, "and am worried that without sufficient understanding and sympathy for personal experience laws will be passed that are so rigid that they will cause more harm than the new LSD that they try to regulate."

The atmosphere was neither hostile nor sympathetic, rather, curious as Ginsberg took the stand. He bowed, a small Buddhist bow, and tried to dispel some of the apprehension among the Senators, press, and spectators in the floodlit, marbled caucus room. "Whatever prejudgment you have about me, or my bearded image, I hope you will suspend it so that we can talk together as fellow beings in the same room of Now, trying to come to some harmony and peacefulness between us."

His efforts were first to establish a common bond with those listening. He noted the common frustration with the lack of a place for the human, personal, individual factor in our society. It is "a feeling of being caught in a bureaucratic machine which is not built to serve some of our deepest feelings . . . a machine which closes down our senses, reduces our language and thoughts to uniformity, reduces our sources of inspiration and fact to fewer channels—as TV does—and monopolizes our attention with second-hand imagery—packaged news, as we're having it packaged now"—and the network cameras whirred softly—"and doesn't really satisfy our deeper needs—healthy personal adventure in environments where we're having living contact with each other in the flesh, the human universe we are built to enjoy and live in."

One More Thing

"All this is inevitable," he said, "especially since we have come to value material extensions of ourselves." But he still emphasized the need for some respite. "Human contact is built into our nature as a material need as strong as food . . . We can't treat each other only as objects—we can't treat each other as Things lacking sympathy. Our humanity would atrophy crippled and die—WANT to die. Because life without feeling is just one more 'Thing,' an inhuman universe."

Ginsberg described experiences he had had using various psychedelic drugs. The purpose of the description was twofold. First, to further attempt to establish a rapport by sharing deepest personal experiences. He often repeated his fears that his candor would be rejected. Secondly, he "wanted to explain why that very personal thing has a place here," that those human experiences might be a possible refuge for a Person in this plastic world.

He spoke first of his early experiences with peyote, experiences which he described in his poem "Howl" (a copy of which he submitted to the

Committee). The peyote vision "felt so strange and yet familiar as if from another lifetime . . . like the myths of all religions, like the graceful appearance of a Divine Presence, as if a God suddenly made himself felt in my old weekly New York Universe." He spoke of his experiences with the psychedelic vine Ayahuasca in Peru, and recounted his conversations with holy men in India. And he told of how the night before the Vietnam Day march in Berkeley last fall, he, the novelist Ken Kesey, the marchers, and the Hell's Angels "all had a party at the Hell's Angels house."

Violent Clash

Prior to this, Ginsberg said, "the public image of a violent clash between students and Hell's Angels escalated in everybody's mind—like a hallucination." At the party, organized by Kesey, "most everybody took some LSD, and we settled down to discussing the situation and listening to Joan Baez on the phonograph and chanting Buddhist prayers. We were all awed by the communication possible—everybody able to drop their habitual Image for the night and feel more community than conflict. And the evening ended with the understanding that nobody really wanted violence; and there was none on the day of the march."

Ginsberg finally told of an LSD experience at Big Sur last fall. It was his first in several years, he said, and was shortly before the Berkeley Vietnam demonstrations. "We were all confused . . . many angry marchers blamed the President for the situation we were in. I did, too. The day I took LSD was the same day that President Johnson went into the operating room for his gall bladder illness. As I walked through the forest wondering what my feelings toward him were . . . the awesome place I was in impressed me with its old tree and ocean cliff majesty. Many tiny jeweled violet flowers along the path of a living brook that looked like Blake's Illustration of a canal in grassy Eden: huge Pacific watery shore. I saw a friend dancing long haired before giant green waves, under cliffs of titanic nature that Wordsworth described in his poetry, and a great yellow sun veiled with mist hanging over the planet's ocean horizon. Armies at war on the other side of the planet . . . and the President in the valley of the shadow—himself experiences what fear or grief? I realized that more vile words from me would send out negative vibrations into the atmosphere—more hatred against his poor flesh and soul on trial—so I knelt on the sand surrounded by masses of green kelp washed up by a storm, and prayed for President Johnson's tranquil health."

Formidable Task

Ginsberg had tried to dispel the apprehension about the psychedelic experience as gently as he had done with the apprehension about himself. It was a formidable task. The hearings to date had had the cold aura of a scientist examining something wriggling under his microscope, a germ, perhaps, a "menace" in the words of Chairman Thomas Dodd. He didn't like the looks of it, but was determined to find out what it was. Ginsberg, to use liberal analogy, was Archy the Cockroach come to life, telling depression-ridden America of the '30s to be gentle and look at themselves. But America still stomped on roaches and Ginsberg's testimony may have been equally futile against the "just the facts, ma'am" scrutiny of the Subcommittee on Juvenile Delinquency. He was not rebuked. More likely, he received the much-taunted "white liberal" treatment. He was smiled at and ignored.

He had pointed out the need for a self-liberating experience, a need which everyone, consciously or not, shares, and he gave examples of personal experiences with psychedelic drugs which, for him, had helped fulfill this need. Ginsberg now went on "to offer some data to calm the anxiety that LSD is some awful mind-bending monster threat which must be kept under lock and key."

Ginsberg offered three main ideas regarding this anxiety. He suggested that "there has been a journalistic panic exaggeration of the LSD danger," noting wide discrepancies in the news reports on the young Brooklyn girl who accidentally swallowed a cube of LSD. He provided statistics showing that "there is negligible danger to healthy people in trying LSD and comparatively little danger to most mentally sick people." And he urged the Committee not to disregard "the appearance of religious or transcendental or serious blissful experience through psychedelics" and suggested that they "treat LSD with proper humanity and respect."

When he had finished his statement, Ginsberg was questioned by Senators Jacob Javits of New York and Quentin Burdick of North Dakota, who was acting chairman in Dodd's absence. Many of the questions seemed to be standard ones asked of the "pro-LSD" witnesses in these hearings—for instance, on the source of the drugs. One could not help but get the impression that such questions were asked merely to get them on the record. When asked where he obtained the drugs, Ginsberg replied that "in order to speak freely on the subject, I've had to stop my use. I have heard that the Narcotics Bureau has been trying to set me up for an arrest." Burdick prodded: "You don't know where it comes from?" "I literally do not know," he replied. At this point, Javits reminded Ginsberg of his privilege against self-incrimination. Other witnesses, when asked about the source, almost invariably said that they had obtained the drugs from "friends." The consistency of the "friends" answer became almost a joke to the Committee, evoking some laughter.

Although Javits had amiably spoken with Ginsberg a number of times before his testimony, his questioning became somewhat sharp, though far short of the harsh Teddy Kennedy–Timothy Leary exchange in the same room a few weeks ago. Javits repeatedly reminded Ginsberg that he was not qualified to testify on any of the medical aspects of LSD. "Do you consider yourself qualified to give medical advice to my sixteen-and-a-half-year-old son?" Javits asked. Javits indicated that he was concerned about Ginsberg's influence "among young people" and wanted to make it clear that the poet should not give "medical advice."

As he concluded his statement, Ginsberg suggested that "if we want to discourage use of LSD for altering our attitudes, we'll have to encourage such changes in our society that nobody will need to take it to break through to common sympathy." He suggested that the new generation, many of whom have experienced this "new sense of openness," will "push for an environment less rigid, mechanical, less dominated by automatic cold war habits. A new kind of light has rayed through our society—despite all the anxiety it has caused—maybe these hearings are a manifestation of that slightly changed awareness. I wouldn't have thought it possible to speak like this a year ago. That we're more open to each other is the new consciousness itself: to reveal one's visions to a Congressional Committee!"

_____

From the *Village Voice*, June 23, 1966. Reprinted by permission.

A Conversation between Ezra Pound and Allen Ginsberg

MICHAEL RECK, 1968

I N 1967, Ginsberg's Italian translator, Fernanda Pivano, arranged a luncheon meeting between Allen Ginsberg, Ezra Pound, and Pound's longtime companion, Olga Rudge. Ginsberg admired Pound's poetry, but Pound, essentially silent and living in exile since his controversial anti-Semitic radio broadcasts during World War II, had very little to say to Ginsberg during that initial luncheon, He did, however, agree to meet Ginsberg in Venice. Ginsberg's persistence wore him down, and Pound talked about poetry and, in a stunning turn of events, his regrets about his broadcasts—the first time he had ever spoken about the topic in public.

The following article catches a side of Ginsberg rarely addressed in newspaper and magazine articles at the time: his great patience and understanding. Ginsberg's patience was stretched to the breaking point on countless occasions through his life, when friends stole and sold his possessions for drug money; took advantage of his hospitality by staying in his apartment beyond their welcome; attacked him in public through the media. Jack Kerouac, Peter Orlovsky, Gregory Corso, Neal Cassady, William S. Burroughs, Herbert Huncke—the list goes on and on . . . all tested Ginsberg, but his capacity for patience and forgiveness was seemingly endless. He possessed an insatiable curiosity and, as this article on his encounters with Ezra Pound illustrates, he sought out the humanity in people so easily dismissed by others.

ONE FINE DAY IN VENICE RECENTLY, I saw an apparition that was real: a round face like an apprentice Santa Claus framed by an immense mane of flowing pitch-black hair and beard, its pink nose surmounted by equally black spectacles. From its neck dangled a great silver Buddhist medal. This apparition confronted another real one: a very thin aged face with a minimum of silky fine wispy white hair and beard. Fixed staring eyes of a deep aquamarine, now losing their power, seemed to mirror a dreadful sadness. Two long thin hands, the skin of the knuckles raw, rested on the table before him; from time to time he rubbed one against the other. The old man wore a handsome blue wool suit, tan V-necked sweater, and a bright solid-yellow tie. The conversation that day was of extraordinary interest, and I believe both men were deeply moved. With Ginsberg's help, I recorded it later.

They had met for the first time only a month before when Ginsberg sought the Master out at his home in the hills high above Rapallo. I understood Pound was pleased with his visit. Then Ginsberg appeared to stay near Pound for a week in Venice. He played selected records of the Beatles, Dylan, and Donovan and chanted mantras for him, accompanying himself on a portable harmonium. He dined with the Master once or twice a day. But that afternoon of October 28, 1967, two days before Pound's eighty-second birthday, was, Ginsberg told me, the only occasion on which the Master spoke more than a few words.

Ezra Pound's silence is by now pretty well known. The father of modern English poetry is now, in many ways, "a man on whom the sun has set." The imprisonment in a lunatic asylum for thirteen years after World War II had touched him little. He came out the same ebullient cheerful personality, dead set in his conviction that usury caused the world's ills, especially war and poverty. He never insisted on the value of his own works, but he never appeared to doubt it in the slightest. Since about 1960, however, Ezra Pound is a changed person. He talks very little, is often depressed, and declares that his own writing is worthless.

Those of us who loved the old Ezra Pound, for all his faults, are not happy to see him so negative about his past life and works. But history, as Ginsberg observed to me in another context, makes itself. The new Ezra

Pound has—in over-supply—those qualities which the old Ezra rather lacked: humility and modesty. He is of a gentleness that approaches saintliness. His physical health is fairly good, though his eyes are weakening. He summers in Rapallo, on the coast near Genoa, winters in Venice, and every year attends the Gian-Carlo Menotti festival in Spoleto.

That afternoon the *pensione* near Pound's home was swarming with Italian television people engaged in making a film about him. But we sat almost alone in the *pensione*'s dining hall—Ginsberg, myself and my six-year-old boy, and the English poet and critic Peter Russell. Pound appeared at the door, very thin, with his friend Olga Rudge, and moved slowly toward us. Seen from a distance, his quiet blue eyes were piercing. He seated himself at Ginsberg's right and across the table from me.

Olga Rudge told us that Pound had been working all morning. Ginsberg and I were not sure whether she meant on his own poetry or on the filming, but it was probably the former, because she then declared he had enough poetry for a new book. "Cantos?" I asked. "Of course," she said. Miss Rudge said she did not believe he was discouraged about his work as a whole; when he reads, she pointed out, he recites some parts with much enthusiasm.

There is nothing harder than conversing with Pound nowadays, and Ginsberg and I tried unsuccessfully throughout the meal. Russell sat by Olga Rudge and talked mainly with her. Pound simply did not answer when addressed, and he looked very morose. At one point, however, Russell said, "I have a birthday present for you, E. P. Would you like it?" And he handed him a copy of *It Was the Nightingale,* a long out-of-print autobiography by Pound's dear friend Ford Madox Ford, long since dead. "Yes, yes," said Pound. His eyes lit up, and he riffled through the pages with a pleased, almost excited smile. Then he put the book down and was again silent.

Finally Ginsberg mentioned to Pound that he had been looking up Venetian places mentioned in the Master's *Pisan Cantos* but had been unable to locate some things. The church San Giorgio, where "in the font to the right as you enter/are all the gold domes of San Marco." Ginsberg had found no such reflection in the font, he said; nor could he find "the soap-smooth stone posts where San Vio/meets il Canal Grande." And where was "Salviati"? In a slow, even voice, looking at his hands, Pound gave precise information: the font had since been altered; the posts and Salviati were at such and such a place. Ginsberg asked a number of similar questions, and Pound answered one after the other very painstakingly.

Then Ginsberg leaned over to Pound and said, "Your thoughts about specific perception and [William Carlos] Williams's 'no ideas but in things' have been a great help to me and to many young poets. And the phrasing of your poems has had a very concrete value for me as reference points for my own perception. Am I making sense?"

"Yes," said Pound, and after a moment mumbled, "but my poems don't make sense." Ginsberg and I assured him that they made sense to us. "A lot of double talk," said Pound. And pursing his lips for a moment as if searching for words, then finding them, the Master said, "Basil Bunting told me that *The Cantos* refer, but they do not present." Ginsberg assured Pound that Bunting had only recently pointed out *The Cantos* to him as a prime example of economy of language. And I said, "Presenting means that when someone reads your poetry he is struck with how real the description is, even if he hasn't experienced the thing himself. He says, 'That's it, that's just how it is.' Reading your poetry, I often feel this myself. Your poetry is often shockingly direct."

Pound was silent, and rubbed the back of one hand with the other. Then a moment later: "At seventy I realized that instead of being a lunatic, I was a moron."

Ginsberg said, "In your work, the sequence of verbal images, phrases like 'tin flash in the sun dazzle' and 'soap-smooth stone posts'—these have given me, in praxis of perception, ground to walk on."

"A mess."

"You or *The Cantos* or me?"

"My writing. Stupid and ignorant all the way through. Stupid and ignorant."

And I said, "In your poetry you have an *ear*. That's the most important thing for writing poetry. So it's hard for you to write a bad line."

"It's hard for me to write at *all*," he answered with a dim smile.

Then Ginsberg: "Bill Williams told me that you have a 'mystical ear.' Did he ever say that to you?"

"No, he never said that to me." The Master looked away, smiling faintly, almost shyly.

All this was not sycophancy. Ginsberg and I were simply trying to lift him out of his doldrums by telling him what we (and so many other poetry readers) really felt. I said, "Your work has influenced writers all over the world, even writers who may never have read you. For example, the Russian short story writer [Isaak] Babel said that he had learned to write dialogue from Hemingway, and you taught Hemingway." Pound drew back a bit, and looked doubtful. "You *did* teach Hemingway, didn't you?" He pursed his lips but said nothing. "Well, he wrote that he had learned more about how to write and how not to write from you than from anybody." Pound studied his hands in silence.

Ginsberg had a notebook with him at the table, and now he began to read from the notes he had made during the preceding day, a kind of poetic mental diary of his walks in Venice. When he came to the lines describing—or, I should say, presenting—marble "crooked-mirror'd in the glassy surface," Pound smiled. "That's good," he declared. (And so it was.)

"When are you going to return to America?" Ginsberg asked him. He told the Master of the interest in contemporary poetry at Buffalo University. ("They even offered *me* a job!" he said.) "And San Francisco is lively. Maybe you'd like it there," Ginsberg added. He offered to make arrangements for Pound to read in the States. "Too late," Pound answered slowly. Ginsberg declared it was never too late.

"You have shown us the way," Ginsberg said. "The more I read your poetry, the more I am convinced it is the best of its time. And your economics are *right*. We see it more and more in Vietnam. You showed us who's making a profit out of war. And as humours—using the word in the ancient sense, as a state of mind—the irritations against Taoists, Buddhists, and Jews fit into their place as a part of *The Cantos,* despite your intentions, as theater, the record, of flux of consciousness. The Paradise is in desire, not in the imperfection of the way it was done. The magnanimity of the desire to manifest coherent perceptions in language."

"Any good I've done has been spoiled by bad intentions—the preoccupation with irrelevant and stupid things," Pound replied. And then, very slowly, with emphasis, surely conscious of Ginsberg's being Jewish:

"But the worst mistake I made was that stupid, suburban prejudice of anti-Semitism."

"It's lovely to hear you say that," said Ginsberg. Whereupon he added, "Well, no, because anyone with any sense can see it as humour, in that sense part of the drama, a model of your consciousness. Anti-Semitism is your fuck-up, like not liking Buddhists, but it's part of the model and the great accomplishment was to make a working model of your mind. Nobody cares if it's Ezra Pound's mind but it's a mind like everybody's mind."

Ginsberg went on to tell Pound, "Prospero threw away *his* magic staff at the end of the play." And he recited these touching and appropriate lines, Prospero's, from *The Tempest*:

> Now my charms are all o'erthrown,
> And what strength I haven't mine own—
> Which is most faint . . .
> . . . now I want
> Spirits to enforce, art to enchant;
> And my ending is despair,
> Unless I be reliev'd by prayer,
> Which pierces so, that it assaults
> Mercy itself, and frees all faults.
> As you from crimes would pardon'd be,
> Let your indulgence set me free.

Ginsberg reminded me later that these were probably the last lines that Shakespeare wrote.

Then Ginsberg again leaned sideways to the Master, who stared straight ahead. "But you must go on working, to record the last scenes of the drama. You still have a great deal to say. After all, now you have nothing to lose. You *are* working, aren't you?"

Pound was silent, and Ginsberg continued, "Ah, well, Prospero . . . what I came here for was to give you my blessing—despite your disillusion . . . unless you want to be a Messiah. And you'll have to be a Buddhist to be that. But I'm a Buddhist Jew whose perceptions have been strengthened by the series of practical exact language models scattered through *The Cantos* like stepping stones, because, whatever your intentions, their practical effect has been to clarify my perceptions. Do you accept my blessing?"

The Master hesitated, opened his mouth a moment, and then the words appeared, "I do."

Pound was tired, it was nearly four o'clock, and the television people were waiting at his home for another filming session. He rose slowly, took his coat, his felt hat, his cane. We all accompanied him and Olga Rudge to their home, along a lapping canal bordered by an iron rail.

Ginsberg walked by Pound, and told him that he was at the beginning of wisdom, this being the Buddhist definition of where one is when one recognizes one's own ignorance. Then he threw an arm over Pound's shoulder and said with a large smile, "As it says in the *I Ching*, no harm." (He told me later that he was referring to the statement in the *I Ching*—the Chinese "Book of Changes"—that there is no harm in making a mistake. Ginsberg said Pound knew the *I Ching* well, and would have understood the abbreviated citation.)

As we approached Pound's tiny home, on a side street off the canal, we saw that inside the place was abuzz with television technicians and a black electric cable snaked out the front door and down the street.

We stood before the door, and Peter Russell took Pound's hand in farewell. "Ezra, I have just returned from America. They talked a lot about you there," he said. I grasped the Master's hand and said, "We are leaving tomorrow, E. P." And after a pause, "You have many friends all over the world. You are loved by many people." Then Ginsberg, with his great black rabbinical beard, put his left hand on the back of the Master's neck, looked at him for a few long moments, and said, "I have told you what I came here to tell you. I also came here for your blessing. And now may I have it, sir?"

"Yes," he nodded, "for whatever it's worth."

"And I would also like your blessing for Sherry Martinelli. She needs it."

And with a touching grace and naturalness, Ginsberg leaned over and kissed the Master on the right cheek.

Pound appeared greatly moved by the farewells. He had held each of our hands long, and I thought that tears would start from his eyes. "I should have been able to do better," he said to Ginsberg. Then he slowly turned and walked into the house.

———————

From *Evergreen Review* 12, no. 55 (June 1968): 27–29, 84–86. Reprinted by permission of Barney Rosset and *Evergreen Review*.

Identity Gossip

ALLEN GINSBERG, 1974
EDITED BY GORDON BALL

EVERY YEAR, Allen Ginsberg peppered his calendar with tours of college campuses, where he would give readings, conduct classes, and meet with students in informal settings. Gordon Ball, editor of two volumes of Ginsberg's journals, traveled with the poet on one of the poetry tours. His taped recordings of Ginsberg's lectures and meetings with students, eventually edited and published as *Allen Verbatim,* caught Ginsberg expounding on poetry, social change, the Vietnam War, politics, Ezra Pound, Jack Kerouac, and just about anything else crossing his mind.

"IDENTITY GOSSIP" RECORDS THE END of a long day at Davis, California. It had begun with a morning address to science students and was followed by open-air talks and poetry with the rest of the student body and a late-afternoon visit to gentle mouni Hari Dass (teacher of the former Richard Alpert, Baba Ram Dass). As we returned from an evening visit to a prisoners' writing class at Vacaville State Prison (where Dr. Timothy Leary was incarcerated prior to his transfer to and subsequent escape from the state prison at San Luis Obispo), an impromptu rap session arose in the lounge of the dormitory where we were staying. A cameraman immediately began taking flash pictures, and thus this writing begins with Allen's response to a question about fame, about being a center of attention.

AG: The problem of being the center of attention, like now, or being famous is an identity problem no different from anybody's identity problem because of the vastness of all of our identity problems: "Who am I," like "Who're you?" What's the actual identity, what's the actual inner person, *is* there even an inner self, is there any identity? Anybody's identity problem is the entire universe, it's as vast as the entire universe. Yours as well as mine. So actually in the grand scale with which we're dealing, my identity problem is not any bigger than yours.

Q: *But it seems like you're moving around and surrounded by different people all the time.*

AG: So are you. Aren't you? So are you. Now whether or not you relate to them and are conscious of them and they're conscious of you, on a subliminal level everybody's conscious of everybody including the trees, all the time. It's just that usually you don't acknowledge the tree's eyeball or you're not totally "on" in the communication. But in actuality you are moving around and surrounded by people and relating with people, one way or another. A negative relation or a blank relation is nonetheless a choice. So like when you're high on acid you know that you're surrounded by sentient beings all interrelated all the time except that you choose generally not to notice it, but you realize that you could notice it all the time if you wanted, if you were open.

You all know what a Zen koan is? It's like a verbal riddle or conceptual riddle presented to the body, to the meditator, which he meditates on in order to discover his ultimate nature. And one koan is, What is the face you had before you were born? So I find the problem of being stared at by others or being a center of energy or center of consciousness or "fame," like a koan. It presents me constantly with a mystical riddle of identity, to move through continuously and solve in different ways. The alternative would be to get paranoid about it and think of it as a big drag rather than as a karmaic mystic charming problem.

Q: *Do you feel that people see you as you see yourself? As you visualize yourself?*

AG: Sometimes, amazingly. Often not. I find out later, many years later, sometimes . . . Like I gave a reading in Lawrence, Kansas, in 1965 and ran into someone here today who was at that reading, who said it freaked him out, freaked him out sort of, not in a bringdown way. He was studying business administration at the time, and I came around with Peter Orlovsky, who seemed a bit mad, and also there was the overt homosexual relation between us, plus Peter's catatonic brother Julius came along, so the "entourage" with me seemed to him completely socially displeasurable or socially out of bounds.

Now the point I was making was that socially out of bounds or not, the people I was running around with were existent, were there, were real at least in my life, so why shut them up in bughouses or something, why suppress it all? I mean it was there. The cat who was then freaked out is now sort of satisfied, "Oh, it was just there," you know, the people were just there. He was trying to exclude them from reality at the time because he was trying to make it on a short-hair business scene where a schizophrenic catatonic wasn't welcome—though he existed, he wasn't welcome in that universe.

In other words, at that time he was not seeing me as I saw myself.

Q: *That seems to be a problem right here—*

AG: But that's everybody's problem, too, see. I mean, do people see you the way you want them to see you? Do they?

Q: *No, but most of the people, you know—like when you're on* The David Frost Show, *or something like that, and you start getting letters, then you find out how they visualize you in specific terms . . .*

AG: Yeah; I know. But they send you eye glances, they send you all sorts of fan mail in form of heart throbs, eye glances, little cries, and oo-bop-shebams, and moans in bed. In other words, you get a feedback, actually.

Q: *Isn't there a difference, though, in the awareness which you have of your audience and the balance of awareness coming back to you?*

AG: Uh, don't know. I assume, actually, that there is one consciousness that we all share on the highest level, that we are all one Self, actually, that we are all one Self with one being, one consciousness.

Q: *So the awareness between you and other persons is virtually the same as between me and us?*

AG: Yes. When we all address ourselves to the highest awareness possible, to the highest awareness that we can conceive of among ourselves. So in a situation like this I try to address myself to that one consciousness, I try to pay attention or keep it in mind at least, conceptually if not heartwise, as much as possible, try to keep my body in a condition of the highest possibility of awareness, or keep that as the touchstone of the relationship, and so *can't* go wrong—trusting, however, that others do recognize this gleam in themselves.

Q: *Then you never try to analyze this highest possibility of awareness?*

AG: Yeah, sometimes analyze it in order to explain it for those who feel the heartthrob-gleam-mind-consciousness shared but who don't understand how it can be true.

Q: *But for yourself you don't try to analyze something you're conscious of?*

AG: No, to the extent that analysis requires the babble of language running like ticker-tape through mind consciousness, I try to silence that babble and feel with my body more, exist in the feeling. Because what it is, finally, that highest level of consciousness, is like feeling, really, a feeling-sensation—consciousness. It's a body consciousness as well as a conceptual consciousness. So like in yoga the highest wisdom is centered in the heart.

A yogi today was telling me something I didn't know in yogic terms, that the heart is supposed to be guided by the third eye, or the area here *[points to the center of his forehead]*, the *ajana*, I think they call it, which is like intuition, imagination, too. But at any rate the highest awareness of mammal is heart's knowledge.

Q: *So the highest awareness doesn't necessarily involve a separation between body and mind.*

AG: No. It means a stilling of superficial mind yatter and a sinking of the mind into the heart area. In fact there is a Tibetan mantra that articulates that particular conceptual set that we were just talking about, performed as Om Ah hum. Body *[points to head]* set in head, actually, as if the body were just a mind concept that sprang out of mental conception. Body: OM. Ah *[points to larynx]*: Speech. Mind *[points to heart]*:

Hum. It's a very funny idea, the mind in the heart, as they put the body up there in the brain. Om Ah Hum Vajra Guru Padma Siddhi Hum, at least that's how it's done if you're practiced in that yoga, which is Om Ah Hum, already explained. Then, Diamond Teacher—hard teacher, masculine-teacher, tough teacher, hard: samsara, maya; hardness *[raps table]*—Vajra Guru, Padma (lotus, feminine, soft) Padma Siddhi: Lotus power, flower power. Why don't I chant that for a couple of minutes, because that's an interesting new addition to the American yoga scene. Since Hare Krishna became a kind of pop mantra, you know, penetrated interestingly, this is as far as I know the second important mantra to hit America in the seventies. *[Chants five minutes.]*

Try Om, it's interesting . . . Close your lips at the end of the "Ooooommm" without clenching your teeth: it gives a funny vibrational massage to the front of your skull . . . *[continues with Om]* . . . you have to straighten your backbone to get enough air in your lungs . . . and breathe in your lower abdomen like natural childbirth breathing . . . straighten your backbone and let your belly hang out. *[Ends with Om Ah Hum.]*

If that's done properly, actually you can get a slight buzz, literal physiologic buzz out of it. It's supposed to be equivalent to *kundalini*, what is called serpent power, or *kundalini* power, which is a bodily sensation, and also a mental sensation of the space of emptiness in a body. So, to conclude the question, finally I feel like a radiant but empty body. So that there is no disturbance in the radiant body, which is the same as all body, all consciousness.

Q: *What about Leary and his scene—how do you see it?*

AG: I got a card from him two days ago, said everything's all right, surprisingly. So I don't know. I like him, I trust him; I think he's done heroic work, like he's taken all the lightning and the anxiety and all the shit for the entire nation's change of consciousness, to the extent that psychedelic drugs have catalyzed it. So I think he deserves like a great big reward and a giant professorship of psychology at the Supreme University of Consciousness in Minneapolis. He's done the best formulations of terminology about set and setting conditioning the Acid experience; he is really the best and most acute and most adept psychologist and the most serious psychologist in this area, of psychedelic psychology, and he obviously is being persecuted for his philosophy and his professional practice. You know—sent to jail for two roaches.

Now, when they sent him to jail, when he was sentenced to ten years in California and in Texas—ten years each, twenty years—and when he was denied bail, the judges pronounced that he was being given heavy sentence for small amounts of grass specifically because of his writings and teachings, because his writings and teachings were "a menace to the community." And that's a very important basic fact: he's not in jail for two roaches, because almost nobody except political prisoners get sent up so long for roaches, particularly not a college professor with a good record who's never been busted. He was sent up ostensibly by the judges for his public philosophizing—if you read the trial sentencing record—and sentenced for his texts, specifically a text in *Playboy*. And fragments of text of his testimony at the Chicago Trial were clipped out of the newspapers by the prosecuting attorney, and given to the judge as appendix material to show him why Leary should be kept in jail and denied bail and be given a long sentence.

So Leary therefore is in the class of a philosopher or professional savant who is being persecuted for his philosophy, his language, rather than any action that was illegal, that they could get him on. So I see him as one of the major scandals of the Academy. In other words, any psychology department in any university which does not ardently desire to have Leary on its faculty is a psychology department betraying its academic responsibility. Any law faculty which is not interested in his case as a case of abuse of constitutional propriety is ignorant of its scholarship responsibilities. Any student body accepting the fake materialistic mechanical science subsidized by Department of Defense grants and ignoring the sciences and arts proposed by Leary is doing itself out of an education. So I see Leary's situation as one of the major academic and legal scandals presently floating in the American karma.

He's the only man I know that no country in the world will have. So that means he couldn't be wrong. No bureaucracy in any country will accept him—which means that he couldn't be all bad. Everybody else can go somewhere—Communist, revolutionary, this one, that one, China, Russia, Korea—but he can't go anywhere, except to Algerian refuge under the aegis of Cleaver and Cleaver's very irritable with him, so Leary must be uncomfortable. And I don't know what can be done, but sumpin' oughta be done.*

Q: *I don't know too much about Zen, but how do you feel that complete sense consciousness or sense awareness would mix with Zen consciousness?*

AG: I'm not a specialist in Zen; I know some Zen people like Gary Snyder and Watts and Roshi Suzuki, and I've done some sitting, formal Zen sitting, that involves abdominal breathing, so that's my preparation for any answer. If mind consciousness is stilled, that is if the matter babble behind the ear, yakety-yak ticker-tape conceptual language conscious linear gossip inside the cranium, is shut up—which means a stillness in the vocal cords and vocal apparatus, and a stillness in the body—if by accident or design or practice you're able to turn off the phantasm consciousness that beclouds sense consciousness, smell, taste, touch, optical, because you're not beclouding the doors of perception with preconception, you're not inventing universes which overlie this universe.

To be a little more precise: if I'm looking at you but thinking "Gary Snyder's supposed to get here tomorrow night, what time is he supposed

---

*On January 13, 1973, in the Kabul, Afghanistan, airport Dr. Timothy Leary was kidnapped in Watergate style by agents of the U.S. government and returned to the U.S. in violation of international law. Prior to his escape conviction his bail was set at five million dollars, the highest for any single person in American history.

In December 1973, Dr. Leary was transferred from Folsom Prison to the California Medical Facility at Vacaville, where he is serving a six-month to ten-year sentence for possession of two roaches. He has also been given a five-year sentence (to be served consecutively, not concurrently) for his escape from San Luis Obispo, and the state of Texas has a ten-year "hold" on him for his Laredo arrest.

In the ten years since he first attempted to live peaceably with dignity of purpose in Millbrook, New York (where his privacy and freedoms were initially violated by Dutchess County law officers including G. Gordon Liddy), Dr. Leary has been arrested fourteen times and undergone seven prosecutions. His current legal co-ordinators are Vasilios Choulos and Kent Russell, of the Melvin Belli Law firm, in San Francisco.

to get here?" I'm not seeing you or addressing you, so I'm not in sensory contact with you, simple as that. That's what I meant by phantasm consciousness overlying present moment sense consciousness.

Q: *I was sort of wondering whether you are aiming toward a complete transcendence of the physical world.*

AG: I don't know, I don't know. Depends on which yogi you go talk to. The Zen people don't aim at transcendence—they aim at no-mind in which the question of transcendence or immersion in the world is a piece of conceptual furniture dragged in (from being told to go to the bathroom in the toilet, you know) from conceptual body habit training from childhood grammar school. The Zen people would say that mind is conditioned to manufacture displaced fantasy mostly, fantasy continuously displaced from this Place: where we are right now. And so the whole point of a Zen tea ceremony is precise, accurate, attentive gestures to the object in front of you, to neutral objects like the tea, the tea bowl, and to the pouring and mixing of the tea. So it's sort of like an exercise in the staying aware of just exactly what you're doing instead of drifting off, even to transcend.

Q: *Yeah, because if you completely transcended, you probably wouldn't write poetry, I guess.*

AG: Yep, likely. Except when you say *transcend*—we haven't defined what we're talking about really—

Q: *Well, I'm referring to states in which you leave this, uh, physical . . .*

AG: . . . body. Yeah. I don't know, I've never done that. I've never left the body entirely, so I don't know. I'm not a yogi, either, like that—I mean, I don't have that much *siddhi,* power; I don't have that much experience.

Q: *If you don't indulge in the babble of the mind, how do you verbalize your consciousness into poetry?*

AG: Occasionally I just simply turn on and listen to the radio—it's just like listening to the radio—and then write it down. It goes on, except if you focus attention elsewhere. See, like if I'm chanting, for instance, conceptual language does stop. That's sort of the interesting thing about chanting—so see what it can do to a room. If I can stop my conceptual fantasy by forming myself or my identity into a column of breath that goes Om, vibrating in the body, and if other people do that or it sets up a sympathetic vibration in the sympathetic nervous systems of other people—you know, like if you pluck one chord on a string and the other chords vibrate—so if other people tune in on that, sometimes it can reduce the room to a sort of frankly physical place where everybody is sitting in the immediate eternal present. Without having another thought, except being where they are. Or that's the ideal, that's my fantasy of what I'm doing, half the time. Actually someone told me that was the effect of the singing this afternoon on the quad. But I guess that varies with people. Does that seem like a believable fantasy?

Q: *But it seems like when you're chanting you can't create something.*

AG: No. You simply *are*, without creating any further. You're not creating any more universe than there already is right there.

Q: *What's the advantage of that?*

AG: Um, man, haven't you ever wanted to rest from all your godlike creations? Ain't you created enough? I mean, what's the advantage of creating more? There's already so much here. And if you pay attention to what's already here, like accounting what's already here, being aware of what's already here, then you can go out and create some more stuff to fit in over there, if there's a place that's missing a piece of stuff like a piano or hard-on.

Q: *Then creating is kind of like a relief of guilt.*

AG: It's more a seeking out of an eternal state of consciousness, or trying to articulate an eternal state of consciousness, or seeking a response from other self in terms that I was talking about before—that we are really all one self. Or at least that's how I see creating, that's how I see my poetry. You see it as a byproduct of guilt of some kind?

Q: *Well, it seems to be that people who feel guilty are the most creative. People who fit in perfectly just become blocked, they don't have the rough edges.*

AG: I don't agree with you. There are different varieties of creation, but all those people making those breakable and atmosphere-befouling automobiles are also creating. They sure are creating, and creating real solid objects.

Q: *What do you think about this town, in terms of the technology you were talking about this morning?*

AG: I haven't seen enough of the town. The campus is low, which is interesting. I was at UCLA last weekend, and, gee, it's all these giant monolith buildings, whereas here everything's low. I don't know. I imagine that the agronomic-economics here is like bank capitalist creepy Moloch agricultural technology rather than anything more musical.

Q: *I guess that's the foundation.*

AG: Yeah, and I assume they haven't converted to anything more humanistic in their agronomy, or anything more ecologically attuned.

Q: *I was wondering what you thought about the layout and the architecture of the place, and the way the money is spent. The construction.*

AG: It's nicer than most of the modern U.C. schools I've seen. Partly because it's surrounded by farm fields, so that's sort of interesting.

Q: *Yeah, but aside from comparing it to other places if you had a chance to live here, how would you feel?*

AG: Well, what do you think about it?

Q: *Well, I don't like it a lot of the time.*

AG: Because of what particular details? From what particulars in the construction?

Q: *From I guess the planning of it . . .*

AG: In what particular detail?

Q: *A lot of it's very cold.*

AG: Like where? How about this room, say?

Q: *Well, classes and the administrative building.*

AG: Oh, I passed that by car. I didn't get a close-up look but I was surprised. I was told that was like the big tall building from which you could see the entire campus, so I was surprised to see it was only about four stories.

Q: *Well, nothing else is very high around here.*

AG: Well, it was a relief it wasn't a twenty-story monolith, it was only four stories. That was almost like a—

Q: *Well, the trees planted on campus, I don't think it's natural, like it's all landscaped all the way long.*

AG: Yeah, there is very little wilderness around, that's true. But then this is a flat plain anyway.

Q: *What do you think about the environment in human terms, from a sociopolitical view point?*

AG: The only thing I feel about that, a little, is I wonder if it isn't a little like an artificial paradise in the sense that it's nicer here than Berkeley—it's calmer and more tranquil, but at the same time it's a little island of luxury and conspicuous consumption in the midst of a starving, torn-apart, freaked-out world. And I don't know to what extent the luxury here depends upon the exploitation of the Third World. Probably a good deal. I was at Kent [State University] and a lot of other places the last couple of months (this is the last reading I give for quite a while). So after two months of running around fifteen or twenty schools, I came to a view I hadn't seen before, similar to the hard-hat proposition: which is, basically, that the students in the United States are enjoying a very specialized way of life, compared to the rest of the world. They've really got it easy—you know, they have these great lounges, they can go around in their shorts and be as sexy as they want and get laid all they want, they get fed in cafeterias, and they have an unlimited supply of milk like big babies, and then they get these big jars of peanut butter like overgrown television pubescents, get all the books they want . . . Sort of like—at Kent State, for instance, it's sort of like an old folks' home for young people in that sense. Leading a very cloistered, sheltered, and spoon-fed life, you know, in which all the charming indulgences of American youth are indulged in, like having an unlimited milk supply and having little cars and gasoline they can run around in, bicycles and dates, and nice dormitories—a little cramped, you know, that's the only obvious sort of squeeze on consciousness there, that the dormitory rooms are being made smaller and smaller and the buildings larger.

From *Allen Verbatim: Lectures on Poetry, Politics, Consciousness*, edited by Gordon Ball (New York: McGraw-Hill, 1974), 3–13. Reprinted by permission of the Allen Ginsberg Estate and Gordon Ball.

A Conversation with Allen Ginsberg

JOHN TYTELL, 1974

WILLIAM S. BURROUGHS, author of dozens of books, including the Beat classics *Junkie* and *Naked Lunch*, was a lifelong friend and mentor of Allen Ginsberg. Introduced to Ginsberg and Kerouac by Lucien Carr in 1944, Burroughs, older, more worldly and intellectually developed than Kerouac and Ginsberg, quickly became their teacher, advising them on books to read, places to go in New York City, even offering them amateur psychoanalysis. Burroughs had very little inclination to write, at least in the early years of their friendship, but when he eventually put his thoughts on paper, Ginsberg and Kerouac offered enthusiastic encouragement, both helping with the editing of *Naked Lunch*, Ginsberg acting as Burroughs's agent in trying to find a publisher for his controversial work.

John Tytell's *Naked Angels: The Lives and Literature of the Beat Generation* (1976), a seminal study of the Beat Generation writers, found Tytell interviewing Ginsberg and Burroughs as part of his research. The following interview, conducted for Tytell's book, illustrates the great influence that Burroughs had on Ginsberg and other Beat Generation writers. Carl Solomon, to whom "Howl" is dedicated, sat in on the interview.

INTERVIEWER: *What was Burroughs's impact on you and Kerouac in the mid-forties?*

GINSBERG: Kerouac and I went to see Burroughs in his apartment around Riverside Drive below Columbia, Ninety-second Street. We were curious. We understood that Burroughs was very intelligent and to us mysterious because he had been to Europe in the thirties, and had married a Hungarian countess, we thought, to get her out of Europe. He showed us pictures he had of Berlin friends in 1936, and told us about people going around and saying, "Won't you have some uppies, my dear?" for cocaine, introducing that whole mythology of old bohemian European use of drugs.

INTERVIEWER: *Had you tried drugs before meeting Burroughs?*

GINSBERG: No.

INTERVIEWER: *So that was a crucial introduction?*

GINSBERG: He didn't immediately introduce drugs at all. It wasn't until about a year later, through Huncke and Vicky Arminger, who was in that auto crash with me.

INTERVIEWER: *The one that Jane Kramer describes?*

CARL SOLOMON: *Before you went to P.I. [Columbia Psychiatric Institute]?*

GINSBERG: There were a lot of Benzedrine inhalers so the first drug was speed, which was introduced by Vicky rather than Bill, and then, around '45 or '46, through Huncke and Bill Garver and Phil White, there was morphine on the scene. So I took morphine at about the same time Bill first did, in the same week. He has described that situation, meeting Huncke, and trying to unload some morphine not knowing really what it was. Bill had a gun he was trying to get rid of, and so he traded it for a box of stolen Syrettes of morphine—these were war stocks of morphine that soldiers carried around as part of their first aid. Grass didn't come in until about a year later, in '47.

INTERVIEWER: *Was that the first time grass appeared in New York?*

GINSBERG: Well, for me anyway. Burroughs had had some in the heydays, gaydays of East St. Louis toodleloo.

SOLOMON: *Ronnie Gold and I used to eat benny inhalers in about '49.*

GINSBERG: That's what Kerouac used a lot for writing at first, too. And that's what Joan Burroughs took, but she was taking two or three inhalers a day, finally, when we were all living together a little later.

INTERVIEWER: *In what other ways did Burroughs influence you?*

GINSBERG: With books: Kafka, Korzybski's *Science and Sanity*, Spengler's *Decline of the West* which he gave Kerouac, Blake, Rimbaud, Yeats's *A Vision*, Cocteau's *Opium*.

SOLOMON: *Melville?*

GINSBERG: No, that was Jack's interest. Especially, a little later, *Pierre*, because of the euphuistic, packed poetical Shakespearean quality of the prose.

INTERVIEWER: *And the Gothicism. Were there other books?*

GINSBERG: Yes. Celine's *Journey to the End of the Night*, Auden, Hart Crane, and Eliot, which I borrowed. It was my first introduction to modern literature really, and also to modern ideas.

INTERVIEWER: *Would you say there were similarities between Eliot and Burroughs?*

GINSBERG: St. Louis origins, yes. Going to England, finally. They also had the same banker look, which Bill always had but which he cultivated more later on. Bill actually applied to be in the O.S.S. because he knew Wild Bill Donovan from Harvard, and he was of that elite aristocracy that would have fitted into it, except that he had some early record of having cut off his little finger with a chicken shears to see what it was like.

SOLOMON: *Wasn't that to get out of the service?*

GINSBERG: And Bill's hatred of the American-secret-police-bureaucracy grows from the fact that they wouldn't have him in it. I mean, he *knows* them, that social type and mind.

INTERVIEWER: *When were you introduced to Gnostic ideas?*

GINSBERG: The first time I heard the word *Gnostic* mentioned was when Kerouac and I went to see Raymond Weaver, at Columbia, who had done the first biography of Melville, *Herman Melville: Mariner and Mystic*, and had discovered the text of *Billy Budd*. Weaver was this great scholar who shared an office with Mark Van Doren, and Jack brought Weaver a novel called *The Sea Is My Brother*, his first poetical novel, and Weaver gave him a little list of books to read, like the *Egyptian Gnostics* and either the *Tibetan Book of the Dead* or the *Egyptian Book of the Dead*, I can't remember.

SOLOMON: *Burroughs's first contact with me was when he read my first article. He said the insights were psychological and not deep psychic.*

INTERVIEWER: *I felt Burroughs's influence in your last book,* The Fall of America.

GINSBERG: Thematically, yes. But technically, Bunting, saying to condense more, that I had "too many words," getting rid of extra syntactical fat allows more perfume to verbs and nouns.

INTERVIEWER: *How come you chose as your Preface to* Fall of America *that selection from Whitman's* Democratic Vistas *on adhesiveness? It seemed so ironic.*

GINSBERG: Except that it does point to a goal and an ideal and a human potentiality that America was supposed to fulfill, because that was the prophecy, the need, and the psychological condition of American democracy, and Whitman named it and particularized it very clearly in that passage. Also it gives credence, historical background, and traditional justification to my own adhesive poems.

SOLOMON: *I was interested when I read* Fall *mainly in the sex, being a Bronx boy.*

INTERVIEWER: *In the tender obscenity of poems like "Please Master"?*

SOLOMON: *And in "Graffiti."*

INTERVIEWER: *"Jessore Road" is especially Blakean, its metric, rhyme scheme, and the whole feeling of the poem like a long extended "London."*

GINSBERG: The consequence of three years working on Blake songs. It was the first poem I wrote to music with chords, intended to be chanted and sung. I had finished two albums of Blake's *Innocence and Experience.*

INTERVIEWER: *I think I saw you singing the poem on television last year with a whole room of people?*

GINSBERG: Yeah. With Dylan and Happy Traum. I wrote "Jessore Road" to have something really sublime to present to Dylan to record. So the performance that you saw on TV was a first performance without any rehearsal because I had finished typing the poem that afternoon, and I had written it the day before.

INTERVIEWER: *You have written a number of poems in a very short period of time, haven't you? Didn't you write "Sunflower Sutra" while Kerouac was impatiently standing at your door waiting for you?*

GINSBERG: Also poems like "A Strange New Cottage in Berkeley" and "Supermarket in California" which, incidentally, were part of one composition, and later cut apart.

INTERVIEWER: *How were you affected by Kerouac's notion of no revision?*

GINSBERG: "Sunflower Sutra" is almost completely untouched from the original. It took me a long time to get on to Kerouac's idea of writing without revision. I did it by going to his house where he sat me down with typewriter and said, "Just write a poem!" So I did about the Statue of Liberty, which I never published because it wasn't any good. But I did get the idea of how interesting it could be, the accidents that come up if you commit yourself irrevocably to accepting the traces of your mind during the composition.

INTERVIEWER: *What led you to your concept of "undifferentiated consciousness"?*

GINSBERG: Blake.

INTERVIEWER: *The experience in 1948?*

GINSBERG: Which convinced me that it was possible—just like the Cézanne thing, reproducing the *petites sensations* of experience. That's why I became interested in Cézanne after Blake, because when I looked at his painting I got a sudden shock of eternal thrill, that sensation of eternal space being reconstituted—but the experience of Blake was that through poetry you could catalyze in the reader the experience of *Pater Omnipotens Eterna Deus*, an experience of eternal consciousness; but then later on, reading Zen and other philosophy, I would find different nomenclature for it.

INTERVIEWER: *In which of your own poems do you think you've come closest to achieving this quality?*

GINSBERG: I don't know because it seems to happen accidentally, but apparently in "Howl," where it is sufficient to alter people's minds.

INTERVIEWER: *What about poems like "Journal Night Thoughts" or "Television Was a Baby Crawling toward That Deathchamber"?*

GINSBERG: No, that's like a full chaotic consciousness. There is too much excitement and activity in the consciousness, that's amphetamine partly. So it depends on what we mean by "undifferentiated consciousness" . . . but if we mean empty, *Sunyata*, in which everything comes in quietly, simultaneously, then I don't think I've written anything quiet enough for that—but to get enough excitement to break people's mind systems open, through rhythmic means partly, "Howl" works.

INTERVIEWER: *Burroughs was interested in conditioning, wasn't he?*

GINSBERG: Yeah. Another book that he gave us at that early time was a book by someone named Jacobson called *Progressive Relaxation*, which was a sort of Western homemade yoga—just lie down and begin untensing your whole body from the skull to the toes, muscle by muscle and portion by portion, which is similar to the *Satipatthana*, or body-feeling-mind and mind-object meditation of Burmese Buddhists, which is primary Hinayana Buddhist Yoga.

INTERVIEWER: *What is word conditioning?*

GINSBERG: That was covered by Korzybski's *Science and Sanity* immediately when he pointed out that words were not identical to the things that they represent. And the best example of that was when Lucien Carr and I had this big argument as to whether if you carved a walking stick on the moon, was it art or not? Burroughs said, "I never heard of such a stupid question!" In other words, art is whatever you want to define it as. It's only a three-letter word. Burroughs's attitude was that we were giving the word an essential identity outside of any use we might make of it, so if we wanted to use the word art to describe the walking stick on the moon, then it was art, and if we didn't want to use the word art, it wasn't. He just said: "It's too starved an argument for my sword," so he cut through arbitrary conceptions like a Zen master. It's like a goose in the bottle *koan*: if you put a full-grown goose inside a bottle with a narrow neck, how do you get the goose out without breaking the bottle, or damaging or bruising the goose? That's one of the first *koans* that you meditate on if you're studying Zen. Another is the *koan*, "Does the dog have a Buddha nature" the Zen master Jo-jo was once asked, and he answered, "Wu," which means no in Chinese. Why did Jo-jo say *Wu*? ... Well, how do you get the goose out?

INTERVIEWER: *I don't know. How?*

GINSBERG: *[claps hands loudly]* It's out! Same way you put it in, with words. It's only a conceptual bottle. So Burroughs resolved the problem of whether a walking stick on the moon was art or not in exactly the same way.

INTERVIEWER: *Did Pound reinforce this approach to language?*

GINSBERG: I hadn't started reading Pound then.

INTERVIEWER: *What about when you visited him in '67? Was he talking then?*

GINSBERG: A little bit, in answer to very specific questions. I have a journal I kept on that which should appear in the next *City Lights Journal.* I wrote it a long time back, and gave it to Laughlin [James Laughlin, publisher of New Directions], and he sent it to Olga Rudge who got upset, and I couldn't at first figure out over what. Laughlin said it was because I mentioned in the journal about how I had smoked a stick of grass at the table on Pound's eighty-first birthday. Then I saw Olga Rudge earlier this year in London, and apparently she objected to my quoting something Pound said to me. He said, *The Cantos* are a mess, stupidity and ignorance all the way through, and the worst stupidity was stupid, suburban anti-Semitic prejudice."

INTERVIEWER: *Why did she object to that? I mean, had Pound said it?*

GINSBERG: Uh hum. But she maintained that Pound was not anti-Semitic, and it was a misunderstanding to think of him as anti-Semitic in the beginning.

INTERVIEWER: *Was Pound's statement an apology?*

GINSBERG: Well, she didn't want to see it as an apologia, and it wasn't precisely, I think; he was just being generous and extraordinarily sociable, and Prospero-like, taking some of the burden.

INTERVIEWER: *I know how important Buddhism is in connection with your own work and Kerouac's but is there any connection in Burroughs's?*

GINSBERG: There is often an emphasis on open blue space like nirvana or transcendence, of conceptual mind prison . . . especially in his recent work, the idea of empty space in every direction, which is very similar to the Buddhist view of *Sunyata,* oddly enough. "Out of the body experience," or "escape from the frightened, nagging, aging flesh"—that's Burroughs's phrase—is like the Buddhist view of release of unconditioned beginningless and endless suchness, nirvana—but Bill wouldn't go for nirvana, as it were, he would see that as a con. But nonetheless what he seems to be after recently, and I think it was implicit all along, is another modality or plane of consciousness, where view is unconditioned. The images in all of the books following *Naked Lunch,* like "the blue tide" that comes in on *yage,* or the idea of "rub out the word," "all out of the body and into space," as at the end of the *Yage Letters,* indicate a place that is very similar to the infinite spaciousness of Tibetan Buddhism.

INTERVIEWER: *Still, isn't this search, no matter what its end, conducted along a corridor of brutal self-examination and explosions of pain?*

GINSBERG: In one view, that pain is part of the "apparent thought, feeling, and sensory phenomena," but Burroughs's late theory is that there's a squeeze on the body by a virus coming from Venus to make it as painful a place as possible, purposely contacting everybody into limited space, so Burroughs's remedy is unlimited space.

SOLOMON: *Did Burroughs and Genet have conversations when they met in Chicago?*

GINSBERG: Yes, a lot of conversation, I was with them. They loved each other and cared for each other. Bill talked a lot and Genet listened and laughed a lot, and told me Burroughs was very sweet and tender.

SOLOMON: *We once characterized Burroughs as the American Genet.*

GINSBERG: Genet told me he had read Burroughs in French, and that he liked his work and his person, and they went around in taxicabs together and marched together in tear-gas situations.

SOLOMON: *What happened then, Genet escaped into the sewer or something?*

GINSBERG: No. The guards [in the park during the Democratic National Convention in 1968] said that we had to disperse: So David Dellinger, who was negotiating with the guards, called me up to chant mantras to keep everything quiet which I did for about twenty minutes in this tight situation. Then Dellinger announced that we had been ordered to disperse. We felt we had a legal right to stay; all those who wanted to leave could, and the rest would invoke passive resistance, sit on the ground and offer themselves for arrest. Genet, being in the country illegally, having come in through the Canadian border, had to cut. So I think Richard Seaver took Genet away, and Burroughs and I stayed . . . And Genet gave a speech to the Yippies saying that he hoped that some day the skyline of Chicago would be covered with vines, that he felt it was necessary for writers to be with the younger people in body as well as sympathy.

SOLOMON: *I remember reading that Genet said at that time that he had had much experience eluding the police so it was nothing to him.*

INTERVIEWER: *I'd like to return to Burroughs's theory of evil. What would you say is its source?*

GINSBERG: Well, originally it was analyzed by William Lee, the factualist (perhaps representative of a trust of giant insects from another galaxy) in *Naked Lunch.* But since then, in *Nova Express* and *Ticket That Exploded,* and more recently in *Exterminator!* and *The Job* and *Wild Boys,* the agency of the hallucinating Word is a virus from Venus so it's not other galaxies anymore—it's an external, extraterrestrial threat from within our own solar system.

INTERVIEWER: *Would you go along with the notion that madness is the norm in Burroughs's fiction?*

GINSBERG: I would say the norm is metamorphosis. In Burroughs's fiction, madness is the normal behavior of the political world, but it's also a medium that A. J. Benway and the factualists are able to handle and deal with and use as the material for their examination ... and sometimes get caught in, as is possible for an explorer to get caught in a sticky wicket, or as Burroughs himself feels that he has been caught in certain areas that he could not handle, with drugs like psilocybin and LSD, or *yage* originally. But madness is *not* his ultimate goal, just the obstacle. This is why Burroughs's geography is so similar to Gnostic and Tibetan procedural maps. The wrathful deities are the guardians of the gate to *Sunyata,* blue space ... except Burroughs is ascribing all these wrathful deities to a plot by the Control Forces. So his books really are investigations of his consciousness to "trace along the word lines" to the *source* of the control.

INTERVIEWER: *So he has a greater conspiratorial sense of history than even you do, I guess?*

GINSBERG: Mine is a little more mundane, like investigations of CIA involvement with dope trafficking in Indochina (which was, I think, a successful investigation).

INTERVIEWER: *What about applying Longfellow's remark in the transcendentalist utopians, that they expressed the "divine insanity of noble minds"?*

GINSBERG: I think Burroughs would reject that as sentimental rhetoric because he feels that he is more of a precise scientist investigating regions of consciousness forbidden to common understanding by the Control agencies, and the *danger* of such investigation is physical pain, madness, "the Ovens," but the factualist investigator armed with various antivirus exercises such as rubbing out the word can ultimately resist, though there may be certain aspects which you can't resist ... and what you can't resist that most dismays him at present comes in the phrase "At Hiroshima all was lost" ... or so he said this year when I went to see him to find out what he was thinking lately. He said that the project was to get out of the body—as the soul or spirit gets out of the body—but that the problem with the atom bomb is that is temperature is so high that it's a "killer of souls." So human beings have arrived at a situation where they can be the Killer of Souls. So I said, traditionally, with the Gnostics or Buddhists, there is no soul to kill, the void is impervious to the metaphysical heat of the bomb. He answered that all that Buddhist and Hindu mythology was very amateur, compared with the kind of precise investigations that might be conducted now in a highly chemical and technological age. For Burroughs, yoga and Buddhism are primitive methods of achieving detachment; it can now be done more immediately through electronic means.

INTERVIEWER: *But less intuitional.*

GINSBERG: Well, just as he uses the physical table as a place to put his mind to cut up—putting the words on the table rather than inner meditation only—so he sees mechanical aids, like a Yankee inventor, as a possibility; and also he says we can't turn back, we've already advanced into a highly mechanized, electronic dimension, and that may be the Path. So he puts down the rural commune, back-to-nature aspect of what Gary Snyder and myself are doing, saying that it's retrogressive, that we're too deeply plunged into the science-fiction reality situation now. For Burroughs, the problem is not so much the fact of science or experiment, as it is that it's being *controlled*, that secrets are being kept—like the Army is the only one that has real license to experiment with acid anymore, and maybe Scientology is another extension of the CIA network. So his idea is "All secrets out" now.

INTERVIEWER: *So resistance becomes openness?*

GINSBERG: Right, by making use of secret material and turning it against Control Agencies, and by realizing that there are a few simple principles of technology that everyone can understand and master which had been obscured by the authoritarian Controllers. That's why he's been experimenting with the cutting up of sounds and playing them back: in other words, feeding back the control images to the Control Central, in the hope of setting up anti-image consciousness feedback that will explode their Control machine.

INTERVIEWER: *That's in* The Ticket That Exploded.

GINSBERG: And which he practiced at Chicago when he came into the Convention Hall with his tape recorder with all sorts of riot sounds from Tangiers—like shutters slamming—and started spraying all these sounds out on the balcony of the convention, and within an hour the place was in an uproar.

INTERVIEWER: *Is the terrifying chaos in Burroughs's fiction purposeful?*

GINSBERG: I think so. He would maintain that he is making propositions and hypotheses, which he examines by means of language and imagination. So chaos—transfiguration is a better word, really—is only the preliminary guardian of the sacred extraterrestrial area of consciousness. The end is no *dérèglement de tous les sens* but clear vision, not chaos but total silence and calm like a great blue tide flooding the body. And *dérèglement de tous les sens* is not even so much a means as it is a by-product of the pursuit through to the other side of phenomena, the disruption of the apparently normal order determined by the CIA and the Control Forces. In fact, he feels that they are responsible for the chaotic apparitions, the fear, the Ovens, the images of death. What he is saying over and over, also, is that death is the greatest con, that it has been created by the Controllers to scare everybody, and there's really nothing to fear.

INTERVIEWER: *Is he still involved with the Scientologists?*

GINSBERG: Only in denouncing them. He wrote a long attack on them as a fascist organization in *Rolling Stone*. I went to supper with him and Giordias and heard another terror story about the Scientologists— which is that Giordias published a book attacking Scientology, and they sued him to try and stop the book and they lost the suit, so they organized a letter-writing campaign to the British Home Office complaining that Giordias was a pornographer, and so the Police raided Giordias and seized 125,000 volumes and drove him out of business in England. So he couldn't defend himself because his assets had been seized. And many things like that have happened, so Burroughs has stacked the Scientologists as an extension of the control apparatus that offers people hints of exercises that are useful, but which hangs them up in the middle of the exercise.

INTERVIEWER: *How does Burroughs see his own function as a writer relating to this control system?*

GINSBERG: The virus from Venus (as before a trust of giant insects from mother galaxy) or as in other times the CIA, or the economic control monopolists, or the antisex forces, are all resumed in terms of Power Addiction. So Burroughs wants to discover the source, where the original imposition of brainwash comes from. He sees his job also as an explorer and inventor of how-to books, how to combat brainwash, how to liberate consciousness from the condition imposed on it by the Control Forces.

INTERVIEWER: *So if the reader can read his books, he is along the way to violating that conditioning by virtue of experiencing Burroughs's own techniques, just as the readers who read* The Waste Land *learned a new kind of perception?*

GINSBERG: Yes. Throughout his books there are all these suggestions on how to observe your own speech and behavior to see who were the people who influenced you, and to trace your attitudes, gestures, styles, words, and tones of voice to the original people you were imitating—it your father, teachers, lovers, or whoever was leaving an impression on you. Last time I saw him, he told me that "whoever leaves an impression on you is a vampire." His statement was so impressive . . . striking, I mean . . . curious . . . that I went home that night and had a dream of William Blake as a vampire because Blake had in a sense invaded my consciousness, left an impression which struck me and stuck me there revolving around the corpse of that impression for decades . . . which was a violation of the Tantric injunction not to cling to any impression. So Burroughs is saying that for his own role he wants to make "himself" obsolete.

From *Partisan Review* 4, no. 2 (Summer 1974): 253–62. Reprinted by permission of John Tytell.

An Interview with Allen Ginsberg

JAMES McKENZIE, 1978

ARTHUR AND KIT KNIGHT deserve much more credit than they received in their lifetimes for their work in championing the lives and work of the Beat Generation writers and poets. Their journal, *unspeakable visions of the individual,* in which this interview appeared, featured previously unpublished poetry, journal writings, photographs, letters, and interviews that presented the Beats in a serious light.

This interview, published as part of the Knights' *unspeakable visions* series, was conducted when Ginsberg and nearly every other influential Beat Generation figure were participating in a conference focusing on Beat writings and history, and caught Ginsberg in an expansive mood. As usual, he was able to tie together a wide-ranging list of social and literary topics, including an in-depth discussion of his friendship with Gary Snyder, a poet of considerable influence on Ginsberg.

***

THE FOLLOWING INTERVIEW took place at Dan Eades's home on the last day of the Fifth Annual Writers Conference at the University of North Dakota, March 1974. The scene before the interview began was a miniature of the week-long City Lights Conference of which it was one of the concluding parts. Gregory Corso and Kenneth Rexroth had taken turns noisily walking off a fractious, sometimes stormy marathon Open Mike discussion, each protesting loudly the other's words and conduct. Each time it was Ginsberg who patiently reknit the ragged threads of the panel discussion: "Now, Kenneth, come on. The problem is that what we're dealing with here is only a sample of the difficulties that we have in America in getting dialogue going, Kenneth, in which we have to deal with all sorts of aggressions, and control our own aggressions in order to come to some resolutions where we act in the community." Allen's entreaties prevailed and Rexroth and Corso rejoined the panel, the discussion proceeding with only little less anarchy.

With just a few hours between his final Open Mike session and the Ginsberg–Orlovsky reading that night, there was not much time for the interview, and a similar chaos reigned: technicians tested sound equipment, people wondered where we could all get lunch, Peter continued his seamless web of exhortations against smoking and drinking, urging everyone to begin organic gardening and explaining how properly to chew peyote. Again it was Ginsberg who focused the activities. Without a word he began foraging through Eades's kitchen as though thoroughly familiar with it, opening drawers, rummaging through the refrigerator, clattering around until he had collected the ingredients for an enormous chef's salad, which he then assembled and served us all. Someone turned on the tape recorder as we ate, and the talk gradually crossed whatever the theoretical boundary is between conversation and interview.

—*James McKenzie*

JAMES MCKENZIE: *In our conversation on Tuesday, Gary [Snyder] spoke about how he was being influenced by you again and saw both a personal and—the way he put it—a movement-wide recognition of the Beats that was related to your recent serious study and turn towards the East, though he did go as far back as when you were with him in India. And I wondered how you would respond to that.*

ALLEN GINSBERG: Well, of course, I have always had Gary in mind so partly I'm taking a formal Buddhist meditation discipline in order to please Gary, and make him feel secure. That's sort of a minor shrewd extra reason—to keep the scene together and to continue the scene. I mean, all of us have an esthetic and dramatic, even melodramatic, view of ourselves as history, and what we've done as history; and we want it to come out all right. We always *did* want it to come out all right.

JM: *He talked, too, about his influence on you earlier to give up graduate studies, which I think Kerouac alludes to in* Dharma Bums. *Snyder has for a long time been someone that you said you wanted to "please."*

AG: Yeah. I learned from him a great deal. I learned mountain climbing from him, love of nature from him. When we went through India, he already was experienced in Buddhist iconography, and place histories, so that the two months we were there together at the beginning of my visit with Peter, we were able to take advantage of his Buddhist knowledge and go around to Sanchi, Ajanta and Elbra; and I think the first time I heard the Prajnaparamita ("Highest Perfect Wisdom") Sutra chanted was in a cave at Elbra, I believe, or Ajanta, where Gary sat down on a rock in the middle of a cave and chanted it the Sino-Japanese style. Before that Kerouac had laid Buddhism on me because he had studied that and was really quite a deep Buddhist and quite an adept Buddhist intellectual, according to Gary and according to other people who are expert. He was the one that turned me on to the Sanskrit form: "Buddha, saranam gochami, Dharma saranam gochami, Sangha saranam gochami," which he used to croon, sort of like Frank Sinatra *[here AG croons the Refugees],* which I think he was singing in '54 or '53 or maybe even earlier. I remember him singing in Berkeley when we were all living together in a cottage. Gary was always sitting, already back then.

JM: *Sitting?*

AG: Meditating, sitting is the technical word in Zen for meditating. Jack did some sitting at that time, also, and has recorded his experience of a sort of satori he had in a text called "The Scripture of the Golden Eternity." But when we went to India, we went to the historical places of Buddhism that Gary knew . . . we went to see Lama Govinda, and went to see the Dalai Lama, and so we touched certain Buddhist home bases that he knew about that I didn't know about. And then when I left India I went to see Gary in Kyoto where he lived near his temple, and I did some sitting there in his temple. I took part in a four-day sesshin with him. So Gary got me sitting in Kyoto. Then I did a lot of other experimenting with different forms of Hindu mantra chanting from the time I left India and left Gary and spent in the United States from '63 to '68 or so. I did all sorts of Hindu mantra chanting, and developed that—vocalization and concentration and finally got a good Hindu teacher who gave me a mantra for sitting—around November, 1970. And then finally we met a Tibetan teacher, Chogyam Trungpa, in 1971, after about a year of steady sitting. And then we sat with the mantra that *he* gave me, and finally last fall went to a Buddhist academy and did long sesshin—about ten hours a day—twenty-five days, as part of the seminary studies that we were doing, so that by the time I got out of there I was more familiar with what Gary had been talking about all along. So that now that I've been doing that I'm more able to transmit that than I was before, because I was transmitting mantra and ideology of Buddhism before and Hinduism, and now, sitting, I'm able to be like a little firmer and quieter and securer in what I'm proposing to students in audience or in poetry. And lately I've been including sitting sometimes as part of poetry reading. In other words, doing some mantra chanting, bringing it down to a low slow breath, and then maybe doing a ten-minute meditation with the audience.

JM: *You've talked about Gary's spiritual influence on you over the years; I wonder if you'd care to comment on any influence his poetics have had on your poetry?*

AG: We still haven't covered like the mutual thing in the Beat Generation in relation to the acid freak-out and the acid illumination in relation to meditation, which is what he was concerned with.

JM: *And Gary's sense of responsibility—O.K.*

AG: Yeah . . . well, we all had that sense of responsibility that way; we'd gone out and shot our mouths off and made public manifestation of our own private lives, which included acid and acid friendships as with Leary, for myself at any rate, or peyote, and all felt that since we had broken through early, and had experience from the early '50s with peyote, that we should be able to share that experience with any younger people that were turned on by our own behavior or articulations or symbols or poetries or dramas or public theory. And that got increasingly hard as police state closed down, particularly in the drug area, and as the regular respectable professors refused to deal with that area—well, doctors and psychiatrists gave it over into the hands of the police, or the police grabbed it out of their hands. So it was left to some extent to the poets to formulate some sort of public knowledge, to transmit granny wisdom about those things. Gary always knew all along, and I slowly came to realize, that the safest way of preparing the mind, people's or young kids' minds for psychedelic experiences is training in meditation to give them firm ground and firm balance and firm awareness of mind, clear mind. No trip, to cut down the horror tripping as well as the celestial tripping. The teacher I'm working with now, Chogyam Trungpa, is very strong on this particular point, not as a put-down of acid but as, you know, like finding an equilibrium.

JM: *When you say "no tripping," is that related to what you were saying on the panel about clutching after something, either good or bad, holding on to it?*

AG: Yeah. A choice statement of Dudjom Rinpoche, the head of the Hyingmapa branch of Tibetan Meditation Study, told me when I went to visit him in India bringing with me a tale of all sorts of LSD horrors, you know, bum trips. And he said, "If you see anything horrible, don't cling to it; if you see anything beautiful, don't cling to it," which is a straight Buddhist position, Manjusri's sword of intelligence cutting right through the mental knot. So we all felt that dramatic and historical responsibility for what we let loose, to the extent that we were responsible for letting anything loose on America, in terms of opening of consciousness. I mean, nobody knows whether we were catalysts, or inventing something, or just the froth riding on a wave of its own. We were all three, I suppose— froth on the wave of biological consciousness consequent on the over-crowding and the over-industrialization.

JM: *Is that something you've come to think about recently?*

AG: No, we knew that back in 1948–49. You see, Gary and I and others by '48 had had some kind of psychedelic breakthrough without drugs—that is psychedelic mind manifestation—which I've talked about at great length at other places [see *Paris Review* interview, 1965, and Preface to *Jail Notes* by Timothy Leary (New York: Douglas Books, 1970)], so no need to go through that here. There already was that; and by '58, around the time when the media began coming around really heavily, exploring what we were having to say and distorting it and projecting a Frankenstein vision of it all over America, by that time—I remember there was one night I lay in my bed, in the middle of the night, realizing that if all those people were coming around, we must have touched some nerve, and if what we were saying had any truth to it ... and then I shuddered in bed, realizing that America was going to take some awful fall and go through some great transmogrification and change because if other people's minds were going to be opened as ours were, or they were going to glimpse some of the nightmare of Moloch, of the money bank capitalist earth-eating monster realization that we already had, that everybody was going to go through a funny change. Like it took me to go through a bughouse to get adjusted to it, so I realized that in a sense we had an awesome responsibility that we had sort of intuited but hadn't asked for, but which I took very seriously, and realized it as a sort of national shiver around 1958—that it was really serious—that what we were talking about, though it seemed light and funny and, you know, beatnik humor and angels in the valleys and "High on the peak top, bats! And down in the valley the lamb," though it was all poetical, that there was strange penitrant awareness that we had been gifted with or latched on to.

JM: *Can you say what made you see that then?*

AG: We'd already had, by '48, some sort of alteration of our own private consciousnesses; by '55 we made some kind of public articulation of it; by '58 it had spread sufficiently so that the mass media were coming around for information, and by that time I realized that if our private fancies, our private poetries, were so serious that they absorbed the attention of the big, serious military generals who write for *Time* magazine, there must be something strange going on.

JM: *You're speaking of the discovery of the Beats, and that made you know it was ...*

AG: No. I'm speaking of the *exploitation* of the Beats—the Beat discovery is '52 or something. I'm talking about the mass media spread and exploitation, actually, in the stereotype characterization, the Frankenstein image that they put down. See, and as I saw Frankenstein image being laid down by everything from Congress for Cultural Freedom, *Encounter* magazine, through *Partisan Review*, through *Time* magazine, through the *New York Daily News*, you know, sort of like a yellow press image of what was originally a sort of ethereal and angelic perception of America, and the world, and the nature of the mind, I realized early that if they were going to do that to us who were relatively innocent—just a bunch of poets—if they were going to make *us* out to be the monsters, then they must have been making the whole universe out to be a monster all along, from the Communists to the radicals to anarchists to the Human Being in America; so then I began reflecting back that what we were doing had some kinship with what Whitman was doing in announcing large magnanimous full-consciousness of American Person. Then I began digging Whitman's use of the word "Person" and linking our own struggle back to the tradition that was immediately contractible in the Populist good heart of William Carlos Williams, with whom we were in direct contact; and that linked us up, both by study and personal contact and letter, with Pound and his struggle with America; and through Williams to a great extent with Alfred Steichen and the Bohemians of the '20s and An American Place Gallery; and forgotten figures like John Herrmann of 1932 who won a literary prize with Thomas Wolfe for a proletarian novel; and Sherwood Anderson for his examination of the beating heart of lonely souls in Winesburg, Ohio; and the strange, cranky privacy of Melville in his old age writing love stories to Billy Budd, the handsome sailor; and Thoreau pondering in the woods about his overgrowth of competitive materialism in his own time as distinct from solitary study of minute particular detail of nature of which he accomplished by himself; and Thoreau going to jail not to pay war taxes for the Mexican War. So when the mass media began creating a hallucinatory image of the poetry activity that we were involved with and took that as sort of like something to mock and make an enemy of, then I realized that the whole country had a false mentality built up which was almost on the scale of mass hallucination. And so in 1958, Independence Day, I wrote an essay ["Poetry, Violence, and the Trembling Lambs"; see *A Casebook on the Beat,* Thomas Parkinson, ed. (Crowell, N.Y., 1961)] saying that America was going to have a nervous breakdown, and that part of the cause of it could be located in that year's thirty-billion dollar military budget and the growth of military police state; that one aspect of it was the persecution of the junkies and the drug people who were basically sensitives who may or may not have been fucked up but needed compassion and medical care rather than Swastika-like police agencies chasing them down with guns, calling them "fiends," which is a terrible violation of the human spirit, to create a class of people in America called "fiends"—I mean, it's diabolical . . . once you realize that you've got a class of armed police calling another group "fiends," you've really got a situation so surrealistic and hallucinatory and violent that there could be no outcome but some massive nervous breakdown in America when people find out that they've not only been lied to but drawn into a dream of reality which is not only false but painful and bitter and murderous. So I began seeing very clearly a line of transmission, Gnostic insight—I think I picked up the Gnostic aspect of it very early from Raymond Weaver at Columbia, who was a friend of Kerouac's and mine, who suggested Kerouac read the Egyptian Gnostics. I never explored it until maybe '67, and picked up on the actual tradition, except through Blake as of '48 and Blake was also a Gnostic, and I had some direct transmission there. But I was seeing the transmission, in America, as a transmission of person, the concept of person, the feeling of person, as a breakthrough, a *reasonable* breakthrough, beyond the purely conceptual mind that had gone mad with the fake conceptions of thinking head cut off from the body and cut off from affective feeling. So when I was lying in bed one night in 1958 I shuddered, realizing that America was taking a fall, was going to have to take a big fall.

JM: *That's before the July 4th essay?*

AG: Probably around the same time, you know . . . yeah, the July 4th essay was written in [Michael] McClure's house in San Francisco. We had said relatively the same thing before. There's an early interview in the first City Lights *Journal for the Protection of All Beings* talking about . . . I wrote a whole bunch of essays around that time, one was for the *London Times*, one was published in *Evergreen* and also *San Francisco Chronicle*, and one was in the *Journal*—which were pretty good statements, prophetical—sort of summaries of what I felt it had been all about, that is our poetic activity, and the breakthrough into public consciousness of that; why I felt it was almost inevitable and historically charming and real and why it had some significance and what it represented. In other words, I think I was able to figure it out early, and I think everybody knew pretty much what it was all about. Rexroth certainly did. Gary did very clearly, in much finer detail than myself because he was already into not only realization of natural man as distinct from capitalist, or police-state man, but he also had a realization of birds, beasts and nature. He already was into nature and so was McClure. It took me a long time to catch up to that; not till '67 did I really get into ecological perspective as Gary already had.

JM: *What did it in '67? Was there something?*

AG: Yeah. I went to London to a Dialectics of Liberation and there I met Gregory Bateson and R. D. Laing, and a whole bunch of people; and Bateson gave a great lecture on ecological mind and perspectives, and just presented the information that Gary and McClure were talking about with our discourses on the Club of Rome about *Limits to Growth*. And Bateson said, you keep the heat up the way you're keeping it up and the fog gathers up, and pretty soon you have a cloud over the sky and you have the greenhouse effect and the earth will heat up and melt the poles and the poles will melt and drown the cities with 200 feet of water. I mean he was just pointing out the natural consequences of over-activity and thoughtless feedback. Of course Kerouac has a lot of statements like that, and essays like that in *Lonesome Traveler*; he's got quite a few social statements, which are really good. His realization of the fact that something really hard and terrible was coming to America was the realization that the road was no longer open for the wandering hobo saint. In its place you find police cars prowling up and down in strange shark-like science fiction faces and police with steely glint of murder in their eyes, stopping people and feeling them up. So Kerouac had a very clear and direct picture of that hard military police-state that was descending on America. The machinery is so big now that it's built that it would be impossible to uproot, just because of the drag of inertia, and the fact that there's so many people whose paychecks are dependent on their work as police or police aides, now—secret police. It's an industry worth several billion dollars now, and if you put on top of that the dope bureaucracy, it's a billion dollars—seven-hundred-fifty million dollars in the dope bureaucracy now just for the social workers and the police and so forth, the cost this year for suppression of dope. That's just the dope aspect. Then there's billions of dollars that go to Army Intelligence, Navy Intelligence, FBI, National Security Agency, and CIA and what other agencies we don't know. It's an economic interest now, like a cancer—and to cut it out might be a rather violent operation. Nobody's yet X-rayed the government to see how large the cancer is and how fast and far apart into all the nodes of the body the metastasis has spread.

JM: *Where's the X-ray machine for that?*

AG: Well, the X-ray machine is you have to get access to all the computer material, find out who's on the computers and see everybody's files. I have a solution for the problem actually. I think rather than attempting to destroy the computers and files, there should be a move to make all that information public, to open up the libraries of dossiers on everybody so that anybody can see anybody's dossier, which means that not only can Nixon read my dossier, but I can read his. *[Laughing.]*

JM: *Is that what Gregory [Corso] means by talking about truth in the '70s?*

AG: Yeah. In other words, the only way to confront this technological monstrosity is to make it all open and make everybody's head transparent. Just like Watergate disillusions everybody and brings them back to reality, so if everybody's dossier was available with all of the raw data and all of the gossip, fine, sure. As far as I'm concerned I got nothing to lose. But anybody that's got something . . . some secrets *[laughing]* they are the ones who started all this secret collecting and now let them take the karmic consequences of it—that is, the police agencies themselves. So, that's one way that, I would think, would be working with the negativity of the computerized police state, working *with* that negativity, and making it an asset instead of a liability by bringing all that information out.

JM: *You have that essay in* Naked Poetry *in which you trace the development of your poetic—it's only about a page—and I wondered if there's any . . .*

AG: Changes since?

JM: *Yeah, or if Snyder has any influence . . . you know, you were tracing Snyder's influence on your thinking; how about your poetics?*

AG: No, not too much because I relied more on "spontaneous mind" that I got from Kerouac. From Snyder I got the sense of "riprap," or just hard, tough facts, and some idea of Chinese poetry which was useful to supplement what I had gotten out of Pound's Fenollosa essays. From Snyder it's more like a life-influence, you know, like climbing or sitting or taking Refuge and working with Buddhism. Now I've been wondering, I don't know where I brought that up to in that *Naked Poetry* essay, probably up to mantra chanting ... O.K., so by then, from mantra chanting then I began doing like devotional homage to my guru, Blake, by putting his words to music. And that's an outgrowth of long experience with monochordal music in the mantra chanting, and then extended to "The Lamb" in Blake or other poems which just required one or two chords, one chord, at first; and then I did about twenty songs on one chord. And then I discovered a second chord, from C to F. Then about 1970 I got much more influenced by Dylan, and then as a result of working with the musicians recording the first Blake album that I did, which was '68, '69, '70, I discovered a third chord; and then by '71 ran into Dylan and he gave me some more information about three chords, and encouraged me to do improvisation. So he and I worked together and made an album and did a lot of recordings together. I started doing my first complete improvised poems on that occasion. And so I got then into studying blues and blues forms as a proper modern minstrelsy, and from that went into ballads and rhymed verse for singing. And from experience with Dylan, who was interested in Peter's gift and mine for improvising, there was a reinforcement from Chogyam Trungpa, who said that what I ought to do was be able to make up poetry on the spot, like the great poets—like Milarepa and his tradition, rather than depending on a piece of paper— that I should be able to trust my natural mind to provide the language and the ideas. In other words, it was just natural mind and finally came, with him, to another apothegm as good as an earlier one that Kerouac and I had worked out, which was "Mind is shapely, art is shapely"—this is an early thing that Kerouac and I figured out; and with Chogyam Trungpa came to "First thought, best thought"—first thought is best thought. That was last year. So, you know, was a combination of Buddhist influences and jazz influences and there were Kerouac influences.

   To continue what I was talking about in the development of poetics in that *Naked Poetry* thing, what I've been doing lately is songs and blues as well as regular writings (regular open page poetry), songs and blues and ballads and then improvisations. So I took *some* instruction from Dylan, as I took instructions from Kerouac, as I took instructions from Chogyam. So it's really nice because it's feedback from a younger generation, feedback from people who learned from us, then feeding back to us. Even Peter's picking up on the banjo now—doing banjo songs and improvisations on his guitar.

The point of *Howl* that Rexroth made at one time or another, that was historically interesting, was that it was a return to the vocalization of the poem, a return from the page to the voice in which everybody was interested—Olson, Creeley, Williams, all the Black Mountain Poets, Snyder, Whalen—actual voice. With *Howl* it was from voice, to spoken conversation voice, to chant or to long breath chant, tending to the bardic-chanting direction, the ecstatic direction, and then from chanting it actually moves to song with Dylan in the next generation, and then returns to us as song.

JM: *You're talking about your poetry getting this new input from your influence and the return of your poetry from the printed page to voice; have you talked anywhere else about using a tape recorder? I think I heard you say today or yesterday that you've abandoned that now.*

AG: Well, Dylan gave me four hundred dollars to buy a Uher tape recorder in 1965 as a Christmas present, as he gave Peter enough money to buy his first guitar and . . .

PETER ORLOVSKY: Amplifier—forty dollars for an amplifier.

AG: No guitar?

PO: No, no. No. The guitar I bought for twenty dollars; amplifier I bought for forty dollars.

AG: Amplifier, yeah—and McClure, enough money to buy McClure an autoharp. And he told me I should learn an instrument. So I bought a Uher tape machine and I used it for like talking into it to make up the poetry like "Wichita Vortex" and the travel poems in *The Fall of America* are taken from the tape machine, transcribed, edited quite a bit (not a great amount, the main body is just as given but blue-penciled for repetition), stitched together somewhat, as are the interruptions in conversations—the "Wichita Vortex Sutra" itself is almost intact, except one problem with the tape machine is that at the climax of "Wichita

Vortex Sutra," the calling on all of the gods, in that part, the battery went dead while I was dictating that, and I had to reconstruct it later on. *[Laughing.]*

JM: *Oh—how awful!*

AG: No, it gave me a chance to reconstruct it stronger. But the original one had a funny kind of force that I don't know if the second version has. So from about '65 to about 1970 I had a tape recorder around; it wasn't the only way I wrote poetry, I wrote a lot of nice poems on it like the "Elegy for Frank O'Hara," the "Elegy for Neal Cassady," most of the "Auto Poesy," the traveling things; everything except the stuff in airplanes. But then, well, it was just too much to carry around—notebooks are easier, and sometimes the batteries fail; not as reliable as writing it down. There was one time I went into the field, laid down in a meadow with the tape recorder in Cherry Valley and wrote this exquisite long pastoral poem, cricket chirps and star twinkles or something, you know it had everything together. I was laying there in the fields and assembling all the sounds and describing them and putting them together. Then I came home and I found out that the machine hadn't been turned on properly and the whole poem was gone. And I said, "Well, fuck this. From now on, I'm not going to depend on that machine anymore." It's too much. But it gave me some confidence in improvisation. You realize that if you can talk it, why not just write it; you just talk slowly, you know, talk one line at a time, just like you wrote one line at a time. It's no different, except there's more work transcribing. But then I got to be very artful at transcribing and doing that. But then it's too much trouble carrying it around. And also my Uher got ripped off in 1970 or so. A friend of mine was living at my house in New York, and a couple of guys with knives came in and ripped out the telephone wires and tied him up with telephone wire and stole the Uher and a good Sony I had, ripped off all the tape machine equipment, which was like a real blow because I was just *then* getting into working with Dylan and I needed all the equipment. I had to find cheaper replacements but they've never been satisfactory. So I haven't been using tape anyway, lately. But now I'm in an interesting situation where a lot of the material I do, write compose, the only *exact* extant manuscripts are chance tape recordings of poetry readings I improvise. So almost every poetry reading I do some improvisation, you know, at one point or another—sometimes extended, sometimes generally rhymed blues form or ballad form, and I'm just slowly verging toward trying to improvise without music, you know, and do my regular forms like *Howl* or "Sunflower" or something like that, but without the crutch of music, or rhyme. Haven't gotten to that yet. Almost did the other day, though, because I went to a lecture of Chogyam Trungpa, and he said, "When we finish with the Refuge Ceremony, would you improvise a poem?" And I figured out, let's see now, *[semi-chanting]* "Krishna has left the light bulbs, but the illumination shines by itself. Allah is gone out of the Holland Tunnel ..." And I figured out four or five lines to begin with—then he forgot to call me up *[laughing]* after the ceremony. But it made me think of how to do it without music, you know, just thinking fast; I had to—for that situation, to improvise sensible Buddhist imagery, on the subject of there being no god but our own empty mind.

DAN EADES: *Have you yet transcribed any of those, or you plan to transcribe the ones that you have improvised?*

AG: Yeah, a couple of things. But I've been so busy that I haven't had a chance. I have like maybe several hours of untranscribed verses on tapes and a lot more that other people have that I haven't ever gathered together. So now I have to make more effort to gather my tapes together in an archive, but it's an awful lot of work; unless there's a reason, I don't think I'll do it. But I'm digging that as a form and I'm discovering that's a most classical form of poetry, the bardic improvisation. That was the old form. And it's one that's almost fallen in complete disrepair, and disuse. And it really shows the differences between the rigidification of mind in poetry in, say, the '40s when we came on the scene—which was totally a question of scratching rewriting and rewriting and rewriting—that is presenting a poem for just a page, as against no more fear of embarrassment at the possibility of simply even forgetting to leave a record behind, but just simply giving forth inspiration into the air. It's a whole transformed attitude, and it's more Neolithic. *[Chuckling.]* The latter one is more Neolithic—and may ecologically be absolutely necessary when we run out of paper, then people will ...

JM: *But you are still concerned with leaving a record behind, surely?*

AG: Not enough to make sufficient effort to gather all the tapes I've made and transcribe them. I'm more interested in being able to compose spontaneously. If I felt that I were just able to do it all the time with no check or hindrance, then I think I'd just forget about the whole problem of books and just go around being a minstrel. And I think it would be an exemplary thing to do, actually, insofar as I could fill out my life from here on out, working toward that—that's the next stage of exemplary poetic activity. There's one thing I did try and do once I realized I was going to be famous and that *Howl* was fixed—I thought it would be nice to really present the persona of a poet "without death as a consequence" (a phrase of Apollinaire), without fuck-up as a consequence, with a really good . . .

JM: *As a consequence of the persona?*

AG: No, without death as a consequence of high poetics, as the old Dylan Thomas, Hart Crane, Baudelaire, Rimbaud tradition was. It would be nice to do something else, without death as a consequence, without fuck-up as a consequence, with just increasing spread of consciousness, and increasing powers of a gentle nature that didn't require mass murder, violence, war or anger or aggression. And to really open up some territory that would be usable by other people, but to set a good example. I figured that was one of the best things I could do with the powers that I was given in terms of fame and poetic inspiration. I figured, well, you know, why fuck it up. I've got my health, why not do something nice—like answer every letter, and go around and read free for a long while and develop that into music, or develop it into improvisation if necessary. But that also meant cutting the ground from under myself a lot, like reconciling myself to my father in rhyme again, taking lessons from younger kids like Dylan, and not coming on like a haughty old dogfather, avoiding some of the corniness of dignity and fame, and just developing into something that would be encouraging, rather than a blank wall or a death trap. I'm referring back now to what Gary was thinking of in terms of like what we could do since we were given a Movement, so to speak; it was a *donnée*, a gift.

JM: *I was just going to ask you if you see Gary as part of that?*

AG: Oh, sure. Gary is conscious of it too. I don't think it's a question of being too conscious of our roles, in fame or history, because that's just part of the general reverberations of eternal consciousness which is much larger; it's part of the understanding of life as a dream or an illusion or a play, and it's not quite a corny matter of making a good act. It's more involved with Bodhisattva's vow in Buddhism, which is "sentient beings are numberless, vow to illuminate all; attachments are inexhaustible, vow to liberate all; nature gates, Dharma gates are countless, vow to enter every one; Buddha path limitless, endless, vow to follow through." And there's a certain natural impulse towards that, which then becomes more conscious as you study Dharma and meditate, but that Bodhisattvic compassion aspect was something that was very clear very early in Kerouac, and was really the basis of my feeling of love for him; and his tenderness to me was the realization that we were going to die, that we're here a very brief time, and that the body, the situation we were in, the houses we were in were all full of tears of mortality. And with Kerouac, the realization of the existence of suffering was very strong; and the briefness of it, the mortal clouds over it, the skies brooding over the pitiful lonely short brief man vanity puppet-doll sense in his prose, that was really clear in his person and his prose. That perception in Kerouac, which he awakened in me, is very similar to the substance of the Bodhisattva vow. Then there's the problem that if you calculate too much esthetically in terms of careers and in role-playing, you obviously can make mistakes . . . you obviously automatically *will* make mistakes if it's all calculated like that. So it then comes back to dependence on spontaneous mind for inspiration and trust in the heart as the teacher, as the guru, poetically and cosmo-socially, and playing it by ear. I mean both the public activity in imagery—which is a poem, the public role is a poem for everybody, not just the poet, everybody invents their existence and their theater except poets are aware of doing it, sometimes— and maybe are even able to cut through it and show it is theater rather than try to hypnotize other people. And Gregory certainly does that, you know, like really shows the back of his theater and breaks the spell that he makes all the time, and breaks anybody else's spell who's trying to hypnotize you. So he's very valuable that way, painful as it is—it cuts deeply, exposes the raw nerves, the suffering that he goes through, and that you go through to bear with him, and to bear with yourself.

JM: *Before we started this tape, you were expressing, understandably, your concern about the chaos of some of the things that are happening in the conference, but on the other hand, Gregory is functioning that way [*AG: Yeah.*] and it's been important for me, I guess.*

AG: Yeah. *[Pause.]* It's funny, it's both repulsive and at the same time absolutely necessary that there be somebody completely mad, as they used to say, but completely sane also, in a funny way. It's the old question of, you know, don't commit god-slight, if the god is Dionysus. Do you know that little canto of Pound's where they commit god-slight? All the sailors mock the young god Dionysus who s there in disguise and he turns them all into leopards and the vines grow over the scuppers.

JM: *Yeah, that Second Canto.*

AG *[to Peter]*: So from what we're all saying, do you have anything you want to lay out?

PO: To grow your own food, to start your own orchards: I'd like to, as soon as I can, start growing apple orchards—write away to the government to get some information on how to grow apples and fruits and nuts and grapes and rose hips. I want to grow a lot of rose hips. They're very easy to grow, they're very easy to harvest, and they're very easy to dry in the sun, they're very easy to store for the winter, and they're full of natural Vitamin C. And they probably stop you from getting colds so they are very, very good for you. So I'd like to do that. And Gary was saying that up where he lives at Kitkitdizze it's so hot up there in the summertime that they've got a lot of dried fruit stored away, and that he harvested 300 pounds of wild apples.

AG: They also have acorns there; he knows a lot about acorns. I'll come back in a few minutes. Why don't you ask Peter some historical ...

PO: Let me say, to finish this. So Gary harvested 300 pounds of apples, then cut them up and dried them all, and he's got a couple of big jars where he's got all the dried apples in them. It's good. He says he doesn't go into the garden though; his wife does the growing of the food. Gary does the hunting. Well, I'd like to try to be a vegetarian, you know. I don't hunt animals; I don't hunt deer. Gary believes in hunting deer with a bow and arrow; I don't think that's fair. If you're going to hunt a deer, you got to do it with your hands, not with a bow and arrow—that's not quite fair; you know what I mean. So in that sense I would be a little worried about Gary; but then again, I've broken my own rules. I've been eating meat lately, meat and chicken and stuff. But I'm planning to get back to vegetarianism, you know. It takes a little while but it's good to be a vegetarian—you're supposed to live longer, I think. You live longer and it's probably more healthy for you. It makes your shit smell clearer and better. And I think also it's probably better for your stomach to be a vegetarian, it's easier on your stomach. That greasy stuff, you know, takes your stomach and ties it up into knots. And stuff like that, you know what I mean? But you ever tried being a vegetarian?

JM: *No, I haven't.*

PO: Have you, Dan?

DE: *No, except for very brief lengths of time.*

AG: Don't you have any historical . . . because Peter was in on most every scene. Peter knows lots of detail.

PO: I was with Neal Cassady at the Six Gallery reading, and Neal Cassady said to me, "Come over here, Peter, come stand next to me." I said, "Why? Why, Neal?" And he said, "Well, I don't know anybody here." So I was standing next to Neal but then I moved over and stood next to someone else because, you know, I was a little embarrassed. I was very, very bashful and embarrassed—very self-conscious, you know, in those days. And Neal was there, dressed in his brakeman's uniform. He had his vest on—his watch and his vest.

AG: He was very proud.

PO: He was very proud, smiling, very happy—he was very happy, full of smiles and bowing . . .

JM: *About what was going on?*

AG: Yeah; he came up to me and he said, "Allen, my boy, I'm proud of you." *[Laughter.]* It was really nice—it was the nicest thing I heard that night. It was completely, unabashedly, friendly, happy approval.

JM: *For a historical question, I'd like to know how you first got to San Francisco.*

PO: The Army—the Army sent me over. I was in Letterman Army

Hospital, military hospital, in San Francisco, as a medic. And I got to meet Robert LaVigne, an artist in San Francisco. And then I was LaVigne's boyfriend for a year, and then Allen saw a painting of me, naked Cleopatra-type painting of me, with a bottle of wine on the painting couch, and fell in love with me through the painting [AG: Right.] and wanted to come up and meet me right away. And so Allen stole me away from Robert LaVigne. I looked at Allen and said, "My God, he's very smart—he talks very nice, he knows about the world and everything. Boy, it's so good to hear Allen talk." So I really felt intrigued by listening to Allen talk all the time. So I went and lived with Allen; we made love and played with each other. And then we all went to Mexico together—with Allen, Gregory, Jack and . . .

AG: To meet Jack. We were on our way to Mexico and we wanted to give a reading there on the way. We figured . . . let's see, Gary and I had gone up and given readings in Portland and Seattle already and spread the poetry up there, and then I came down. Gary went to Japan and Peter and I and Gregory took off for the south to visit Kerouac who was living in Burroughs's old flat (Burroughs was gone) in 210 Orizaba Street in Mexico.

DE: *What was Kerouac writing then?*

PO: Kerouac was writing then? I think he was writing a poem every day.

AG: He may have been working on *Desolation Angels* already.

DE: *How accurate do you see Kerouac's characterizations of yourself and other people and your friends?*

AG: I see myself somewhat caricatured, but very tenderly so, and sometimes very penetratingly, critically right, in a way. His criticism of my vanity and egotism was really right, I think. It was a good view—and my general superficiality, actually, as a person. He didn't have a very comprehensive or sympathetic eye on my cock and my love life, or anything like that. He was very reticent about our own relationship sexually, or any sexual relationships that weren't idealizable in his own terms, so he never really wrote in depth about my relationship with Neal or Peter or himself or anything that involved like a heart-throb sexuality, tenderness, or Gay Lib, so to speak—what it would be called now. So there was a whole area left out there that would fill things out and make me more sensible. As it was, he had me as a sort of thin, nervous heterosexual, I seem to remember, basically. He knew more than that.

DE: *What about Cassady?*

AG: I think his portrait of Cassady is very full and very genuine and really solid. There were three or four people that he was always completely good on, people that he really respected and loved and idolized. One was Burroughs, he's got really good pictures of Burroughs; one was Cassady; one was Herb Huncke; and a couple of others, probably Gary . . .

JM: *Yeah, Gary in* Dharma Bus?

AG: Yeah, Gary; it's really a good picture. That's right. Then there are the minor characters, the secondary characters who are not the heroic ones in his books, which includes myself and Peter Orlovsky—well, many, many others—John Montgomery—in which he saw the slight crazy vanity within us; and so that was the main tone. But I didn't mind it; I still think it was nice. I once wrote a letter saying: "Why ain't I a hero?" but I said, "What you do with your heroes is that you really get them full, and with us less ignu characters, you have a thinner characterization, more cartoon-like."

JM: *To continue with the history, I was wondering if you care to say anything more about Ann Charters's biography than you did in that little introduction. Are you pleased with that?*

AG: Well, I wrote that little introduction only on the basis of reading a couple of chapters of the manuscript which had turned out to be the final manuscript. She had a better version before it was edited and there were a lot of troubles. One main trouble was, of course, that there were a lot of little tiny mistakes, which she had corrected in the paperback. But one problem was Kerouac's estate did not cooperate with her and wouldn't let her see many necessary documents, including the original manuscript of *On the Road,* so she's got the whole *On the Road* story upside down because *On the Road* really is mainly first draft.

JM: *It's mainly first draft, not revised, as she told it?*

AG: Not as she tells it. It's revised slightly, you know, tacking a couple of trips together, and weaving and looping a few things in together.

But the kind of extensive revision that she described, she describes on the basis of his letters to his publisher, which were letters to keep the publisher busy and make the publisher think that Kerouac was working hard because they wouldn't know the difference. And they thought that if you did a lot of work, it would make it nicer. So he just wrote them letters saying, "I'm working on it, I'm working on it, I'm working on it." But I read the original, in the original, and I've also read the final version, and I know they're not very different. It's divided into paragraphs and sentences instead of one long continuous sentence—that's different, of course. But she has it as enormous revisions, you know, stage after stage of superimpositions just like a regular novel—and it's not so. And also she wasn't allowed to quote directly from most of his published texts, which were owned by the estate, because they had another biography— official—scheduled by somebody else.

JM: *Do you know who that is, or how reliable it's going to be?*

AG: What's his name? Oh, Aaron Latham, who is an editor of *New York Magazine,* who has written a biography of Fitzgerald, and they had gotten an expensive contract with Random House or Scribner's, much of which went to the Kerouac family, or a percentage of which went to the widow. So the contract said that they couldn't cooperate with any other biographer until that one was published, and Charters had already started working on her biography sometime before, a year before; so they shut her out from access to materials and letters. And they wouldn't even allow her to quote from Jack's letters to me which I gave her to read from my archives. So the direct quote in nine-tenths of the cases has had to be paraphrased, was paraphrased. And she was having a baby at the time when the news came through that there were no reprint rights allowed, no quotes allowed, so the Straight Arrow Press assigned some secretaries to do the paraphrases. And so they've come out like all botched and messy; so they don't realize that she is quoting Kerouac's own intelligence on himself, his own language and attitudes on himself. It sounds like she, the lady biographer, is kvetching about his neuroticism, his failures and stupidities, when it's *Kerouac* ruefully commenting on his own foibles. In many, many cases you get a really gross view of Kerouac, when it's Kerouac's own view, which makes it a very refined view, actually, and you know, self-critical. You think it's the biographer being critical than the author including that insight—the most striking passage that I remember is when she's describing his return from Big Sur, and he got out on the highway where all he could see were middle-class housewives staring straight ahead into their cars and didn't notice the bum on the road. Well, it's actually Kerouac saying, "Then, I got up on the highway and all I saw was a bunch of middle-class housewives looking through their car and wouldn't even look at me cause I was just an old bum on the road." Well, from the prose point of view of the present biography, it sounds like Kerouac was limited as some sort of jerky beatnik that got out on this big highway and all he could see was middle-class housewives staring through the windows of cars; whereas when *he* says it, it means something different and much funnier and much more ample, much more Spenglerian, much more aristocratic almost, you know, it's more elegant; whereas it sounds very inelegant—like he's just got some kind of cruddy beatnik view of all the human beings in the cars. And unless you know it's a quote, you really think, Oh, this is sort of a drag; this guy, you know, he gets out on the highway and all he can see is middle-class housewives, and he's got all these prejudices. So it's the thrust of the whole book and it brings it down; it doesn't credit Kerouac his own intelligence, is what it boils down to. So I regret that little blurb I wrote, because I wrote it on the basis of the original manuscript and quotations, and only on a few chapters that I'd seen rather than the whole book.

JM: *That's really helpful to know . . .*

DE: *Yes, it is. Would you care to comment on one of the implications of her book, that is that Neal Cassady's letters were the start, in a way, for Kerouac, who . . .*

AG: Kerouac always said that. I mean, there's no implication. Neal wrote a long, long, long letter which I lost.

JM: *Oh, that forty-page letter?*

AG: Yeah, well, I loaned it. See, there was a time when I was carrying all this literature in San Francisco when I got there, which was what is now published as *Visions of Cody*—in '53, my own poetry, pieces of Burroughs's *Naked Lunch*, *Yage Letters*, Neal's letter, and some other poetry. And I brought it around to Rexroth and other people, and Duncan, so that everybody could read it, and I loaned it to various people in Mill Valley, and having less sense, and not have Xeroxing in those days, I didn't have copies; so when one batch of all the stuff was returned, Neal's letter was missing—and it's never been found since, except I think it will turn up ultimately, but . . . I noticed it was gone immediately and went back . . . it was in somebody's car trunk on Montgomery Street up where we lived, and went back to ask about it and they said, "Oh, what? What? I don't remember." So it's still lost. The guy is still lying—and I keep blaming him for it and he keeps saying, "But I don't remember." Jack kept blaming me for it. Anyway, there was this long letter, part of which was recopied and is in *The First Third*: the description of making it with a girl and then squeezing out the bathroom window when her mother comes in. That's from that letter.

Neal had read Proust at great length and was very good at Proust and could read him aloud because it was very similar to his own mind, that is operating in long lines of simultaneous free-association in Proust, while contained and balanced in a sort of mobile of long sentences with subordinate clauses. So he was really good at reading Proust because it fitted his own mind and tongue. And so his own prose was sort of American-Denver talk, but with Proustian detail. And so he wrote Jack this long buddy-buddy letter, beginning how he was going to tell Jack all about his first flushes of consciousness in adolescence, the first time he got laid, and his first discovery of the universe and his first discovery of consciousness, basically, which is probably something he wrote over the weekend, or in two days, or maybe a week of writing a little every night—forty thousand words, I think. He sent it to Jack, just as Jack was trying to write a book about Neal. So the portion of the book about Neal that Jack was writing is now embedded in *Visions of Cody* as that long scene ending with Cody . . . did you read that at all? *Visions of Cody*? It's Kerouac's greatest work, I think, written right after *On the Road*. Well, anyway, there is a scene in *Visions of Cody* in which Cody Pomeray, in a business suit, does a flying tackle on the field outside the high school just at sunset when his old teacher is in the schoolroom slamming his desk shut with a grieving heart, car speeding by with some friends going to a party on the other side of the road, near the football field. It's all sort of like a flash photo in the dying red sunset with Neal, flying forward, and then the tackle. Well, Kerouac had completed that passage which was done in sort of Proustian-Wolfean prose, sentences and all—in the last gasp of a style he had done in *The Town and the City,* his first novel. Then he got this long letter from Neal in which was all this excited talk with all that kind of simultaneous information but done as if he were talking in one long endless sentence without commas, but with dashes for interruptions, and it turned Jack on to the fact that he could just use his natural spontaneous mind, recalling everything he remembered all at once, in the order of memory. So he called the book *Visions of Cody,* meaning his illuminations or visions of the hero, not in chronological order, not in story order but in terms of the most intense flashes of recollection. Like if you have a friend, a close friend, you don't remember your relation to them as a story, you remember it as the most intense moments—you know, and they come up, outside of chronological order but linked together with a structure, the development of feelings between you. So what he did was *visions* of Cody ...

JM: *Almost to say, poetry, not fiction.*

AG: Well, *On the Road* was not fiction either—it's simply ... I mean, you could tell a chronological story and it not be fiction but poetical or autobiographical. But this was non-chronological, spiritual autobiography; non-chronological in the sense that it just dealt with the most intense moments, moving back and forth in time. And the most intense moment, I think the two of them were taking a piss together in some bar after knowing each other five years, and they were both sort of hating each other—you know, ragged and tired—and Neal was like completely beat out and sort of vulnerable, and suddenly looked over at Jack and said, "You know, Jack, I really love you." And Kerouac was so surprised that he had opened up. So, well—read the book. Oh, he handled it nicely, I mean, that was like an intense moment when the whole façade of their personalities cracked open and they had ... so it's *visions* of Cody and there are a lot of other ... maybe the next chapter would be something that happened five years earlier, some similar recollection five years earlier, that linked up to that moment. So it was non-chronological, right? But the story, anyway, in terms of flashes. That was his idea. And I think he was turned on to that by Cassady's letter.

JM: *You described that vision of the flying tackle in the sunset and it reminded me very much of a poem of your own, and that's the "Sunflower Sutra," because of the sun going down . . .*

AG: Well, I got most of my style from him, from Kerouac; that long line style is from him. That's Kerouac's development of Cassady's eager, excited, high fraternal talk.

JM: *So there is a direct connection?*

AG: We were all influencing each other, I mean everybody influences everybody; you get close to people spiritually and physically and mentally and pick up their habits of mind and you begin to see things through their eyes. I mean, is there anybody in whose eyes you see things? You know, like when you see something you say, "Wow, what would X think of that if he were here, what would he say?" So we were doing that about each other all the time. Kerouac was saying, "What would Allen think of this way?" I was thinking, "What would Neal say if I told him this? What would Kerouac think of this?"

JM: *The other poem that I was thinking about when I asked you about "Sunflower Sutra" in connection with Kerouac's interpretation of Cassady's experience, is "Crossing Brooklyn Ferry" because of the sun going down in that poem, too, and the stream of associations that are going on there.*

AG: Well, I read Whitman in high school, but I wasn't thinking of him when I wrote "Howl" too much. But then, *after* I wrote "Howl," but before I wrote "Sunflower Sutra" and a lot of other poems, I laid down in bed for a week in Berkeley in a little cottage that we all lived in, and I read through Whitman from beginning to end, all of *Democratic Vistas* and the whole of *Leaves of Grass,* and really got turned on—totally turned on, because it was like a complete revelation of the same consciousness cutting underneath the culture and every once in a while with a full dazzling breath and body and basic common sense—basic humor and common sense and natural mind. That really turned me on because, in other words, I'd written "Howl," and then I went and read through Whitman and just went on to "Sunflower" and all the other poems of that period—"Whitman in the Supermarket," and things like that. I realized that what we were into was right, and it was right in the very basic rightness of attitude that we were into—mood and content.

DE: *Jim has mentioned before that in many ways he thinks that you have become almost the persona that Whitman was projecting, that actually in your travels and in the sense that you really encompass most of the world, it seems like, and bring it together in your poetry . . .*

AG: Well, I was working consciously to do some of that, but it was more like the natural thing, like we've got airplanes now so it is inevitable. I was working consciously out of the Whitmanic tradition, once I read him, thinking, now what did he do that needs to be fulfilled and what did he prophesy that would be useful to do, that would be *sensible* to do, and did he make any prophesies that made common sense that would be useful, you know, to continue a tradition of, without getting too heavily into it because I had other . . . I mean, there were a lot of other things to do, but it would be nice to fill out the blank areas.

JM: *You made the "Passage to India" that he said.*

AG: Mmmm, yeah. But I wasn't thinking of him when I went. I mean, esthetically speaking I *might* have been doing it; but at that time I just wasn't. Kerouac was mad at Whitman for saying, "Older, wiser Brahma; younger and tender Buddha," "indeed . . . That stupid Whitman faggot." *[Laughing.]*

JM: *What was he objecting to?*

AG: Oh, Buddha is immeasurably older than Brahma, or something. *[Laughing.]* Buddha is much more important than Brahma, and Whitman was making Brahma older and wiser and Buddha younger and tenderer, and Kerouac thought that showed how little Whitman understood real Oriental stuff.

DE: *When I read* The Fall of America, *and I read it very closely after reading* On the Road, *it almost seemed that it was an updating in time through a different consciousness of much the same things that had happened in* On the Road *and that* On the Road *was almost a celebration of a kind of dying part of America [AG: Yes.] and your poem is almost a lament for the death of what had happened and I wondered how conscious . . .*

AG: Yeah. Right, but I wouldn't say for the death of what had happened, but the death of the hope that we were all . . . but which is not our hope but the old Whitmanic hope for America, so it's like a recognition that that hope—at least in the form that it was proposed—was now frustrated and the whole situation might be turning sour; that if the hope was ever to be accomplished it would require the fall of America as a nation.

DE: *Did you consciously structure* The Fall of America *in any way?*

AG: If you notice, it's absolutely exactly chronological. It's just all the poems I wrote during that time. It isn't really one single book or epic or anything like that; it's just fragments of funning around on the road with a tape machine, then interspersed with just poems I wrote sitting at a desk. I tried to separate out all the material, but there was so much cross-reference, like a lot of stuff on the road—you now, the travel poetry with sometimes elegies for Neal, or sitting at home poem with sometimes references to Kerouac or Neal; or references to the megalopolitan industrial machineries, so that finally I just put everything exactly chronologically, divided into sections, covering different eras of time and travel. So in a way it's a little bit of a deceptive title. But it's one that I was sort of cherishing as a title for years, but I never wanted to use it because it seemed like too much of a curse, but seemed final and inevitable after awhile. There's still more of that around, I still have more to publish of that—several conclusions to it. And more—but I just keep adding on to it like a tapeworm. My original conception was that it would go on as long as the Vietnam War went on, and when it was over that would be the determining thing.

JM: *In the first part of* The Fall of America, *are you consciously thinking of Gary Snyder's* Mountains and Rivers Without End? *Where you start down from Oroville?*

AG: Mmmm. I guess that's a little bit, too. Yeah. I mean, the idea of the long scroll poem. But then also I was thinking of the *Cantos* and *Paterson*—but also I was thinking of just the tape machine.

JM: *The reason I say Snyder is because of the situation—your coming down through the Northwest is like the second or third poem in* Mountains and Rivers without End, *in which you are a character . . .*

AG: Oh, that's the same trip! No, no, no. That's not the same trip. We made two trips: there was a trip—a hitchhiking trip north and back that we made in 1956. And then, in 1965, after the Berkeley Poetry Conference, we took the Volkswagen and drove up to Canada and back down through the desert and Pendleton on the other side of the Cascade mountains, the western side, down through Pyramid Lake, back to San Francisco. I think Gary's poem refers to the first trip; and my poem actually begins and was written during the second trip coming down. But he may have pieces of both. He mixes it up in time, see.

I think some of the anecdotal material involving me is from the first hitchhiking—anything involving hitchhiking would be the first trip; anything that involves driving a Volkswagen or a white Volkswagen coming down would be the second trip. I began mind on the second trip. But I wasn't thinking of *Mountains and Rivers,* no, because I wasn't really aware that it covered that territory.

There was another poem I wrote on that first trip, which is, I guess, in *Reality Sandwiches* and called "Afternoon Seattle," which is a description of the first trip, going to the Wobbly Hall with Gary, and that was in Seattle—the Wobbly Hall in Seattle on Yessler Street. But my influence from Gary was much less really, basically, than my influence both in terms of Buddhism and spontaneous mind; the big influence, the soulful moving thing was Kerouac's heart. Because I was in love with him, I was sort of romantically in love with him for about six years when we first knew each other, or longer . . ?45 through '55, or so, at least. It was sort of a direct, regular crush, so I was taking instruction from a lover so to speak, from someone I loved at any rate. But it was a very frustrating love affair in *that* sense, because it was a love affair on my part. He loved me in a different way; he was very tender. But it wasn't a physical thing with him except every once in a while we made it. *[Long pause.]* He was very shy about that—more than, I guess, what people are now. There seems to be more of an open scene, now. Maybe partly because of our constant imagery propaganda.

JM: *Partly because of your propaganda?*

AG: Yeah, a little bit, I think.

JM: *Well, Beat poetry had propaganda effects on us all. Just to connect that with Corso's reading—the reason I had Gregory Corso's "Bomb" when he needed a copy, you know, was because that was the first book of poetry I ever bought. It just happened that I had never bought poetry before and the first one I saw was that, and I knew there was something there for me. I did not see* Howl *at the time because my reading was still very accidental. In Dan's case, I believe* Howl *was the first book . . .*

PO: Getting back to City Lights, I knew Neal before he died, you know. I saw him . . . he came to New York City before he died. Sad—he was taking a lot of amphetamines and stuff, you know, but he was very bad. Then Jack was worried, calling us "Communists" . . . Jack was always calling us "Communists," you know, and stuff, in 1969 or '68 or '67, or something . . . '67 . . . '66, because we were going on demonstrations and stuff, you know, being arrested. He was always saying, "Well, I'll be up in my tree with a gun and shoot you Communists—shoot you Commies when I see you riding by."

JM: *What do you think caused that in Jack?*

PO: What I think caused it is him staying around his mother and looking at TV and the radio and the news, though he was writing a lot then, he developed like a very persistent on-path attitude, which was "Commies, I'll be up in the tree with a gun, waiting for you."

AG: Later on, he began writing for his mother's ear rather than for Burroughs'.

DE: *Did his mother actually dislike as many of his friends as Charters reports in the biography, and especially you?*

AG: Well, no, I think the key was that his . . . the story I once heard from Jack was that his father, on his deathbed, made his mother promise to protect Jack from the evil influence of me and Burroughs and maybe Cassady—I don't know about Cassady. So that was like a really heavy paternal instruction, you know, so that really gets internalized—so he internalized that family view. You know, but he also had an inspiration, like Dylan and other people, which is really necessary, which is to include the redneck, hard-hat view. And there's a real view there, too.

JM: *We're running short. I wonder if . . . would you be interested in talking about your own father at all? Or have you done that elsewhere? You mentioned . . .*

AG: My father has a book out, which I wrote a preface to. And it's pretty much there. My father was relatively friendly to people. Though, at first, all the parents are offended by their children's friends. Mrs. Kerouac was apparently bugged by us, and my father was bugged by Kerouac, and Lucien Carr and Bill Burroughs, and everybody was misunderstanding everything. That was another instruction for us because we were all such friends, and our parents all thought we were all monsters seducing their sons, or leading their sons into iniquitous ways and unwholesome influences. That lasted ten years, but then they got over it. I finally had a reconciliation with Mrs. Kerouac after Jack's death. I went to see her in her sickbed in Florida, and sang her Blake's "Lamb." She cried. So did I. And that was the end of our ...

JM: *That's nice.*

AG: Yeah, it was nice to resolve that ghost. It also turned out that she was afraid of my beard. I went to see her at a time I had shaved. I happened to have shaved at the suggestion of Chogyam Trungpa, the lama, who said he wanted to see what I looked like without a mask ... wanted to see my face. He said he loved me, he wanted to see my face. So I shaved my beard that night, in a big drunken conversation, because he reminded me of Kerouac. And maybe a month later, I was in Florida and saw his mother and I didn't grow a beard. Apparently she was phobic about beards on account of some German uncle.

From *unspeakable visions of the individual, volume 8: The Beat Journey* (1978). Reprinted by permission of James McKenzie.

"Slice of Reality Life"
An Interview with Allen and Louis Ginsberg

STEPHEN M. H. BRAITMAN, 1974

L OUIS GINSBERG, ALLEN'S FATHER, was a moderately successful lyric poet. He published three volumes of poetry and was a regular contributor to respected newspapers and magazines. Not surprisingly, he was enormously influential in his son's interest in writing poetry. He read and critiqued Allen's early rhymed poetry; he debated some of Allen's decisions after his breakthrough with "Howl." He was thrilled by his son's success, even when it became very clear that, in the Ginsberg family, the student had passed the teacher in talent and influence.

By the mid-1960s, when the division between generations was reaching its peak, Allen and Louis Ginsberg were giving joint poetry readings, much to the amusement of those who could not imagine the compatibility between the young poet with his long black hair and beard, given to using language not usually associated with poetry, and the older bard, conservatively groomed and dressed, looking the schoolteacher he was, issuing groan-inducing puns as part of his reading. They might have been polar opposites in many ways, but those attending their joint appearances would end up appreciating their differences.

The interplay between father and son is apparent in the following interview, conducted by Stephen Braitman and syndicated to newspapers across the country.

WHEN ALLEN AND LOUIS GINSBERG gave their reading on campus last May 9, most people felt a sense of love and unity between the two poets that went beyond their filial bond. The closeness of father and son was further strengthened by the mutual pursuit of poetic self-expression. In the following interview, conducted the previous afternoon in their Holiday Inn hotel room, the Ginsbergs revealed more of their closeness and differences than their formal reading suggested.

ZENGER'S: *How do you feel about presenting two worlds in these father and son readings? Do you think about it as making a statement of poetry's possibilities rather than your own particular ideas?*

ALLEN: It's just the inevitable mess of reality-glory. Whatever happens is real anyway. Whatever harmony there is, is real; whatever difference there is, is real, and it's typical of the culture. It's sort of inevitable. That we can stand it is the miracle. Or that the audience can stand it. Or that America can stand it. Any split between us just very much [reflects] reality in America, psychologically anyway . . . In other words, it's just like a slice of reality life, rather than a manifesto in one direction or another. Unless you can consider it being able to coexist.

LOUIS: That's what I say, that we practice peaceful poetic coexistence.

ZENGER'S: *Complementarity, as it were.*

LOUIS: Complementarity, yes. Not really in opposition, but each one presenting a viewpoint which, put together, gives a more rounded view of life.

ZENGER'S: *What sort of response have you had to these readings?*

LOUIS: In general, I'd say the young cluster around Allen, while the "mature" cluster around me. Finally there's an intermingling; some of the young see something in mine, and some of the mature see that Allen has a great deal to say that is relevant.

ALLEN: Besides, they're generally overwhelmed by the closeness of death.

LOUIS: And also the necessity for relating to each one in harmony in one world. Sometimes when we have flights of fancy we both are soaring above in some cosmic union, you know, in which the individual pulses with the universe. And when we come back to earth we believe in harmony and mingling and peace on earth, the old shibboleth which should really be practiced. As someone said, "Any religion is good if you practice it."

LOUIS: Here's one of my puns: Poets are born, not paid. But a lady poet can be made.

ZENGER'S: *Now, now, now, that's not very nice. Does that appear in one of your newspaper columns?*

LOUIS: That's an influence of Allen's. Here's another: What's a woman's best quality? A man's imagination. How much is a smile worth? It's face value. I'm loaded with them.

ZENGER'S: *We were talking earlier about the risks involved in your poetry. Your poetry, which so often is politically oriented and is almost a call to action in what you're saying . . .*

ALLEN: Not quite. My poetry is primarily a record of my consciousness. The basic principle relies on spontaneous and non-revised transcription of thought forms as they arise during the time of composition.

ZENGER'S: *Non-revised?*

ALLEN: Primarily non-revised. For the most part. They're touched up here and there, but the basic principle is to catch the bird on the wing rather than construct an artifact.

LOUIS: But the point it . . .

ALLEN: Uh uh oh, I am just trying . . .

LOUIS: Well, go ahead.

ALLEN: Just am trying to talk about why politics in my poetry. I wasn't trying to say this is good or this is bad, I was just trying to answer your question.

LOUIS: Very good, very good. Go ahead, go ahead.

ALLEN: I wasn't trying to get into a polemic about what type or another . . .

LOUIS: Oh, far be it from me to . . .

ALLEN: I wanted to avoid it, right now. I wanted to answer his question.

LOUIS: I thought the gentleman was soliciting my responses . . .

ALLEN: I want to answer his question.

LOUIS: Very good, I'll give you all the time ...

ALLEN: I want to answer his question ... ONLY want to answer his question.

LOUIS: You see ...

ALLEN: I *only* want to answer his question. So, since the political activity—notice such as Watergate, police state, or the wars for the last ten to fifteen years—are a part of the contents of my mind, it inevitably enters into the poetry, to the extent that it's part of the recurrent thought forms in the mind. Probably more basic than political are thought forms about meditation, and about processes of awareness themselves, meditational awareness. So that's probably a heavier element in the poetry than the political. So I was just answering your question as to why there's political matter in my poetry. It's not that it's intended to be a call to arms, at all, it's just the opposite. It's only a record of what's going on in my head, and *only* a record of what's going on in my head ...

LOUIS: But at the same time when you make exhibit of your consciousness of political depravity and injustice you arouse indignation among people who don't see it that way, who are sleepy and sluggish. And then they are alerted and to them it is a call to action, to say, "Why, why should this injustice exist? Let's do something about it!"

ALLEN: But that's called concomitant potential ...

LOUIS: Maybe you don't mean it that way ...

ALLEN: Rather than the intention.

LOUIS: That may be, that may be ...

ALLEN: And it is really important to make that distinction. A lot of younger poets thinking that the purpose is a call to arms than write poetry which is a call to arms but ignore what is going on in their minds, and only take account of what's going on in the newspapers, or what they think should be going on in their minds rather than including what *is* going on. And that is a very basic error, so that I constantly keep coming across younger people saying, "Well, you're calling for a call to arms, aren't you? That was the purpose of your writing, wasn't it? Now my writing is imitating yours and I'm calling for a revolution, and violence, and throwing rocks at cops and windows. Isn't that what you said and isn't that your purpose? And how can you deny your own purpose?" On account somebody wrote something about me saying my poetry intended to be a call to arms when it's not. It's a call to awareness.

LOUIS: That's right, and ...

ALLEN: And recall of my own awareness.

LOUIS: That's very good, but the repercussions of what we say continue, and we don't know where we begin and where we end, because the repercussions of what we say fall on fallow soil and some people that will be more alerted, and people, more indignant than others, are turning over the page. I am aware, too, of the injustices, though not as much as Allen. He's younger and pays attention to them more.

ALLEN: You lived a more sheltered life.

LOUIS: Yes, I would say that, and besides, in my day, in the '30s and '40s and '20s, we didn't have this turbulence, this domestic intolerance and turbulence, of all those wars. But nevertheless, my being, my nature responds more to a philosophic bent and to an interpretation of nature as an exploration of the purpose of life as far as you can get to it, you know; of an intense awareness of beauty. I'd say, too, my mind is a record of my observations, but my inner nature, my inner compulsion, my inner upbringing, my milieu, the circumstances that shaped me, the writers I read, my own inner nature, the combination of, permutations of my chromosomes make me more sensitive to philosophic probings than Allen. And so while I say what Allen is doing is wonderful and noble, still, that's one part of life. Who's to say that life is only this. Life is so mercurial, so manifold and so uncomprehensible, that to say this is life is like coffining it.

ALLEN: I'll say this, the only thing that I know of life, or can possibly know of life is what I know of life. I couldn't know of life what I don't know of life. That right? That right?

LOUIS: Except that some people are more intensely aware of things ... I'd say the difference between a poet and an ordinary person is that the poet feels more intensely and sees more, and at the same time the chief difference is the poet is a voice for the voiceless. He can articulate what many people find trapped in themselves and can't express.

ALLEN: You're going to mislead people if you say that. He's a voice for his *own* unvoiced thoughts . . .

LOUIS: Nevertheless . . .

ALLEN: And *if* he's accurate it will also touch a common chord that other people . . .

LOUIS: Well, that's sort of the same thing . . .

ALLEN: If he starts out intending to be a voice for other people, he will always make a mistake and finally synthesize what he thinks other people should . . .

LOUIS: I differ from you, if I am true . . .

ALLEN: There's a tendency . . .

LOUIS: If I am true . . .

ALLEN: There's a tendency . . .

LOUIS: If I am true, then writing a love poem exactly the way I feel, I am sure that a lot of people have the same feelings and say, "Ah, that's the way I feel." Not only poetry, but literature in general. If you hear a good speaker with soaring eloquence express what you can't express, you feel inner expansion, say, "Ah, that's the way I feel!'

LOUIS: Now, to go on to a different subject, where we differ. Allen feels that anything that wells up in the subconscious is O.K. in art.

ALLEN: Now I don't feel that way. That's your version.

LOUIS: What's your version? He says, "Catch it on the wing . . ."

ALLEN: I only publish a fiftieth of what I write. Your formulation of anything that wells up from the unconsciousness is incorrect.

LOUIS: But the fact remains that you think anything that you well up in the unconscious is poetry.

ALLEN: Now Louis, Louis, now this is all the writing I've done in the last year, of which I . . .

LOUIS: You believe in conscious revision?

ALLEN: One moment. Here is all the writing of the last year, which is a hundred and seventeen pages, of which I have published only five.

LOUIS: Then you do practice conscious revision.

ALLEN: No, I select out of all the material that I write what is most concrete. And hot.

LOUIS: Is anything you publish consciously scrutinized and selected?

ALLEN: Everything I publish is selected from the totality.

ZENGER'S: What do you use, what do you depend on to make the choice?

ALLEN: Whatever makes sense, finally. I write a lot of things that are complete nonsense.

LOUIS: I would put it this way . . .

ALLEN: I write a lot of crap. But once I write it down, I don't *revise* it. I don't go back and do it over again.

LOUIS: But you omit certain things to prevent them from being public.

ALLEN: I omit ninety-eight percent of the things I scribble.

LOUIS: I call that selection, too.

ALLEN: That's selection but not revision. I'm just using words precisely as a poet should.

LOUIS: Do you ever decide this verb is weak, and not concrete, that you need a more vivid, alive, palpitating word?

ALLEN: Occasionally, very rarely.

LOUIS: That's revision!

ALLEN: Occasionally, very rarely.

LOUIS: That's revision.

ALLEN: But the basic principle and the practice of ninety-eight percent of the time is not to make alterations of the original transcription of thought. That's a discipline in itself.

LOUIS: If you examine the manuscripts of Keats and Shelley, all the great writers, you'll see their original manuscripts have been revised and scribbled over till you can't recognize them. The theory is this, I think: the wedding of conscious scrutiny with unconscious welling-up. Milton had a phrase, music and wanton heed and giddy cunning, the musician seems to be writing in a fine frenzy and fine tempest. But that's the result of a great deal of practice and imitating, naturalism. Life is indiscriminate, Art is selection. Life is a welter of impressions, Art is choice of essential elements, and the smearing of what is important, of course, than an embodiment into an harmonious for. By the way Allen talks, you'd think that everything that wells out, that's art.

ALLEN: I think you're being unfair to me.

LOUIS: That may be, but . . .

ALLEN: In fact, I think you're misquoting me. I think that that's unfair for you to misquote me.

LOUIS: Well, uh, I'm giving you . . .

ALLEN: You said *everything* and I said maybe five percent. You're misquoting me now, and it's just sort of . . . it's not fair. It's just not fair!

ALLEN: The discipline or revision should take place in the mind itself. One disciplines one's mind to be attentive so that, at best, at best, during writing, attention is completely absorbed and focused and there's no wandering fantasy so the mind is clamped down on objects.

LOUIS: The magic union that took place in the unconscious is where the natural born ability of the poet manifests itself. Stendahl, in "The Salt Mines of Salzburg," said if you put a branch in the mines and leave it there overnight, the next morning you'll find a lot of crystals and spangles on it. In the same way in the subconscious of the poet, that's what we mean by "he's a born poet." These images flash up and you have great power welling up from your interior. Natural spontaneous concrete details. But you're only human and everything that wells up may be tainted a little bit with the prosaic. So, I think out of a thousand critics, 99.9% would say it's a wedding of scrutinizing of what poured out spontaneously. Period.

ALLEN: Kerouac said if there remains the possibility of changing it later, then very often during the time of composition the poet won't give 100 percent attention to getting it right the first time. His theory was if you know you've burned your bridges behind you, you can't touch it again, then you have to say it once and forever, as if in eternity.

ZENGER'S: *What concern do you have that* Howl *or* Kaddish *or any of your books will be available after your death, that people will be reading your poetry long after you survive? How does that affect you?*

LOUIS: Are you pleased by it, or displeased? Tell the truth.

ALLEN: Pleased but, you know, I'm not necessarily pleased by my pleasure . . . as long as we are tied down to values, then we're prisoners.

ZENGER'S: *Isn't poetry a value you're tied down to?*

ALLEN: Two weeks ago, I was tied to smoking. Being tied down to preconceived notions of value may blind us to the actual freedom and openness of the space we move around.

ZENGER'S: *I want to ask one final question. What do you feel when you read each other's poetry?*

ALLEN: When I read my father's poetry, very often there is a tremendous melancholy awareness of how much he is aware, an almost tearful realization that I should have been kinder when we were around together.

LOUIS: Well, I feel, first of all, when I read his poetry I am stimulated by recognizing more than I'm aware the injustices of the world, because he lashes and excoriates the world with its injustices and blackness and greed. But I realize that's a part of its nature and it stimulates me to that. And I'm proud, of course, that he's fulfilling his nature, that he's successful, and has fame and fortune. A father's natural pleasure of seeing him soar high. But in the end it's sort of complementary—he sees things, I see things a different way, according to our inner compulsions and inner natures, But who's to say only this can be written, only this is written . . . the world is too infinite for the finite mind to make absolutes.

From *Zenger's,* May 22, 1974, 8–9. Reprinted by permission of Stephen M. H. Braitman.

Visions of Ordinary Mind (1948-1955)

Discourse, with Questions and Answers, June 9, 1976

ALLEN GINSBERG

EDITED BY PAUL PORTUGES

I N THE SUMMER OF 1948 Allen Ginsberg, while living in Harlem, experienced some of the most important and influential moments of his life
when he had a series of "visions" that became his obsession for the following fifteen years (and, arguably, to some extent for the rest of his life).
In these visions, Ginsberg "heard" the prophetic voice of William Blake,
reciting his work directly to him through the ages.

He tried to use poetry to explain—and even attempt to re-create—these
experiences. He was never satisfied with the entries in *The Gates of Wrath*,
poems written immediately after the visions, or, to a lesser degree, "Empty
Mirror," poems that began as journal entries. The visions and their after-
math were eventually recorded in the poem "The Lion for Real."

Ginsberg spoke extensively about these visions in interviews (most
notably in his interview with Tom Clark in the *Paris Review*), but never to
the length and depth as in the following interview, in which he tied in the
visions with his poetry prior to the writing of "Howl."

ALLEN GINSBERG: My father wrote what was called in the twenties "lyric
poetry," and I got my ear from him to begin with. Some major exponents
of that kind or poetry were Eleanor Wylie, Edna St. Vincent Millay and
Edward Arlington Robinson. A. E. Housman was a big influence then, in
the standard anthology used by poets that belonged to the Poetry Society
of America, an organization in New York that had kicked out Maxwell

Bodenhein after he pissed on the floor at a public meeting in 1927 (or something like that). The Poetry Society of America had a standard notion of style. At its best, it was the Edward Arlington Robinson genre, *Miniver Cheevy*, or *Eros Tyrannos*, great poem:

> Meanwhile we do no harm, for they
> That with a god have striven
> Not caring much for what we say
> Take what the god has given,
> Though like waves breaking it may be
> Or like a changed familiar tree
> Or like a stairway to the sea
> Where down the blind are driven.

That series of linked stanzas has a very powerful clanging rhyme.

Louis Untermeyer was, I guess, the anthology king and taste maker (as Oscar Williams's *Little Treasury* was the standard anthology circulated in colleges in the fifties, and Don Allen's *New American Poetry* set other standards post-sixties), and Untermeyer's taste was for his own style of poetry, lyric, similar to my father's, like his *Caliban in the Coal Mine*, a very simple rhymed statement. I picked up on the iambic, rhyme, stressed verse; I was brought up on it. For my high school graduation book, I wrote a sonnet which I've forgotten by now, but which went something like, "We face the glorious future, da da dee and we're off into our pomp maturity." Just a goofy high school sonnet, valedictorian's pentameter. So all the poems I wrote when I was sixteen or eighteen were sleepwalking repetitions of sounds I'd heard in Robinson or Edna Millay. And their sounds were like sleepwalking repetitions of sounds they had read in Wyatt and Surrey or Shakespeare. The whole form has degenerated, yet it was still called "lyric poetry." Originally "lyric" because it was done with strings, with a lyre, those forms were songs at the time. Then people stopped singing poems in these forms for the general public, until Dylan, probably, as far as most poets were involved. Yeats wrote lyric poetry, but he always had "a chune in his hand," but he was one of the very few people who did.

So by the time I was twenty-two, I was still writing that same kind of verse except that all of a sudden I had a funny kind of visionary experience (or a "psychedelic experience") which completely changed my attitude toward poetry. I was examining Blake's pages and heard Blake's voice in a sort of interesting hallucination, without any drugs, in 1948. So I realized after that it was possible in a poem to reproduce some body rhythms which, if inserted in other peoples' bodies, might catalyze a similar experience, 'cause that's what happened to me.

PAUL PORTUGES: *Were there some specific Blake poems that caused your visionary episode?*

A.G.: The particular poems that turned me on in Blake were "The Sunflower" and "The Sick Rose" and a couple others. *[He sings Blake's "The Sick Rose."]*

P.P.: *Did your experience have much effect on your own poetry?*

A.G.: Having had a visionary experience out of these little poems—Blake's, my initial reaction to getting turned on, mentally, poetically, spiritually, was to create little mysterious verses similar: "Many seek and never see / anyone can tell them why . . ." (from "The Eye Altering All"). I thought I was making a sort of mystical riddle as to the nature of consciousness, but actually, the whole—there's no content to it. It's just sort of like a paranoic reference. Like going around staring at people's eyes, saying, "Many seek and never see," but I thought that's what poetry was supposed to do. Sort of penetrate the skull by some eye stare or some hypnotic rhythm. "I cannot sleep. I cannot sleep / until a victim is resigned; / a shadow holds me in his keep / and seeks the bones that he must find." The same kind of rhyme like, "Though the waves breaking it may be / or like a changed familiar tree, / Or like a stairway to sea / Where down the blind are driven." An echo of that insistent, prophetic, very abstract sound with no specific imagery, no automobiles, no fingernails, no noses. I thought of poetry then as hermetic, containing some kind of mystical secret of consciousness, which would be referred to by symbols. If you talked about "bones," if you talked about "light," that would turn people on to the area of consciousness you were talking about; it might even catalyze that consciousness in them. By "that consciousness" I mean some kind of big open mystical consciousness, like on acid. (I hadn't had acid at the time.)

P.P.: *Did you hear Blake's voice reading or singing his poems?*

A.G.: Yeah. I had my eye on the page, and I heard a big solid, solemn earthen voice saying, "Ah, Sunflower, weary of time . . ." My voice *now*, actually! I had a much higher voice then. What I heard was my own voice now, or, say, about five or ten years ago, when I was in stronger voice—the peak of health. By hindsight, I've always been mystified by that experience; I've never really figured it out. It was actually an auditory hallucination, I heard a voice, and went around for weeks and months and years telling people I heard Blake's voice. "I heard Blake's voice!" like an acid head who's had some transcendental vision and goes around trying to beat you over the head with it and insisting that it come true right now! Like everybody take their clothes off right now, or like revolution now! Or like what—electricity now! CIA now! Breakthrough now! You know that syndrome.

P.P.: *Could you explain it some more?*

A.G.: It's a realization that there is one common consciousness, and that if only everybody would refer to that consciousness simultaneously, there would be some universal cosmic consciousness breakthrough—so that everybody at the same time would be the same sublime self. And would be telepathizing the same perceptions back and forth!

P.P.: *Was your vision a classical visionary experience, like St. John of the Cross? You know, hearing voices, having a feeling of light . . .*

A.G.: Well, yeah . . . but what to do, what are classic visionary experiences like?

P.P.: *Like in St. Teresa, or in other famous visionary accounts—they all heard voices, like you mentioned with Blake, and there were sensations of light . . .*

A.G.: Okay, as far as light—I had a sensation of that everyday light as becoming some kind of eternal light. So it was like an eternal light superimposed on everyday light, but everyday light wasn't any different than everyday light! It was just, "the eye altering alters all." My eyes, having altered, everyday light seemed like sunlight in eternity. So there was a sensation of awe, spaciousness, and ancientness as in some eternity, but actually people get that everyday. I mean, aren't we now in eternity?—by "now" this is years later—I don't know what was so striking about it . . .

but it seemed to me like a complete break in nature, or a break in the normal continuum of my consciousness. In classical religious experience, like in James's *Varieties of Religious Experience,* there's a reference to light, as if it's something special. And there *is* a sensation of something special! Like in acid, when you go out in the day, and you're not hallucinating, you're just seeing the normal air and light of the day. You can't say it's any different than everyday light, can you—really?

P.P.: *Well, the acid, the acid . . .*

A.G.: It may seem different, but basically the big discovery is that everyday light is supernatural! Does that make sense? Is there anybody that disagrees with that? So if everyday light seems supernatural—thus the line of Blake's—"the eye altering alters all." So, change your brain, change your eyeballs, and the light seems awesome. So what are the characteristics of the light? It seems like it's eternal, in the sense that it's always been there, timeless, translucent, you can see through it . . .

P.P.: *Like the later afternoon light through the leaves of trees . . . Bright . . .*

A.G.: Gracious, because it allows you to see. So there's a certain kind of intelligence in the light because it's built to allow you to see. It seems like some intentionality to the light. It's cooperating with your consciousness, 'cause without the light you wouldn't be able to . . . whatever it is . . . words . . . but . . . the particular experience I had without drugs.

I was taken completely by surprise. I was overtaken because I hadn't expected anything like that.

P.P.: *Do you ever think of having prepared yourself, in some unconscious or conscious way, for the visions?*

A.G.: I hadn't been seeing friends, I had a sort of social breakdown. I was living alone in East Harlem and eating mostly vegetables. I had kind of gotten into a nervous breakdown, given up on my life, and just didn't know what or where I was, I was living alone, so there was an absence of preoccupation, absence of plans, a dead end. I had come to a dead end, like most kids do when they get out of college, got to make it in the world, get a job, they don't know what to do, don't want to confront the anxiety of unemployment office, "getting your shit together," suit of clothes, reality becoming real. I was in a kind of limbo period where I had no security, no assurance of what I was headed for. An open future. The only special thing on that specific occasion was that I had just jacked off. I don't know if you've ever done that, but jacking off while reading . . . sort of an absent-minded jacking off. Sort of special kind of pleasure, masturbatory pleasure, being distracted in the mind, and the body having its own life.

P.P.: *Do you think the rhythms or rhymes of the poems you were reading affected your state of mind?*

A.G.: Well, the particular poetry I was reading was Blake's, which has rhyme . . . *[He reads and sings Blake's* "Ah! Sunflower."*]*

P.P.: *This modern poetry, uh, it doesn't have to rhyme, is that right?*

A.G.: Modern poetry? We'll be talking about that later, right now I'm just talking about old-fashioned rhymed poetry, for which Blake was exemplary; and some rhymed, old-fashioned-style poetry that I used to write when I was eighteen to twenty-five.

P.P.: *Had you been reading a lot of mystical literature prior to your Blake visions?*

A.G.: Yeah. I was going to say, St. John of the Cross. I was reading a little bit of Plato's *Phaedrus,* and some Plotinus, a little Luther—I had a lot of theology literature at hand, set up in egg-crate bookshelves by a student whose apartment I'd sublet. And St. Teresa of Avila, Blake, a little Marvell.

Let's get back to the *quality* of that kind of breakthrough experience—Has anybody here in class had visionary experience, what they *thought* was visionary experiences, outside of drugs? Really raise hands so we get some clear signal. *[Majority raise hands.]* Outside of drugs?! Well then, OK. How many people *don't* feel they've had any visionary experience outside of the drug scene? *[Scattering of hands.]* How many people have had some sort of visionary experience *with* drugs? *[Majority raise hands.]* How many have had *no* visionary experience of any kind? *[Few hands raised.]* Raise your hands! *[Still few hands are raised.]* That's terrific! OK. These are probably the saints here . . . so (nearly) everybody's had some light—It's amazing. I didn't realize that it was so common for people to have had—

Q: *But the quality of the vision may be different?* . . .

A.G.: I don't think so; probably I'm more loud-mouthed about it.

Q: *How did you feel after visions? What were your first reactions?*

A.G.: "Many seek and never see / anyone call tell them why / . . . I ask many, they ask me / This is a great mystery." . . . A slightly paranoid element's there because I was secretly asking everybody else: have you seen *the light*? Have you seen it? That's why "I ask many, they ask me / This is a great mystery." I had the idea that all conversation—even about the butcher shop—secretly referred to the infinite light of the mystical experience.

P.P.: *And you changed your mind?*

A.G.: Well, I . . . yes, sure, why not. Yeah, I'll get to that later. My immediate thought was, "Many seek and never see." Meaning: many people have the idea of looking for a God, truth, looking for beauty, but actually never attain some breakthrough of consciousness into a totally fresh eternal awesome-world visionary experience. However, everybody does experience it, whether they know it or not, but most of the people push it to the back of their mind. Or've had some glimpse, but put it in the back of the mind and don't bank on it, or don't count it as social currency, don't talk about it. For that reason: "Anyone can tell them why." "Anyone" is practically the majority of this class; the majority of this class could tell them why. "And never take until they try." I thought that perhaps there was some element—you could catalyze it, if you were willful, or if you really threw yourself into the search for vision, you could bring it about. "Unless they try it in their sleep"— How many people had visionary experiences in their dreams? *[Muddled speech from class.]* Has anybody not? . . . You haven't had it in your sleep? You can't remember. First thing in the morning, check back. So: "And never take until they try / Unless they try it in their sleep / And never some until they die." That's because I'd assumed that death was complete consciousness. There's a line in T. S. Eliot: "The complete fire is death." I thought he meant that when you die, everything opens up, and you see ALL! So: "I ask many, they ask me, / This is a great mystery." I titled it, "The Eye Altering Alters All," out of Blake, a direct reference to a visionary experience; actually, it was the first poem I wrote immediately after that Blake audition.

P.P.: *Can you spend some time describing the visions . . . after almost thirty years, do you remember what happened?*

A.G.: What happened to me was: one afternoon in Harlem, I had been reading the Blake poems. Heard, as I say, an "audition," of a very deep voice reciting three or four poems—first "The Sunflower," then "The Sick Rose," and then "The Little Girl Lost." I wasn't quite sure about the time span involved—there was the sound of a voice in the room that didn't seem to be coming from inside my head. Seemed to be a voice in the room. But nobody was there. Recognizably Blake, simply from the Ancient of Days feeling about it. I thought it was the Creator, God, I associated it with a God, some anciency, prophetic. At the same time, there was outside the window a sense of extraordinarily clear light; the everyday afternoon sunlight, but with extraordinary clarity as if the light itself were some sort of bright intelligent substance, revealing all of the intelligent handiwork of the Ancient of Days, the working of ancient days. And the first thing I noticed outside the window were the cornices of the buildings in Harlem—1880s, 1890s, 1910s apartments. In those days there was quite a bit of handiwork, hand work. Like stone chiseled—

Q: *Friezes?*

A.G.: On apartment houses . . . friezes . . . the special metal artwork for the roof, overhangs, done in slight Greek or Roman style. Little cornucopias, or cornices, or scrollwork—I don't know architectural terms. Do you know what I'm talking about? Well, it was the first time I looked at the roofcombs of those old-fashioned tenement apartments—very carefully—and they were silhouetted against the bright living light of the sky, which sky-light seemed endless in blue. Standing up like buttresses in eternity! Somewhat as in the Magic Squares, paintings of Paul Klee when seen optic in 3-D. Giant foundations and buttresses were the cornices of the buildings, and I suddenly realized that an enormous amount of conscious intelligence had gone into their creation. A great deal of care, a great deal of planning, a great deal of love, in the sense that people put their bodies to work, six flights up in the air creating these sculptures, which nobody ever noticed, in the street, generations, nobody noticed them, or I had never paid any attention to them. And I suddenly saw them as signs calling for my attention. They were signaling to me from 1890, intelligible comments. Anonymous, thousands and thousands of invisible workmen all over New York in 1890 had made intelligible comments throughout the building tops of the city. Street after street, there was all this sublime cosmic intelligence, made out of metal.

P.P.: *Intelligence: what do you mean?*

A.G.: Intelligence in the sense that—of writing for the eyes. Signals that they were there. Workmen were there and they were quite conscious in 1890, and had built something in eternity for me to look at fifty or sixty years later. It'd never occurred to me that people were full of wisdom, or that there was that much transmission of consciousness in material forms throughout the civilized world. And then I looked further, say, at the clouds that were passing over, and they too seemed created by some hand to be conscious signals also—just like the cornices. Signals of some kind of intelligence. An intelligence much vaster, more far-reaching than a workman's hand because there's the Whatever accumulation of energy and force and suffering and consciousness that would have taken for animals to die and their blood to dry and be evaporated and brought up into the skies and the oceans to be drawn up into the skies and formed into clouds and then drift over New York and drop rain. See, that enormous amount of work had gone into making clouds. Millions and billions of years of work to make the entire structure I was sitting in the middle of, an entire planetary solar system! And then, all of a sudden, I looked up beyond the cornices into the sky, and the sky seemed to be a creation of a great Ancientness and a much vaster creation than anything I had thought of as Poetry. So I had the impression of the entire universe as poetry filled with light and intelligence and communication and signals. Kind of like the top of my head coming off, letting in the rest of the universe connected into my own brain.

Q: *Can you get any sense of expansion by retelling, by recalling that experience now?*

A.G.: At the moment, yes, because it seems so obvious. While talking, I've been looking out and seeing very bright greenery, bright golden light outside the green door and trees swaying in a very gentle muscular wind. If I look for it, I can . . . Well, I don't want to get into analysis yet, I'm still trying to get to the Suchness . . . some poetic description. By hindsight,

I think that I was, in adolescence, so limited in my view that what I discovered was ordinary consciousness! What I was discovering was mere ordinary everyday consciousness, or ordinary mind, so to speak. The sky is big, the light is bright! It's just that I'd never noticed it, never appreciated it. In other words, what I took to be supernatural vision was just natural growing up, I was just becoming conscious, waking up to what was ordinary. By this time, I'm so used to it that it now seems ordinary, it doesn't seem supernatural at all; maybe then just waking up to what I thought was supernatural, which everybody else had been seeing all along. It's just that I was the only one in the universe that never noticed that, see. So that's why I made such a big deal out of it. It was my nightmare, that I was the only one that never noticed the sky. I had been so limited and dumb that what I was discovering was what everybody knew already, and I was *afraid* that that was the truth. And probably that was the truth, for nowadays I've come to decide maybe it's best that I alone was Blindman, because thus everybody's already living in Eternity and I don't have to worry about it anymore. Rather than claiming it as my exclusive territory ... I've never really talked about this in a class before— interesting, kind of mind-blowing, see, because I asked how many here had visions. And two-thirds *have* had. Actually, I'm curious: what have other people gone through?

Q: ... *The reason people don't talk about these ... because it tends to dilute the experience ... Although talk about it realizes the experience ... or else talk about it [and] you lose the experience ... Also, there's the pain of being separated from that experience ...*

P.P.: *Didn't your experience, state of heightened consciousness, last over a period of a week or two? ... It wasn't just a day?*

A.G.: No, it was intermittent. It actually was quite limited. The first day, there were three separate occasions, and I can't measure the time. I've been baffled by that. Because it might have been just a second, but it seemed like a long bath of time, twenty minutes, half an hour. And as I became conscious of experiencing it, it closed down, and my ordinary consciousness returned.

P.P.: *What do you mean?*

A.G.: See, as I was sitting there in a sort of state of suspended mind and suspended awe—no, suspended decision, suspended mental activity—then, when I said, "Oh, I'm Allen Ginsberg. I'm having this particular visionary experience, isn't that great? I'm a poet, I'll be able to use this for the rest of my life." Then, all of a sudden . . . "Oh, let me see, what was I having, what was going!" . . . It was very paradoxical, and immediately you become self-conscious, immediately you think, your Eye closes down. Very similar to meditation experience, too . . . later.

Q: *Isn't there a conscious cultivation of these experiences now? That's why everyone raised their hands . . . everybody has visions but not everybody knows it?*

A.G.: "Many seek and never see, / Anyone call tell them why." My theory then was that everybody knew all along and everybody was, in a sense, in a permanent state of heightened consciousness. Or, that there were several consciousnesses going on at once. Which you can say is true: when you recall yourself, when you do enter a state of remembrance, you realize that you remembered all along. That's one of the tearful and great things about mind: you realize that you've known all along. Maybe on the death bed or drowning there's that awareness: "Ah, all along I've been aware of this, it's just that I didn't pay attention to what I knew most deeply," and basically, "Yes, yes, / that's what / I wanted, / I always wanted, / I always wanted, / to return / to the body/where I was born."

P.P.: *Back in 1948, people would think you were crazy if you told them how sublime, how visionary they were or could be.*

A.G.: Oh, yeah. There's an acknowledgment in our culture now of those areas of experience as being real. At the time, 1948, when it happened to me, it wasn't anything that people discussed, and it was not part of the background of the culture. There's an extraordinary difference between the consciousness of consciousness of the seventies, and the consciousness of consciousness of the forties. One didn't—there was no real examination of the nature of consciousness, or the suchness of consciousness, or the varieties of consciousness, or alterations of mind. They didn't have the terminology like "alternative mode of consciousness," "modalities of consciousness." They didn't have the terminology to discuss it; or they had a mystical terminology, like "I saw light." So I rushed into Columbia College's English office, Mark Van Doren's, saying

"I just saw the light!" The only one who asked me what I meant was Mark Van Doren. The others just thought I was just a nut, you know, a typical college kid who'd freaked out finally, not gone out and got a job, instead freaked out. I thought, "They're right, I'd better get a job."

CYRUS [*Aet. 72*]: *People back in those times were afraid. They were afraid. They thought they were going crazy or . . .*

A.G.: Precisely . . . do you remember that? Talking now about the forties.

CYRUS: *The forties, sure. Thirties.*

A.G.: Did you have any special experience in those days?

CYRUS: *Yes, I? I went crazy sometimes.*

A.G.: Any kind of illumination feeling?

CYRUS: *Illumination, that you're talking about, didn't come till later, here . . . the seventies.*

A.G.: His Bodhisattva name is Patience.

CYRUS: *Where'd you find that out?*

A.G.: We took vows together.

CYRUS: *Oh yes, so we did.*

A.G.: . . . I'm knocked out, just trying to figure what's the actual common ground between us here, in the room . . . I'd been talking Solitary, as if vision were just my own property. But obviously now everybody owns a piece of that property.

P.P..: *Anglo-Saxons had a language for it . . .*

A.G.: McClure has descriptions, borrowed from Anglo-Saxon, Aelf-land and Aelf-sheen, a sort of hermetic language referring to magical experience, also good practical nature mind description—Aelf-skin, a glow, "there are Halos around each being . . . the aura of the past that is beauty." His terminology lately is Beauty, just simple, and his detail's minute, like nature . . .

P.P.: *It's hard to make others understand a phenomenon strange as Visions.*

A.G.: It's most interesting if you can see something visionary about this room, for example, and point it out to other people so they can get a vision. Rather than see something visionary somewhere else that nobody can see, and you can only describe it to the corridor of nerds! But you can actually point to the peculiar flicker of light of the electric machine hanging from the ceiling—make people see it so they suddenly realize a fluorescent tube as a kind of Raw Intelligence beast hanging from the ceiling—that was my raw intention, then, anyway.

p.p.: *Are you, or were you, sure that everyone had the ability to see in a new way?*

a.g.: Are we all seeing, having the same vision? Or are we all having different visions in different universes out of different brains and different eyeballs, and are they all discontinuous? That's one thing I don't know either; it's something to discuss in public, and somewhat clarify. My original idea was that what I was seeing was what everybody must see, or will come to see, or has seen, since "Egypt" on. "Go back to Egypt and the Greeks . . ." *[He reads "A Mad Gleam."]* That was one of those early poems, trying to *refer* to the vision. But it was still "reference" to the vision, rather than "presentation" of detail. (Ezra Pound's terminology.) So I concluded, finally, that only presentation of detail—what you *saw*—speaks and transmits to other people the mental quality of visionary realization. You can't communicate accurately by conglomerating abstractions. Poetry's power is that you can remember, and then write down little details . . . sometimes even while you are seeing. I always speculated that William Carlos Williams, a modern common-sense naturalist poet, was really recording a high moment of perception—Vision— when he said: "So much depends on a red wheelbarrow glazed with rain water beside the white chickens." As if he made a little symbolic icon of a moment of heightened consciousness. Probably he was just saying to himself, "let's see what kind of detail I can write down." Now I doubt that he was, in fact, making a representation of a special moment of *my* kind of visionary detail.

p.p.: *Did Williams see any of his poems in terms of visions or illumination?*

a.g.: I never asked him . . . it may be that this "Vision" is just ordinary consciousness, and people are so daydreamy and neurotic that they're just not in their bodies, not seeing what's in front of them most of the

time, anyway. So Williams was experiencing it as *ordinary* everyday Rutherford consciousness, while I, for long decades' time, thought it was special heightened consciousness, even visionary.

p.p.: *Did you relate your visionary experience to that Blakean concept
of "eternity in a grain of sand," the eternal in the ordinary?*

a.g.: You find eternity in the roof-cornice of a Harlem apartment. I
see that that's what he meant, to see in any part any place in the universe
some fragment of an infinitely vast design. Whether it be the red brick
or seven-colored squares of wall-facing *[pointing to the classroom wall]*,
which were assembled from many corners of Colorado, or God knows
where all the sand and water came from to plaster up on that wall, and
where the hands came from that put it there. Like an assemblage of phan-
toms to get just that wall up, and the wall itself still here shining out. So
that's part of a larger design, eternal, all the way back.

q: *Did you think you're the ultimate perceiver, or that there's an outside perceiver perceiving you, or you're someone else's hallucination?*

a.g: All those questions came up later. At that moment, however, my
impression was that someone was perceiving me, and I was perceiving
that someone had perceived me all along: that the Ancient of Days was
perceiving me and had been perceiving me, and that I was just waking
up and perceiving back.

p.p.: *What*—

a.g.: There was a sense of an Eternal Father completely conscious
caring about me, in whom I had just wakened. I had just wakened into
his brain, or into his consciousness—a larger consciousness than my
own—which was identical with my own consciousness, but which was
also the consciousness of the entire universe. So basically it was a sensation of the entire universe being completely conscious.

A little historical poetical footnote: there seemed to be a number
of significant poetic visionary experiences in that year, 1948. Gary Snyder reported similarly—in 1948 he'd finished a big essay—his mental-
scholarship rational work, his Reed College senior thesis—and then
went down to the banks of the Willamette River and sat down before
sunrise in total silence, exhausted, with this year's long intellectual effort
completed—finished all that night. And just as the sun rose, in a com-

plete dead silence and his own body exhausted, just as a crack of light appeared in the sky, thousands and thousands of birds arose up out of the trees by the river—birds which had been totally silent—he hadn't even noticed they were there—filling the air with sentient squawks. He suddenly realized that "everything was alive"; that was his description, everything in the universe was sentient, the entire universe was alive. It was '48, soon after the bomb. I'd relate this historically, to some sort of large-scale planetary awakening of consciousness, some vaster sentient-consciousness, or less anthropocentric consciousness, a more biocentric consciousness, as a result of the tolling of the great iron gong of doom throughout the planet into any consciousness that read the newspaper. Maybe the birds didn't know, but all the humans knew that it was finally possible to destroy consciousness, too, or destroy brains all over.

I started to try to trace the curve of my own development. I remember "revolving around my own corpse"—that is, revolving around the corpse of the vision for many years. The visions themselves came to an end abruptly within a week or so, after several other episodes I won't describe, with a final breakthrough or a final experience: I was walking around Columbia College campus at night, with one of Blake's poems going around in my head, "O Rose, thou art sick . . ." I had a distinct impression of that vast conscious sky I'd glimpsed the week before; that it had now turned on me and was going to eat me up, that this enormous power of consciousness that spread through the universe had taken a dislike to me, so to speak, or now that it had noticed me, it was going to call me into it, devour me. So that I, Allen, was going to disappear, absorbed into this giant octopus serpent-monster consciousness. I think that's a pretty common bad acid trip, probably it's a common visionary experience, too. I mean, it's completely real, that you realize that you, the individual self eyeball, are *going to die* and be absorbed into a much larger intelligence. I had a kind of shuddery experience, bad trip, so to speak, which turned me off. I thought I was somewhat in control of my consciousness and could invoke a "breakthrough" at will, for about a week, but the last time I tried invoking it, what I got was the horrors, and I got frightened, and thought, uh oh, I've gone crazy, I'd better not play with this anymore. Or I'd better find out something reliable about this breakthrough. Unfortunately, I didn't have any Tibetan lamas, Swamis, Gnostic esoteric poets, or rock musicians to turn to at that point. There was nobody to talk to, that was the problem, there was absolutely nobody to talk to who was, like, sane or clear—more difficult than "coming out of the closet." The few people I talked to told me to see a psychiatrist, or just turned off, so I got very splenetic, angry and irritable, thinking that other people were resisting acknowledging what they themselves knew. So it was a typical, visionary misjudgment—you run across that kind of acid hallucination—kid who insists that his vision be immediately understood and accepted—walk in front of automobiles naked, revolution overnight, don't eat material food, etc.

Jump cut to London, 1973, Burroughs in St. James Street: "Anybody who makes an impression on you is a vampire." Dream that night: I was looking out of a pub window in London—a mullioned window, with old, unclear-glass leaded squares—and I had an uncanny feeling that some vampire was approaching down street. Sure enough, as I looked out the window, there was a long-haired balding-top round-blue-faced figure, with black circles under his eyes, fanged but human teeth, and a malevolent expression—and I recognized it was William Blake, come to get me again. So I said, "Ah! At last, I'll go out and get that bastard, check him out now. Vampire, eh? He'd been feeding on my consciousness long enough." And when I went out, he got scared and ran away. That's the end of the dream.

I had come to the conclusion, within ten minutes of the original 1948 visionary experiences, that any rationalization or thinking about them would automatically interpose a screen and get between my own consciousness and open reality and fill it with thought, so I would be substituting memory of vision for vision. There's the vampire aspect. But I also had said—to myself at that same time—"Now that I've seen this heaven on earth, I will never forget it, I will never stop referring all things to it, I will never stop considering it the center of my human existence and the center of my life which is now changed into a new world, and I'll never be able to go back, and that's great; and from now on, I'm chosen, blessed, sacred, poet, and this is my sunflower, my new mind. I'll be faithful the rest of my life, and I'll never forget it, never deny it, and I'll never renounce it. So finally, years later, I found I had to shit on it and renounce it to get the monkey off my back. I'm not speaking clearly enough . . .

P.P.: *You mean trying to get back to it kept you away from it?*

A.G.: As the visions faded, the actuality, there was nothing left but memory. I kept trying to go back in memory, to reconstitute the vision by staring at cornices or at trees, or thinking that somehow I could re-catalyze it. Take drugs to catalyze it—and acid does approximate that sensation of eternity. Well, on acid most of the time I also got the horror trip, because I was trying so hard to get back into the Eternity that I'd seen once before; so that every time I got high, when the first doubt came that I might not see "Eternity" . . . or the fear came that I might get eaten alive by "God," then the trip immediately turned into a hell. So my first thirteen psychedelic years were vomiting hells. And I didn't actually get out of that until I tried to combine acid with meditation. I got to India and saw Dudjom Rinpoche in 1963, and presented him with my psychological history, visionary history, my acid and peyote history, and he said very sympathetically that some images I described were similar to meditation experiences: "If you see anything horrible, don't cling to it; and if you see anything beautiful, don't cling to it." That formula actually cut the Gordian Knot of my mind there, because I realized that I *had* been clinging constantly to the memory of the vision. Because of my insistency, filling my head with thought about it, I cut myself off from direct perception—whether it was visionary or ordinary. In any case, I wasn't seeing what was in front of me, whether it be an eternity or just ordinary old Boulder. It's the same very simple situation you all know when you're young and trying to get laid: you think about it so much and make so many awkward efforts you don't get laid, whereas, when you do relax, you let things go their own way and do what comes naturally. Everybody knows that feedback of self-consciousness. So there's the old traditional statement, "Unless the seed die, it won't grow again." Or: "Only by renouncing, will you get what you want." Or what you thought you wanted. Death-in-life, the obvious order is to give up your *idée fixe*. Die, give up, let go, rather than force the issue.

p.p.: *Are you talking about an experience of renouncing Blake visions on the train from Kyoto to Tokyo?*

a.g.: That was a more superficial mental event, 1963, coming back from India. I realized that I wasn't going to make it back to heaven by forcing and insistency, and by continually churning over and over again that original 1948 experience, so I just started crying on the train in Japan—realizing I wasn't going to get to heaven. And the minute I began crying, I found myself in Heaven again, very briefly. So there's a poem called "The Change," which records that. That's just one more poignant moment in disillusionment, of the slow process of getting the visionary monkey off my back. The remarkable thing is that I stupefied myself from 1948 to about 1963. A long time—that's fifteen years, preoccupied with one single thought.

There's some early poems that recorded early takes on this kind of experience. I immediately saw poetry as a hermetic or secret way of talking about experiences that were universal, cosmic, that everybody knew about, but nobody knew how to talk about, nobody knew how to refer to. Nobody knew how to bring it up to front brain consciousness or to present it to social consciousness. So there were these poems from 1948 and after, where I first found myself a poet with something to talk about. Thus "Vision 1948": "I shudder with intelligence and I / Wake in the deep light / And hear a vast machinery / Descending without sound, / Intolerable to me, too bright. . . ." That was a description of the last experience of terror, a fear that the universe was turning inside out. In "Refrain," a month later, I was beginning to realize I was getting hung up on my visions. "Shadow changes into bone" was my symbolic language, slogan, meaning that Thought (high intellectual thought, ambition, idealized desire) actually comes true, and you do get to see a vision of eternity, which kills you. So "shadow," mind insight, changes into three-dimensional "bone."

I had just been in the middle of a broken-up love affair with Neal Cassady, which had come to an end at the moment, I thought, and I was desolate. And so, combining the end of the love affair and the visionary experience, I wrote a song called "A Western Ballad," that was influenced a lot by Blake's rhymes. "I wandered in an endless maze / that men have walked for centuries" is a paraphrase of Blake's "The Voice of the Ancient Bard": "They stumble all night over the bones of the dead / And wish to lead others where they should be led."

P.P.: *Was music part of the poem ("A Western Ballad") when you wrote it in 1948?*

A.G.: No, I put that in—maybe twenty years later. Actually, I'd heard it in inner ear. It was actually there, but at the time, I didn't have an instrument, I didn't play music, but it was built into the rhythm and tones of the poem. The exact notes, probably not, but *[sings]* "I ain't got no use for the women / A true one can never be found / They'll stick with a man when he's winning / And laugh in his face when he's down. / My friend was an honest cowpuncher, / Honest and upright and true, / And he'd still be a-ridin' the ranges / If it weren't for a gal named Lou. / He fell in with evil companions / The kind that were better off dead / And I couldn't help think of that woman/when they filled him full of lead. . . ." *[Laughs.]* That was the only "western ballad" I knew how to sing around that time.

Blake's advice on the subject of how you deal with the terror was: "To find the Western Path, / Right thro' the Gates of Wrath / I urge my way. . . ." Well, I thought that Blake's instructions meant delve right into the terror, cultivate the terror, get right into it, right into death. I said, "Die, go mad, drop dead." So I thought for many years that my obligation was to annihilate my ordinary consciousness and expand my mystic consciousness through death. I thought "the path" was through the Gates of Wrath; Fear, and Wrath, and Terror. So actually, for that fifteen years, I was in a kind of quandary.

P.P.: *Are there specific poems that work with that problem?*

A.G.: So my first prayer—I got into looking at things in terms of I'd better beg for mercy or something, "Ah still Lord, ah, sweet Divinity . . ." By the time of this "Psalm" a year later [1949], the actual experience had become solidified into the symbol of a god, the notion of a central divine Lord that I was trying to get to. Thus, after a while, I wrote big masochistic psalms of the divinity, saying I want to die and be part of You.

Which is a classic poetic position a lot of people get trapped into and finally die, too. Thinking, well, I'm going to pursue the beauty to the tomb. Saying the body has to drop down, the body has to die, and the mind has to die: "When I think of death / I get a goofy feeling: / Then I catch my breath: / Zero is appealing / Appearances are hazy. / Smart went crazy, / Smart went crazy." Christopher Smart. Then Kerouac and I collaborated on a really mad ditty, referring still to the subject of "frantic light"—the basic idea was that only by being torn apart, dying or being cracked open, or going nuts or making a breakthrough or being turned upside down or inside out or ass by mouth or finally sort of mind suicided, would there be any breakthrough opening: "Pull my daisy / Tip my cup / All my doors are open."

P.P.: *Your interpretation of the vision changed as time passed?*

A.G.: Yeah. By 1950, I was already sufficiently disillusioned to be hip to the fact that I was stuck on a broken record, mentally. So there are a couple of sort of self-pitying poems, in a way, saying good-bye to the whole experience, like "An Imaginary Rose in a Book." See, by this time I was seeing the experience as failed, passed, imaginary or hallucinatory, began to be *willing* to see it as that. "Oh dry old rose of God . . ." (ah, "The Sick Rose": "O Rose thou art sick . . .") "that with such bleak perfume / changed images to blood . . ."—changed poetry to reality, changed, you know, prophetic mind thoughts to three-dimensional, stuck-in-the-universe actuality. I just finally had to cut that whole set of thoughts out. By 1951, "Ode: My 24th Year" is all done in like symbolic language, but I was thinking in terms of getting grounded again: 'Time gets thicker, light gets dim . . .' Borne into my body again, "the weaving of the shroud goes on." I was faced with an actual death rather than an imaginary spiritual death. Actually, I just gave up about that time, age twenty-five, having gone through a whole cycle of inspiration and dead end. A lot of people go through that traditional characteristic cycle.

P.P.: *So trying to conjure Blake symbolically was a dead end? What happened after that whole phase of abstraction and metaphysics?*

A.G.: The next stage was a funny compromise. Thinking that, OK, I can't make it by juggling symbolic language, referring to roses, light, spiritual ward, ineffable visions—so the only thing I can do is attempt to describe what I actually see, or actually saw, to pay attention to detail. To pay attention to minute particulars—so that I could have my cake *and* eat it, in a way. Like look out at the world as if I were having a vision and see the sort of details I might observe if I were having a vision. Maybe not look for the entire vision, but at least check out little details like the particular pale greenness of the buds on the south end of the tips of branches of trees in the backyard here, they're pointing at the sun. The pale budgreen budding of a new bud, as distinct from the older, thick, dark green of the regular leaves. So, noticing detail. Around that time, 1949 on, I ran into William Carlos Williams. Naturally the same thought came to me—was Williams living, actually living, in eternity? Observing the detail of eternity, refusing to point to it as eternity, refusing to talk about it in "poetic" terms, refusing to talk about it symbolically—but just directly perceiving what was in front of him? And I realized that's what Blake also said to do: Blake said poetry's in "minute particulars." And Williams said, No ideas (about eternity!) ... "No ideas but in things themselves. No ideas but in the facts." So I began accidentally picking up on Williams's work because he lived near me, I began writing poems that were an imitation of his style, which were little short notations of detail. That book, called *Empty Mirror,* I wrote about the same time as *Gates of Wrath.* I'd sent a bunch of these poems [from *Gates*] to Williams, and he wrote back that they weren't very good. What he said was, "In this mode, perfection is basic"; these are imperfect. I understood that to mean that there was very little actual concrete detail in them; it was all a sort of refining of the imagery of roses and light and mystical references—rehashing of it over again. I'd thought maybe if I could concentrate all my mind's focus into these few symbols and juggle them around a couple of times—you know, make some crystal-like perfect symbolic statement that could turn other people on and catalyze the same vision in them. But it didn't work, it didn't seem to work. So what I did was to turn to prose, so to speak, to little prosaic observations. In Buddhist terms this would be *Vipashyana,* i.e., paying attention to mindful detail, a sharpening of focus to a finer clearer Zennish perception of a black scrape on the floor where a chair has been pulled away; that one detail indicating a whole path of previous activity. Seeing what's in front of the eyes, seeing where the eye strikes. Or, "sight is where the eye hits," a phrase of Louis Zukofsky. The action in *Empty Mirror* was something that I've noticed applicable to a lot of younger students now: the difficulty they have in turning their minds aside from an idealized notion of visionary perception or social revolutionary perception that they're seeking. Turning away from an abstract reference of that, and settling for presentation of what's "closest to the nose." Settling for what they can actually see in front of them as a subject for poems. Settling on something they can say without humorless exaggeration. I see a lot of poetry, floods of visionary revolutionary poet-beatnik, post-hippie, post-psychedelic poetry coming across my desk, and the problem is almost everywhere the same problem that I had, of using referential language pointing to some other vision out of mind; or something that has been realized but the poet is not presently in that state, and is violently demanding a breakthrough into a state of universal consciousness but is not presenting any *details* from that state of universal consciousness. So the only strategy to get to that visionary poesy, to approximate it, is to slow down and fake it, so to speak—it might be interesting to try and fake it—by simply settling for whatever detail you could actually see right now, anytime, with ordinary mind.

So (here in *Empty Mirror*), my comment on my previous poems was "Seven years' words wasted . . ." [He reads "Long Live the Spiderweb."] That was a comment on the whole *Gates of Wrath*. Further, "I attempted to concentrate / the total sun's rays in / each poem as through a glass, / but such magnification / did not set the page afire." So I had to move on.

"How sick I am! / that thought / always comes to me/with horror . . ." See now, here's a shift of diction and an approach to poetry that's more realistic—I'm still daydreaming, still talking about my own thoughts, but at least talking about it in a normal tone of voice that you can understand. "It is December / almost, they are singing / Christmas carols / in front of the department / stores down the block on / Fourteenth Street." That was my big breakthrough, finally; it's called "Marijuana Notation." It took a little grass to make me realize I had been "ignoring other parts of my mind." In "attempting to magnify the sun's rays in each poem as through a glass," I'd been ignoring everyday perceptions, the more

familiar perceptions. Here, the mind-poem shifts from daydreamy intro-
spection as to the nature of consciousness, directly to: "they are singing
/ Christmas carols . . ." I remember this poem as being like a big deal for
me, because it was the first time that a real literal physical object from my
own world entered into a poem. At this time I had got out of a bughouse
and was living on my own—actually, a very good state, aware of the situation and moving toward more realistic approaches to my mindthought.
Looking at the worst! "Tonight all is well . . ." At that point, there was a
certain humor entering in, about my own situation, and dealing with
it a little more observantly—the terrible idea of being so totally freaked
out that "my head was separated from my body" seemed all right as long
as I could talk about it sensibly!

P.P.: *Didn't you write another poem in that same room, the room where
in "Tonight all is well . . ." you're lying sleepless on the couch?*

A.G.: Yeah. In the same room, on the same couch, looking out the
window. There's a line by Yeats, a title in his essays, called *"The Trembling of the Veil."* I took that to mean the trembling of the veil of perception, trembling of the veils of eternity. So I put that title on one short of
homely everyday instance of the trembling of the veil of maya, change
of perception, and wrote "Today out the window / the trees seemed like
live / organisms on the moon . . ." *[He reads* "The Trembling of the Veil."*]*
I was just looking out the window, trying to describe (as in "Marijuana
Notation") a little piece of actuality in detail. I intended to fix my mind,
to root my mind, ground my mind somewhere—in a common place that
other people could see. And I figured that if I was in Eternity, or if I was
a poet, or if I was a spiritual angel, or if mind was open, there wasn't anything I could do about it, except maybe look at something specific. And
describe that. If other people could see though my eyes, whatever Virtue
I had would shiver in their brain. In other words, the only way I could
actually communicate the sense of eternity that I had, or might have, or
wanted to have, was through concrete particular detail grounding my
mind, like taking the opposite direction of the superhuman apocalyptic-
light-hunger poetry that I'd been churning out before: taking exactly
the opposite direction by turning around to face everyday universe, BE
HUMAN! So I wrote a series of real simple poems dealing with that, and

also looked over all my old writing to see if I had anything in my poem-journals that was real—that actually did cover day-to-day perceptions.

P.P.: *Didn't you send those to Williams—after you arranged the journal entries into verse?*

A.G.: Yeah, I found a couple of prose things I'd written and arranged them into "modern poetry" lines and sent them off to Williams. His immediate reaction was, "This is it! Do you have any more writings like this?" So among the poems I sent to Williams, which to him seemed to demonstrate a grounded mind or someone who'd finally come down to earth, was "A Poem on America." *Acis and Galatea,* those images are all from Dostoevsky's *Raw Youth.* It was a really terrific book, about this Russian kid who has a vision, just like me. I was still referring to my visionary experiences, "filled with fire / with the appearance of God," but at least I got my mind grounded enough to: "The alleys, the dye works, / Mill St. in the smoke, / negros climbing around / the rusted iron by the river . . ." I think that actually may be the best poetry I ever wrote! Just absolutely pure clear modern—you know, one hundred years from now it'll be like looking down the wrong end of the telescope into the past, and you'll see the present time, looking into the eternity of 1949.

P.P.: *Allen, how could you have been writing the abstract poems in* Gates of Wrath *while simultaneously writing prose observations in a clear, detailed style? Wasn't that kind of "schitzy"?*

A.G.: It was. It's really interesting: a homely poetic schizophrenia. These were written in notebooks, you know, little journals that a lot of us keep. And I wasn't trying to write poetry. So, [in] not trying to write poetry, I wasn't, then, obsessed with writing the eternal-image-symbol combination to break everybody's mind open. I was just describing what was in front of me. Because I was doing that, my notes were less obsessional, less hung up, they were just detail. After I met Williams and understood what he was doing, I separated a couple paragraphs with word-pictures out of my journals and arranged them in lines like him—sometimes counting syllables, sometimes counting breath, sometimes balancing it on the page to see what it looked like—visually. These are just the ordinary, unself-conscious notebooks, prose, and I just took the nuts out of it, the intensest moments of prose, pushing everything else aside, isolating it, framing it on the page. It's like a painter paints a big painting— You know the abstract expressionist era? They paint a big painting, and then there are one or two little spots on the painting that they thought had funny kind of tension and space. They'd white-paint out everything else and leave the reds and blues in just a few areas. Remember? That's what I did with my journals. I just sort of got rid of everything except a couple of lines that were active. That was Williams's advice. He said, better have one active phrase—by "active," he meant alive, focused, precise, grounded, no ideas—things—but not ideas. Better have one active phrase than pages of inactive opaque poetry—poetry that doesn't move. Better isolate just the one thing that's active. That's what poetry does, some kind of mental action . . . contact with reality, rather than waiting, rather than more babbling vagueness. I just eliminated hundreds of pages of subjective scribbling about when will I see Blake again, or I'm crazy, or when are they going to love me, is blank ever gonna come back, what is the nature of the world, curves of phenomenology . . .

P.P.: *Didn't you mention other incidents like the Williams one—the other night—that helped change your direction from abstract to the concrete?*

A.G.: Another thing that I did, a big lesson to me, was I spent several years keeping journals and then left them months in a friend's apartment on 8th Avenue in New York in 1947. When I came back, I found he'd read through all my secret journals. I was ashamed, [because] it had all this sex stuff and love babblings about Cassady, and Blake and everything. So I asked him about it, and he said, "Well, it's awful. Can't read it, it's unreadable." There was only one page that was readable. I asked what was that? And he pointed to a page, the only page of actual description of something outside of my head. So I took that out of my journals and rearranged it as "The Bricklayer's Lunch Hour." *[He reads "The Bricklayer's Lunch Hour."]* It's just sort of like looking out of the window—sketching. It was something—actually, I got it off Kerouac, the idea of making a verbal picture. Like making a little pencil sketch. Detail a cat, a hat, a tree moving in the wind, etc. Oddly enough, right now, looking outside, "it's darkening as if to rain and / The wind on top of the trees in the streets comes through almost harshly." Without even intending it, there is that little shiver of a moment of time preserved in the crystal cabinet of the mind, a little shiver of eternal space. That's what I was looking for. Simply by looking outside of the window and seeing what was there. That ['The Bricklayer's Lunch Hour"] was probably the earliest text I published which makes real sense. I wrote it in Denver, in my journal, 1947.

p.p.: *So you were settling for a more realized, clearer-detail style?*

a.g.: See, this entry is earlier than the *Gates of Wrath* even. This ordinary consciousness was available all along, except I despised it and thought it was not important, or didn't avail myself of my own intelligence, my own direct detailed perception. This is 1947, and all other symbolic churning doesn't have the "Bricklayer's" clarity. Which is better? I don't know. The other kind, in *Gates of Wrath,* is a kind of mantric magical onanistic, masturbatory sing-along power.

p.p.: *Wasn't there another incident, with Kerouac, I think; you mentioned it the other night. Along the line of convincing you to turn away from the symbolic style . . .*

a.g.: Yeah. I think about the best, funniest of all poems in *Empty Mirror* is represented as . . . finally I get a look at myself from the outside, like in a movie, a burned-out case, a total flop, failure, that I considered I was. I'd gotten out of the bughouse, and thought I'd finally hit the ground and didn't have anything. I had a job in market research, a little furnished room on Fifteenth Street in New York. And I wrote this: "Walking home at night." *[He reads "Walking home at night."]* "I reached my hands to my head and hissed / Oh, God, how horrible!" The taste of actual mind thought, of self thought, in that is so accurate—it's just like a little flash picture of oneself in a funny moment. And it's clear and familiar. I showed it to Keroauc, he said: "Allen, you really got it there, it's my own little Allen. That's actually Allen. Whoever you are, you're right there. You know—like unashamed, completely free." He bought it, so to speak, and accepted the worst possible image instead of accepting an image of myself as an angel—accepting myself as a soft, white-fleshed failure . . . "creeping / in and out of rooms like / myself." Stuck drab "God,

How horrible!" It was just willingness to be that nowhere man, nowhere self, to be myself, really, and the humor involved in being that—rather than being a divine Blakean angel! I think that finally makes it possible to stand firmly on the ground in poems like this and then begin constructing out of that reality: "I saw the best minds of my generation destroyed by madness, starving hysterical naked." Having accepted all that fact, all that detail, and looking at it sympathetically, rather than totally freaked out, working with that ordinary failure; ordinary magic. Then, after several years, it's possible to build a rhapsody of facts, which is "Howl" [in] a later period.

So, basically what I've done in this talk is cover the development of my poetry up to about 1953, a couple of years before "Howl." How I was preparing for application of basic grounded realistic humor to the practical world. More free energy for that, once having found a place to put my feet, once having got grounded a little—then getting a little playful maybe, or even have big rhapsodies on the people who've lost their visions.

Does this make sense? Does anybody feel that I took the wrong turn? Made the wrong decision spiritually? Maybe I should have held out for more, got into the bughouse and held out for more?

P.P.: *Do you ever wish you could go back to 1948, age twenty-two, and start again with the Blake vision?*

A.G.: Go back to twenty-two or twenty-three and start all over again? Well, in the tantric Buddhist tradition, you do that. It's really miraculous, in a sense, the advent of Buddhism—or, if not Buddhism, at least Gnostic experience, the breakthrough (culturally) of the Gnostic tradition, because Blake is in that tradition, which is parallel to the Oriental knowledge, mind knowledge. It's a whole new movie! It starts a whole new movie in America, where everybody raises his hand and has had a vision. It's really terrific, and what's going to come out of that is something that is going to astound the imaginary angels. Before, maybe people had visions; my theory is that they were just pushed to the back of the brain. They weren't socially usable, they weren't anything you could "work" with. Now you can build a rock band out of visions. Electricians went before you. You could make movies out of it, you could probably build industries out of an ecological vision of everything intertwined in nature.

P.P.: *Like Solari . . .*

A.G.: You could make money on visions, nowadays you can reform the society. You could reconstitute the nature of the society, or direction. One thing Kerouac said in 1961, that I always took as a keystone, one key statement: when Leary visited and turned everyone on to psilocybin, Kerouac, high, turned around and said to the room, "Walking on water wasn't built in a day." And that's basically the situation in America: that having had a breakthrough in the 1940s, it will take decades and decades—cell by cell—to reconstitute the body of America, build a new physical body. It will take as long to "unblow" the old consciousness and recreate a physical world corresponding to our mental picture; it will take as long to do *that* as it took to build up this physical monster building classroom we have here. Obviously, you couldn't transform this relatively ungainly basement cafeteria into a metaphysically appropriate arcade filled with green bower leaves and natural sound systems, without decades of slow, delicate adjustment of the material world to our desire. Well, this very Naropa school conception, or the notion of a Kerouac School of Disembodied Poetics, is something that would have required breakthrough, spiritual breakthrough, freak-out, into groundedness—beginning at the beginning, putting our worlds together, slowly. "Walking on water wasn't built in a day," that was the meaning of that.

Q.: *Why the "Disembodied" poetics, if the emphasis is getting back into the body?*

A.G.: That's a joke. Because he's dead. Kerouac's dead, so he's disembodied, so to speak. Also, because we were fools and didn't know what we were getting into. We didn't realize it would be such a serious body. Also, because of beatnik poetic inspiration, that made it sound funny. I objected for a while, saying, wait a minute, this is contrary to all the basic principles enunciated by Pound and Williams and the imagists, but Trungpa said, "Ah, it's pretty funny, why don't you use it—it's too late to change it. Too late!"

P.P.: *Before we finish, could you tell the story about Kerouac's reaction to your visions?*

A.G.: When I had my Harlem experiences, he was quite matured, already written *The Town and The City,* or was preparing his first book. I, I think, had not yet had quite that prophetic shudder of sixties' transcendental freak-out mind so characteristic—I don't think he'd had a totally "visionary" experience. Mortal human transitoriness was built into his nature, and into his early prose, but I didn't think he'd had a full-scale breakthrough at the time. I wrote him a long, mysterious letter, not quite referring ... telling him that something big had happened to my mind, that I had entered the kingdom of eternity, that I would come through and teach him as soon as I could. He read it, and it looked to him as if I had really gone nuts. "Poor little Allen, he really wants to make something, you know, he's going to come and teach me about eternity? Poor little kid." Except that he *was* struck by this sudden seizure of un-New Jerseyesque, middle-class Jewish-boy-seriousness on my part, that I had suddenly gotten to be a fanatic of some kind, instead of [being] a nice little boy from Paterson, who was always wandering around saying: "Discretion is the better part of valor." All of a sudden, I was dreaming about angels. He sent me a funnier letter than I sent him, saying something like, "America is a permissible dream, providing you remember that ants have Americas." Or eternity is a permissible dream, providing that you remember that ants have eternities, little eternities are had by baby mules in musty fields. Actually, that's not what he said: it's another poem. I recorded this emotional transaction in a poem, "The Lion for Real." The lion is symbolic of that Blake vision; each stanza covers like a different attempt on my part to communicate to the profession, to Kerouac, to my family, to my psychiatrist.

However, a couple of years later, Kerouac had a similar situation of isolation, and was sitting in a field in North Carolina in his sister's backyard, doing a little yoga breathing he'd learned. He describes the seizure he had suddenly, in which his eyes closed and everything turned to gold, and he fainted and fell back, and saw everything in the universe as "golden ash." That's described in a text called *The Scripture of the Golden*

Eternity. I thought I recognized that he'd had some kind of spiritual breakthrough, or incident, or visionary experience, and from then on, we knew what we were talking about back and forth, we began to correlate our mysterious "X" consciousness . . .

From *Talking Poetics from Naropa Institute*, volume 2, edited by Anne Waldman and Marilyn Webb, interview conducted by Paul Portuges (Boulder, Colo.: Shambhala, 1979), 381–414. Reprinted by permission of the Allen Ginsberg Estate.

Allen Ginsberg Talks about Poetry

KENNETH KOCH, 1977

THE FOLLOWING INTERVIEW finds two good poets "talking shop" for the *New York Times*. Ginsberg was at his esoteric best, yet Koch was adept at keeping him on topic. The tone is warm and friendly—a welcome dynamic, given the range of topics discussed in this exchange.

Q. *What do you like best about your own poetry?*
A. Cranky music.
Q. *Meaning?*
A. Vowelic melodiousness, adjusted towards speech syncopation.
Q. *Vowelic?*
A. Assonance, long mellow mouthings of assonance. Classic example: Moloch Moloch. In "Howl," "Moloch whose skyscrapers stand in the long streets"—and so on.
Q. *You like the music in your poetry more than you like the content. Because your content is so striking and so . . .*
A. My ambition for my content was to be totally personal. So it could rest on fact. I mean the world I knew. But the sound in my throat, that mellow music's part of the world I know. So if I get "hot" poetically, the vowels heat up.
Q. *Could you explain getting "hot" in poetry?*
A. I mean inspiration in a literal way, as deep breath flowing out unobstructedly as long vowels, musical.
Q. *What brings on this state, if you can say anything about that? I believe some people have the idea about your work that you get poetic*

inspiration from, or have gotten it from, certain drugs, from certain political experiences, and so on. What's the truth about this?

A. The vowelic heat comes from single-minded devotional awareness of death. And the preciousness of the human body alive. Drugs have been a side experiment, just to cover those classical possibilities—Baudelaire, Gautier, old Bohemia. Buddhist Vajarayna studies reinforce natural inspiration. Because it's practice of breath awareness.

Q. *What helps you most to be in a single-minded devotional state?*

A. Not trying to. It's accident, from resting in ordinary mind.

Q. *What things do you think keep you from having that experience, if any? Do your travels, your political activity, your literary ambitions, etc.?*

A. All those, including the telephone and excessive masturbatory activity as a man of letters—publishing journals, teaching, trying to keep up with punk rock.

Q. *What would you consider an ideal existence for yourself as a poet?*

A. Retiring from the world, living in a mountain hut, practicing certain special meditation exercises half the day, and composing epics as the sun sets. I did that actually, for ten days early September in a mountain hut in Southern Colorado.

Q. *Is that when you wrote "Contest of Bards"* [a long forthcoming poem]?

A. No, I didn't do any writing then, purposely.

Q. *How long would you have had to stay to feel good about writing?*

A. About a thousand days. There is in Tantric study a specific three-year, three-month solitary retreat doing non-conceptual practices.

Q. *What does that do for you as a poet?*

A. It clears the mind of false poetry, let's say. That is to say, self-centered poetry.

Q. *You said earlier your ideal in poetry was to be completely personal. Can one be that and not be self-centered?*

A. That's a problem I have, and I'm working on it. I think there is, though. One would still be looking out of one's ego eyes, without attachment. If you sat for three years not doing anything you'd sure wind up that way, if you had a good teacher.

Q. *About non-attachment—your poetry seems so admirably attached to the world.*

A. I'd rather use the word "involved."

Q. *Could you explain the difference?*

A. *Involved* means present in the middle of, with complete awareness, and active. *Attached* means neurotically self-centered in the activity. That's the way I'm using those words.

Q. *Do you think your poetry may have gotten some if its energy from a conflict between being attached and wishing not to be?*

A. No, I think the biggest energy is probably in the Moloch section of "Howl" and the "Hymns to Death" in "Kaddish" and the dramatic rants in this new "Contest of Bards" poem. That energy, in the first two cases, comes from total belief in the subject—annihilation of civilization, inevitability of death. In the "Contest of Bards," I found a dramatic form to go all-out into total self-belief through the mouths of characters. They can say anything I want. I don't have to take responsibility.

Q. *Could you say something more about "Contest of Bards"?*

A. That poem came in a burst of all-night writing. Thirty pages— later to be touched up, unscrambled a little. A few times my attention lapsed and the page got cross-hatched with corrections. But mostly a continuous stream of improvisation. Symmetric and perfect. Like "Howl," "Kaddish," and another poem I love, "September on Jessore Road" (at the end of *Fall of America*). Poe said a long poem was impossible because he couldn't conceive of a long poem being written in one sitting. He thought you'd lose the lyric impulse if you worked on it over a period of years—month, years. But I think most poets have found that every few years they're liberated into a composition. That they can accomplish a vast epic in one night. Vast thirty, forty pages. I think most poets have that experience—most big poets. How long did it take Shelley to write "Ode to the West Wind?" Teatime? Before breakfast?

Q. *I think he wrote it in a park in Florence in one afternoon or one day.*

A. On the other hand, I write a little bit every other day. I just write when I have a thought. Sometimes I have big thoughts, sometimes little thoughts. The deal is to accept whatever comes. Or work with whatever comes. Leave yourself open.

Q. *What do you have to have, or to be, to start with, in order to leave yourself open to produce good poetry?*

A. A little glimpse of death, and the looseness and tolerance that brings.

Q. *I think I understand about the glimpse of death, but haven't ambition and passion and the wish for fame and power been at least as important in making you a good poet?*

A. No, I think a glimpse of the death of power, fame and ambition liberated me from rigid interpretation of those stereotypes. Not that they don't exist in my head, but they exist side by side with taxicab noises and the gaps in between the sounds.

Q. *To go back to what you need to write a good poem. We've spoken of experience, mental states, and breath. What about the work of other poets? What part has that had in your writing?*

A. It changes from decade to decade.

Q. *Let's talk about this decade.*

A. Right now. This year I read through all Blake—early lyrics through "Milton," "The Four Zoas" and "Jerusalem." And his letters and marginalia. And I read "Paradise Lost" aloud.

Q. *Did you read it aloud alone or to someone?*

A. With a young bard. Next project, read all through Shelley and Spenser. I've never read silently all the way through "Paradise Lost" before.

Q. *I never read "Paradise Lost" in college. I read it when I was twenty-five, and I read all the way through in one night, I remember. It seems one can be inspired to read somewhat the same way one's inspired to write.*

A. Yes. Now I'm over fifty, and I want to read all the great ancient epics. So I can hear their vowels.

Q. *Allen, what you say suggests a great appetite; has a Rabelaisian sound. "All the epics" you want to read. Comment.*

A. Quite. The ones that exist and the ones that don't exist. Beginning with "Gilgamesh."

Q. *We were talking before about what you liked about your own poetry. I know the subject sounds a little egomaniacal and odd but, in fact, what a poet likes about his poetry is what's usually called his taste—or that part of it he uses when he's writing. So what else do you like? You mentioned its music.*

A. The other thing I like is that I think it's witty or funny. That is, the phrasing itself.

Q. *Could you give an example or two?*

A. "Death which is the mother of the universe" (from "Kaddish"). The *which* there is weird. In that it sounds archaic, and it means quite literally an im-person. *Which,* not *who.* And it sounds right in the mouth. Rather than a vulgar *who.* There's a funniness to the manipulation of the syntax.

Q. *You have a way of speaking easily and openly about things (including what you like in your work)—I wonder if Whitman influenced you at all to be able to do that.*

A. In the *Journals,* I put myself down a lot, too. There's a lot of depreciation. I'm just registering what comes in my head. I wouldn't be studying Buddhism if I thought I were ego-less. I wouldn't be such a religious fanatic. As for registering what's going on in one's feelings, it's too much work to do anything else but reproduce as exactly as possible the fluctuations.

Q. *Do you feel this makes you a disconcerting person?*

A. I try to be less and less disconcerting as I grow older.

Q. *Could you tell me another line in your work that has the witty quality you like?*

A. *"Taxi September along Jessore Road / Oxcart skeletons drag charcoal load."* There's a certain nostalgia in the first line, as of some old supperclub lyric ("September in the Rain") followed by a Daumier-like, objectively observed fact—condensed into cartoon, literally, charcoal loads dragged by oxen whose ribs are showing—minute particulars, yet in the first line there's this funny Jerome Kern sentimentality, but the statement I'm making is all newspaper-true.

Q. *Did you feel the Jerome Kern sentimentality at the time of the taxi ride or when you wrote the poem?*

A. Both. That's what I meant by awareness of mortality.

Q. *Please explain.*

A. Part of the sentimental nostalgia of show tunes like "September Song" is a little glimmer of actual feeling of the transitoriness and dream-illusionary nature of our presence here on the scene. At the same time as the gruesome bones of suffering show in the oxcart skeletons. Same time, there's an odd humor in noticing they're dragging a load of charcoal through the mud. I don't know if that answers the question. In some respects, the lines are humorous because they reflect ordinary mind. What actually passes through your head. Which you recollect and accept if you're a poet.

Q. *What do you mean by "what passes through your head"?*

A. I mean that literally: the pictures that occur in an area about two inches before the forehead and the couple of inches into the skull where you see mental images. What Pound called Phanopoeia. Which I'm locating physiologically. There are pictures, and then there are the words. And the words—or soundtrack connected with the pictures—seem to occur physiologically along the surface of the tongue and down into the larynx. And the activity of poetry can include bare attention to those two areas which provide sharply defined detailed photos and a running commentary—spontaneous and, so to speak, unborn (you can't trace their origin)—on the picture show. I'm suggesting if the reader takes a quiet moment to pay attention to his mental activities located in those areas he'll discover that process is going on all the time.

Q. *Do you feel these pictures and sounds are worth reproducing in poetry, and, if so, why?*

A. Well, where else in your head are you going to find matter for writing?

Q. *Some have thought to find it in the experience of passionate love, others in singing of the history of their people, others in writing about flowers, streets, etc.*

A. Well, I'm simply pointing out that extant pictures of flower-power street riots can be observed in detail for such purposes in the mind's eye, which I've tried to locate physiologically, as an *aide-mémoire*. No contradiction. Does that make any sense?

Q. *Everything you say makes sense, but I want to be sure I'm getting the same sense you are.*

A. Really. If somebody wants to write about a love affair they once had, they'll have to remember it in pictures and words.

Q. *Couldn't what the love made the poet feel be used to create a poem about something not the love affair? Or might not made-up pictures give a better sense of the love affair than the "real" ones?*

A. Certainly your statement is right. I was just pointing out the easiest place to look for an objective correlative. But even if you substitute a roller-coaster ride for the flash of belly you kissed, the roller-coaster picture will occur somewhere around your forehead.

Q. *Do you think all words are accompanied by pictures?*

A. No. But for that combination of visual particularity that Pound praises so highly in Catullus, with accurate verbal captions, look to the forehead and tongue. If you go to a restaurant and want to order eggs over easy, bacon and hash browns, you'll find yourself formulating it subvocally till the waitress arrives at your table. So when you're trying to describe your grandmother's amethyst necklace, that pretty detail arrives at your tongue as the picture in the mind's eye. I mean, how do you think I got "amethyst necklace"?

Q. *How would you distinguish "minds-eye" lines like those in "Jessore Road" from those in, say, the Moloch section of "Howl," or from the long Blakean lines in your new poem "Contest of Bards"?*

A. The Moloch section really has accurate pictures, like "Moloch whose eyes are a thousand blind windows." That's giant Chicago buildings. "Moloch whose skyscrapers stand in the long streets like endless Jehovahs." That's the robot vista down Park Avenue. "Moloch whose smokestacks and antennae crown the cities." That you can see entering or leaving Chicago by train or bus—swift sketch panoramic vista. I would say those are directly mind's eye lines. Not as particular as Williams's, because we're dealing with panoramic megalopolis. Not saxifrage cracking a Rutherford sidewalk on Ridge Road.

Q. *Allen, that seems modest in an odd way—your statement that anyone can see, just by leaving Chicago by bus, that vision of yours. My next question is, How do you change mind's-eye material so as to make it into lines like that?*

A. Precisely. Just the right question. By paying attention to the soundtrack along the surface of the tongue. You're riding along on the bus. You see these weird wires, gas flares, industrial smokestacks, antennae, covering the outskirts, surrounding the city. They have names. Listen to what you're thinking in the base of the throat. "Smokestacks and antennae crowning the city." Maybe "Smokestacks and antennae . . . crowning . . . the cities." How else do you think of the words? Listen to your foot? Yes. Rhythmically. But the words march in rhythm through the throat. That's pretty good. What I'm saying is taking off from Kerouac's motto: "Don't stop to think of the words. Stop to see the picture better." Sure, anybody can write all subconscious verbal gossip, but if it's connected with a picture, there's likely to be some substance there. If you can focus on details of the picture, the descriptive words rise naturally.

Q. *Has that always been your experience?*

A. It's not been my conscious experience. I've just tried to formulate tricks of the trade in the past few years, teaching at Naropa Institute.

Q. *Could you tell me briefly which twentieth-century poets have influenced your work?*

A. Most recently, enormously, Charles Reznikoff, for his particular focus on sidewalks, parks and subways of New York. Williams, originally, for a large body of haiku-like concrete particulars in which "things are symbols of themselves." Particularly one poem of Williams lately— "Thursday"—which for me is the intersecting point between Buddhist "mind-fullness" and American poetics. Then, further, Kerouac's spontaneous melodiousness—his long sentence, Melville-like prose paeans to American disillusionment. One line of his, particularly: "Trucks driving forward in a seizure of tarpaulin power." Hart Crane's Shelleylike apostrophes. Their musical structure. Especially "Atlantis." Eliot's nostalgic silent movies—"A crowd flowed over London Bridge, so many." Marsden Hartley's plainness and localism. Creeley's and Olson's mystique of syllables and physiology—that is, the line as an extension of the breath has affected me. In the New York schools, glamorization of the informal.

Q. *I thought I noticed in some recent short poems something closer to Gary Snyder than I'd seen before in your poetry.*

A. Gary's always an influence. Towards muscular Chinese. That is to say, sharp specific images rising from actual physical work and familiarity—with woodchopping, Ponderosa pine, Sierra trails, and carpentry. Other influences, particularly toward music, have been the blues of Richard "Rabbit" Brown (a '20s New Orleans guitar singer) and Dylan's marvelous use of rhyme.

Q. *What's the relationship, as you see it, of your* Journals *to your poetry?*

A. My poetry's more or less autobiographical. My model was Yeats ...

Q. *You didn't mention him as an influence.*

A. Well, here we are again. Yeats, in giving a chronological accounting of his changes, from "Responsibilities" through "Crazy Jane." But there is also all this background accounting (which is what is in the *Journals*)— sometimes ephemera, sometimes traumas central to my life. I had most of the *Journals* around my house and gave them to Grove in 1967. They were all typed up. But there was a problem of editing—accurate typescript, and elimination of boring, unreadable, subjectively stupid dross. Gordon Ball spent two years working over the material, and then I went over every line with him, refining and clarifying and eliminating the unnecessary. It's a lot of work as *Indian Journals* had been. That took five years to get typed and edited. The two books constitute about one-twentieth of the mass of journals I've kept since the early '50s. There's a whole book of South American journals, a book of adventures getting kicked out of Cuba in 1965, conversations with Yevtushenko in Moscow. Now everything's typed up to 1976.

Q. *What is in this new book that can't be found in your other books?*

A. Inside dope on daily life. Early snapshots and drawings. A whole collection of haikus. Old prose sketches of extraordinary people I saw on the subways in New York. Conversations with Williams, Burroughs, Kerouac. A glimpse of Dylan Thomas, 1960s prophetical rantings—about the C.I.A. Outrageous attacks, in verse and prose, on early dopey literary critics of the '60s, that I was ashamed to publish at the time. A sort of '60s "Dunciad." Which includes the C.I.A. Bit musings on heroin. Experiments with laughing gas, acid, mushrooms, marijuana—mostly poetry notations on the moment. Dreams with vast literary casts of characters, including you, Kenneth Koch, and Burroughs and Eleanor Roosevelt and Kerouac and Marlon Brando and Corso and Tibetan lamas. Silly ditties I wrote with Kerouac. An obscene lyric for "The Good Ship Lollipop." One Artaud-like recollection of an appearance of Blake. Instant crazed reaction to the Bay of Pigs. Another series of continuing dreams: a sort of soap opera of premonitions of the death experience. Sketches of the Acropolis and Jerusalem. Sex fantasies. Records of New Year's Eve parties. A little anthology of Swahili proverbs. Everything I didn't put in my poetry books that I thought somebody would like to read somewhere.

Q. *Allen, you're a remarkable man. And I've known you for twenty-five years, and this is our first long conversation. It's been good to get around to it.*

A. It's about time.

———————

From *New York Times Book Review*, October 23, 1977, 9, 44–46. Reprinted by permission of Karen Koch and the Kenneth Koch Literary Estate.

Words and Music, Music, Music

MITCHELL FELDMAN, 1982

ALLEN GINSBERG'S PASSION FOR MUSIC dated back to the days of his youth, when he heard blues and gospel sung in his Paterson, New Jersey, neighborhoods. He loved jazz, which became a sound track for the Beat Generation. He expanded his interests to include almost every type of music imaginable, including rock 'n' roll, world, and folk. His friend Bob Dylan invited him to participate in his Rolling Thunder Revue tour. As he lay on his deathbed, the music of Bessie Smith played quietly nearby.

Ginsberg left behind a wealth of recordings, including music he wrote to accompany William Blake's *Songs of Innocence* and *Songs of Experience*; dozens of his own blues compositions, several albums' worth of his reading his poetry to musical accompaniment; even a sampling of mantras. He recorded with Bob Dylan, Philip Glass, the Clash, and, shortly before his death, Paul McCartney. He once remarked that people could remember several verses of a poem, and he aspired to writing memorable songs, despite the fact that his singing voice and abilities on musical instruments were, at best, marginally passable.

He did, however, succeed in writing some memorable songs, most notably "September on Jessore Road" and the beautiful "Father Death Blues." He was always pleased when journalists included a few questions about his music during the course of an interview.

DURING JANUARY 1982, Allen Ginsberg spent a few days in Atlanta en route from New York to Managua, Nicaragua, where he had been invited to speak and sing at an international poetry festival. While in Atlanta, Ginsberg gave a series of readings and directed a poetry workshop under the sponsorship of The Atlanta Poetry Collective. He also had a number of conversations with Mitchell Feldman, an Atlanta writer whose main areas of interest are Afro-American, World, and New music. What follows is a slightly abbreviated version of an interview Feldman conducted with the poet on January 20 over dinner in a vegetarian restaurant near Seven Stages Theater, where Ginsberg was, later that evening, to give the last of his Atlanta readings. As a musicologist, Feldman was particularly concerned with what Ginsberg had to say about the influence of music on his writing, and about his recent collaborations with contemporary rock musicians, so the conversation began in that vein. But one thing led to another, and within the course of about an hour the talk ranged over a variety of other topics—poetics, politics, meditation, and mind-altering drugs. Debbie Hiers, one of the organizers of Ginsberg's Atlanta readings, and Peter Orlovsky, Ginsberg's fellow poet and long-time companion, also came to dinner that evening, and managed to get a few words in edgewise.

MF: *Can you recall your earliest musical memory?*

AG: Fighting with my piano teacher and refusing to learn when I was seven. I started taking lessons at violin and piano, but I never learned anything. But actually the basis of my music is singing in the shower. And singing on a bridge over 125th Street and Broadway—on Riverside Drive, rather. At Columbia in New York there's a giant bridge where you walk along, you know, when you're way above the street and above the city, and you can make all the noise you want. It's like singing in the shower. You get a good sound out there. That open space is the best, that unobstructed space.

MF: *Like Sonny Rollins. Are you familiar with that story? He went into retirement in the late Fifties and he would just walk the Brooklyn Bridge and play solo saxophone and practice. What were your parents into musically?*

AG: Oh, Rosa Ponsell, Galli-Curci, opera, "Rigoletto," "La Traviata," Mozart. But then I began collecting records through a record bargain program put out by the *New York Post* in those days. We got Beethoven's "Fifth" and Schubert's "Seventh" and Mozart's "41st Symphony," Tchaikovsky's "Pathétique." And then I used to listen to WNYC and WQXR in New York—the symphonies—when I was in grammar school and high school. And then WNYC had a series which included live Leadbelly and Josh White. Leadbelly is my basic blues. Then I began listening to Billie Holiday and Bessie Smith and Ma Rainey, Albert Ammons.

MF: *Sonny Terry and Brownie McGhee?*

AG: Older stuff. The classic stuff from records—Blind Lemon Jefferson. But I wasn't listening as a musician. It sounded like Jewish cantorial stuff to me. I mean, it was great. Then I ran into a kid in '48 when I was in the bughouse, who was a real jazz connoisseur. He gave me a huge course in Bix Beiderbecke and everybody else of that era—all the white bands and a lot of the black bands.

MF: *What's the bughouse?*

AG: A mental hospital. In 1948. He was a specialist kid who was in there because that's all he would do—listen to and collect records.

MF: *Why were you there?*

AG: I was there 'cause I was trying to get out of jail. That rather than jail. A group of friends who were stealing autos—burglars, or ex-junkies—were using my house as a pad. They got busted so I got busted.

MF: *Where'd you go to high school?*

AG: East Side High School, Paterson, New Jersey. And down there on River Street they used to have spiritual churches. I heard a lot of that when I was a kid. That's why I like what Dylan's doing now. They had some very hot, lively preachers and singing on River Street in Paterson. The old, run-down street where you have gypsies, blacks, black churches, pawn shops, old Jewish delicatessens, Salvation Army, broken-down, abandoned factories, old clothing shops, rag shops—the strip.

MF: *When you were in Columbia, or when you were hanging out with those people, did you ever go down to the Village, like the Vanguard?*

AG: Yeah, but I didn't dig the music much. But Kerouac was the main influence. When I was first at Columbia, Kerouac had a great friend named Seymour Wyse, who was working at a music shop called Greenwich Music Shop, which was owned by a fellow named Jerry Newman, an early pioneer in recording bebop, who did extensive recordings of Charlie Christian, Thelonious Monk, [Dizzie] Gillespie, in the very early days. But Seymour Wyse is the most expert expert on modern bop jazz that I know of, and he told me one startling, great, amazing thing about Kerouac and jazz when I was in London in 1980. I said, "There's all this talk about Kerouac borrowing his rhythms from Charlie Parker and Thelonious Monk and Dizzy Gillespie," but mostly the saxophonists—Lester Young—not borrowing, but adapting their breath and their shift of time to speech. So Seymour Wyse told me, "Well, what those musicians were doing was adapting street speech to their horns." It started with speech, rapping on the street. Like *[sings]* "Salt *peanuts*! Salt *peanuts*!" is actually the music following the words. So it was originally language-inspired—traditional street-tribal speech forms, like "rapping" or signifying monkey or a different kind of styling out in speech on the corners. Then the musicians were intrigued by the variable rhythms in that, and were adapting it to their alto saxophones, transferring those rhythms to musical breath. And then Kerouac transferred those musical rhythms back to speech breath, so that *On the Road* is actually returning to speech what the musicians had taken from speech, which is the variable rhythms, and that's a technical point I only found out last year. 'Cause for years I've been saying my line as it comes out of Lester Young in "Howl." You know, mythological Lester Young, chorus after chorus—you know, sixty-nine, seventy choruses of "Lady Be Good" or something. But I always thought it was 'cause I got mine from Kerouac, or he taught me that, or made me listen, and I began getting something. And "Howl" is, in a sense, modeled on Illinois Jacquet's solo on "I Can't Get Started" on *Jazz at the Philharmonic*.

MF: *Oh, yeah?*

AG: You know that record?

MF: *Sure.*

AG: You know that big thing where he gives that long squeal?

MF: *Definitely.*

AG: Well, you know where everything falls into place? *[Sings] da-da, da-da-dada-dadadadda ta!* Remember that? The great Illinois Jacquet solo where he takes off—that's kind of the musical inspiration for "Howl," Though that's hardly bebop. That's country sax, more.

MF: *Arkansas—you know, the gut-... what do they call it? The Chitlin Circuit. You know, Eddie "Cleanhead" Vinson and Eddie "Lockjaw" Davis and those people from the Texarkana area.*

AG: So, a little later—not much later, '46, so I'm talking about the period from '38 to '44, Kerouac, '44, '45, '46. Then the bebop went with Symphony Sid. So for me personally, that was getting familiar with "A Night in Tunisia" and Monk's "'Round Midnight." Then, when Neal Cassady came through town, he was interested in rhythm 'n' blues—Louis Jordan and the Honeydrippers, "Blueberry Hill." Who was that?

MF: *Fats Domino.*

AG. Fats Domino. It was stuff earlier than that. It's sort of like a honking horn, the Honeydrippers' sound. Their particular song—*[sings]* "Open the door, Richard / Open the door and let me in / Open the door, Richard / Richard, why don't you open the door ... *poo-poo-poo-po-boo-boo* ..."—that was a big influence. And in *On the Road* there's lots of description of driving across the country with a radio on full blast, listening to rhythm 'n' blues. And that was like the main sound on Kerouac and me, mainly through Cassady.

MF: *Do you know "The Other One"—the song by the Grateful Dead? That's allegedly their eulogy to Cassady. It's about LSD—"The police came 'round and busted me / for smiling on a cloudy day." Later on they talk about "Cowboy Neal at the wheel / of a bus to Never-Never Land."*

AG: Oh, well, the Grateful Dead are very much imbued with Cassady. He was apparently their big inspiration, as far as energy and attitude.

MF: *Do you see LSD as being an inspiration now?*

AG: I don't know how the young kids use it now. I understand they probably use it more than I did.

MF: *I would say that LSD was the most profound tool for helping open my mind and ears to music. I think I've probably done it two hundred times.*

AG: Did you? And now look how straight he looks.

MF: *Yeah, the first year in college at Penn, I was literally tripping three days a week.*

AG: I never did it like that. I did LSD once every three years or two years for twenty-five years, that's all.

MF: *Now I do it maybe twice a year, and make sure my phone's turned off, or that I'm in the mountains and nobody can bother me. It's really spiritual. I respect it a lot more now. But, you know, when you're in college . . . The first time I did acid I went to a Hot Tuna concert, I had no idea where I was or what was going on, and I really just took it without thinking about what I was doing.*

AG: If the police hadn't interfered at the very beginning, everybody would've had a more sacred use.

MF: *Do you find the effect of the meditation you use is anywhere near close to that of acid?*

AG: The relation between meditation and acid is, as far as I can tell—I mean, having experienced some of both—with meditation you're just following your breaths and examining, getting a glimpse of, Ordinary Mind and experiencing the boredom of sitting there. That's real meditation—not hippie-zappie mystic meditation, where you're supposed to get flashes and visions of your actual mind. As you get a slowdown of mind, and begin to see in minute detail everything that comes through your mind as well as in the room and the sounds outside the window—a slowdown of space, really—and as you get less and less attached to listening to yourself jabber, and let go of yourself, then there is a kind of eternal slowdown or calm in spaciousness, and the phenomenal world begins to speak to you in its own detail without your imposing a message on it. So the creak of the door, the cry of the baby, and the clatter of a dish are eternal things in themselves. It's like in acid. However, it's a method of slowdown rather than speed-up. Rather than turning up the volume of sensation, it's clearing away all the mental debris, so that you get a chance to smell, taste, hear, and touch what you're smelling and tasting and hearing and touching. It's, in certain respects, a convergence. Methods are different, and LSD is extraordinary on meditation. When you're cutting through, constantly letting your thoughts go, cutting through your thoughts to Open Mind not filled with thoughts, any projections that you might have on acid—faces in clouds, C.I.A, over your shoulder—they are cut through immediately. It's a little more sensitive than ordinarily, but still—Ordinary Mind more sensitive, rather than Extraordinary Super-mind. So meditation is more ample, because it includes Ordinary Mind. And Ordinary Mind includes everything. Supernatural Mind or Acid Mind only includes that special part of the spectrum of real high zap. But one is more prepared for acid after meditation. Yeah, you'll have less freakouts. You won't freak out.

MF: *What really legitimized doing hallucinogenic drugs, or psychoactive drugs, for me was reading Huxley's impressions of them in* The Doors of Perception.

AG: In the Forties he wrote. Peyote appeared in New York around '50, so I had peyote in '51 or two. Peter and I had a lot of peyote in the Fifties in San Francisco. Then we had some mescaline in '58—was it?—in Chicago. Good drugstore mescaline. And in '59 at Stanford we had acid, and in '60 ran into Leary, and he had psilocybin, but I had already been trying psychedelics, and Kerouac had, and Lamantia had, and McClure had, and Gary Snyder had it in the Forties. By the early Sixties and Leary's experiments, we were more or less experienced with it, and that's why Leary was interested in talking to us, because we already had some background. See, Burroughs had gone down to South America in 1950 to look for *yage*, which is a hallucinogen. I didn't get there till '60 for that.

MF: *Did those drugs effect your perception of music then?*

AG: Yeah. Actually, the first time I took peyote I put on Tito Puente. I took some notes at the time. Tito Puente was the hottest stuff I could think of, musically, and also, I think, Ravel's "Bolero," or some cornball stuff. I knew the music would be extraordinary. But then at Stanford what I asked for was Wagner. On mescaline, earlier, I had listened to a lot of Beethoven. What I found was the height of music, really, is Beethoven's "Grosse Fugue" and the "Opus 111," Schubert's "Opus Posthumous" piano sonatas, and the Beethoven "Light Quartets." They're my favorite music, music, music. With some Bach "Goldberg Variations" or the partitas and sonatas for unaccompanied violin or cello. Those are my favorite of classical. And I listened to those sometimes. But those are so perfect as they are, you don't need mescaline for them. I don't think they'd really get much better with psychedelics. Where some orchestral music does, like Berlioz's "Requiem" or Verdi's "Requiem" or the "Missa Solemnis." Those are improved, when you've got large choral masses intertwined. So actually my first interest in relation to psychedelics was high classical.

MF: *Can you tell me something about the dates you just did in Manhattan?*

AG: Well, on last Tuesday, January twelfth, I did a gig with Tom Rogers and my favorite guitarist, Steven Taylor—who's on the records, and we've toured Europe—at the Peppermint Lounge for MYPRG, the anti-nuclear, anti-Indian Point, Nader group, with a Memphis band. Remember the name of that Memphis band there, Peter? Were you there, Pete?

PO: In Memphis, Tennessee?

AG: No, no. In New York City on the twelfth of this month. I forgot his name, but he's got a band that used some of "Howl," actually, in one of their cuts on their records. And then the Mudd Club date was the night before I got here to Atlanta. That was a kind of get-together, which Robert Palmer wrote an article about for *The New York Times*, with Ed Sanders and Tuli Kupferberg, who are the basic Fugs. But Sanders has subsequently worked out a lot of electronic equipment that he can carry around all by himself—portable and miniaturized—an electronic lyre … And he's also working on an electronic harp, on which the strings are light beams. So Sanders has been working on Sapphic verse form and Sapphic rhythms, which are [a] unique thing, 'cause Sappho was the first individual poet in the West, and she worked on a five-string tortoise shell lyre, and she invented the mixolydian mode. So she was like a real musician and a real poet. Her first form goes like this: *da-da, da-da, da-da-da, da-da da-da / da-da, da-da, da-da-da, da-da, da-da … trochee, trochee, dactyl, trochee, trochee / trochee, trochee, dactyl, trochee, trochee …*

MF: *Have you ever heard Karl Berger's and Don Cherry's "Gamela Taki"?*

AG: Oh, yeah.

MF: *Taki, taki, gamela, taki, taki*—that's a way to count rhythms.

AG: Yeah, I know. Actually, I've been in their classes when they're teaching that, though I never learned it.

MF: *But that's obviously just a variation on the two- and three-meter line that you put . . .*

AG: Yeah. Sappho wrote in many meters, but she was famous for inventing that stanza, which consists of three hendecasyllables, or eleven syllables, with a tail five-syllable line, which is called the adonic. So, Sanders has a lot of really beautiful songs in that meter, and has some songs to The Plastic People in Czechoslovakia, which is a very good avant-garde rock group, and they're all in jail. They're banned and in jail, and they're very famous. They're in the great Central European band that draws from the Velvet Underground, the Fugs, and lots of avant-garde music of the Sixties. And then Sanders applied it so it sounds like a cross between them and Bertolt Brecht or Kurt Weill.

MF: *Have you studied music theory as extensively as poetic theory?*

AG: No, no, no. I don't know anything. I know four chords. But the great line of Sanders is . . . "There are countries in the world where a man goes to jail for a song." It's a great line there. That's an immortal line of poetry, and it's accurate. So that evening at the Mudd Club, John Giorno read, Kupferberg followed, a group that's working with Sanders—very good musicians—Mark Kramer and his group . . . Kramer went on for half an hour, then I did my set, plugging into Kramer's band with Tom Rogers and another musician, Steven Taylor, whom I mentioned, and then Sanders. And then the other band, whose name I can't remember.

MF: *Kramer came to Atlanta with the Chadbournes. Have you ever heard of the Chadbournes?*

AG: No.

MF: *Free-style country 'n' western bebop. It's like a non-stop set, which goes from Hank Williams tunes into space-electronic music, and into another country song.*

AG: I worked with Kramer on that "Capitol Air" song.

MF: *It was funny last night at your reading, not knowing who Tom Rogers was or where he came from. It was interesting to perceive your interactions with him.*

AG: Yeah, it's a struggle.

MF *[Laughing]*: *Well, for all I knew, he could've been just someone you met a couple of nights ago and worked with and just did the set.*

AG: We met on the street in August or September in Florence, at the Piazza. He had bought a copy of my book, *First Blues*, an Italian translation, came up for an autograph, and I took a look at him and said, "Hey, you've got a good-looking face, what do you do?" And he says he's a musician. So I said, "Where do you play?" And he said, "On the street." He's been playing on the street in Paris for years, and in Rome. So I said, "Are you any good?" And he said, "Yeah." So I invited him over to my hotel the next day. We rehearsed, then we put on a performance there, at Piazza della Signoria. And he was really good, actually. A little wild, but he plays well. Then we went down to San Carlo Opera House with Leroi Jones the next day, got Tom a train ticket with me, and put on a great performance there, sitting in the chair all dressed up, for eleven hundred people, a full house.

MF: *Oh, yeah?*

AG: See, I have a lot of books in Italy. And they're great translations. I've been in and out of Italy for many years, but the last three years Steven Taylor and Peter and I have taken about three tours of Italy and done a lot of readings—before twenty thousand people at one point, at Ostia, at a big international poetry festival with Yevtushenko and me and Gregory Corso and Burroughs.

MF: *Austria?*

AG: No. Ostia—the beach outside of Rome. That was in 1979, the first time we went over ensemble. There's a big poetry festival. So it was Leroi Jones, Anne Waldman, Ted Berrigan, Ferlinghetti, Bill Burroughs, Gregory Corso, Peter Orlovsky, me, Giorno. And then the Russians were Yevtushenko and some other political poet they sent.

PO: And Brion Gysin.

AG: Mmm-hmm. From Paris.

PO: Desmond O'Grady.

AG: That was just the English contingent. There were seventy poets in about a week. That was the first big poetry festival from Italy. And the next year they had one in Rome that we all went to, and last year they had another one. I wasn't at the Rome festival last year, but it specialized in black poets, Third World poets, African poets . . .

MF: *Did they recite in their native language?*

AG: Yeah, and everything's translated. Everybody works with a translator and does their thing. So, the first year there was a big riot, or an attempted riot. One group that called themselves street people anarchists, but were certainly well-backed, tried to start a riot, 'cause it was the first successful mass meeting for culture that had taken place in Italy in about eight years, because of all the anarchy. They tried to invade the stage with a big pot of soup, saying they were gonna feed the public—twenty thousand people, or five thousand that night, the next night twenty . . . They invited the public on the stage, which was a big stage, but it would've caused the stage to collapse and hurt a lot of people, so they were apparently trying to start a riot. Peter went up, got the microphone, and cleared the stage almost single-handed. And I came up and started chanting. The whole audience started chanting, and we said, "Anyone who wants the poetry reading to go on, just sit down and let's shut up, and anybody that doesn't want it to, make all the noise you want." That night there were about five thousand people on the beach, and about four thousand nine hundred and seventy-five sat down and shut up. And it turned out all the chaos was coming from a small group who were calling themselves street people, but who were battling the entire majority there. So they shut up, finally. And we called Yevtushenko, who had been driven off the stage, back, and all the French and Italian poets that hadn't had a chance to read because of the chaos came back and finished the reading. And the next night we went on with all the Americans and the rest of the Europeans who didn't get a chance. So that was like a big turning point in Italian cultural festivals, 'cause before it had always been too risky. That was '79. There was all that publicity, and there were movies made of it, and it was on television. I have about eight books in Italy, and the books I had over the last twenty years were the best-selling poetry in Italy by anyone, the translations.

MF: *Is that the country where you sell the most books?*

AG: Oh, probably, after the United States. And I have better translations there than anywhere, 'cause my translator is a great woman named

Fernanda Pivano. She was a girlfriend of Cesare Pavese, who was the sort of dean of American studies when it was considered anti-fascist to study American literature, back during the war. And she was a friend of Pound and Hemingway. She was Hemingway's translator and friend. And certain high society literary—you know, Pavese and Montale were all friends, and Mecurecro, the painter . . . So she's worked with me and Kerouac and Burroughs and Corso since 1961. So we've had like twenty years working together, line by line, going over the footnotes— you know, American references: who's Charlie Chaplin, W. C., Fields, who're the Beats, who're the Marx Brothers? Last year we took a tour to Italy with The Living Theatre. Me and Peter and Gregory and Steven, the guitarist, and Julian Beck and his boyfriend and Judith Molina and her boyfriend all got in a big tour bus and did a tour of four Italian cities. The tours are organized and sponsored by the communist governments of cities' communes, 'cause all the cities had Communist Party mayors. And since the communists came in, they started a giant cultural program to bring poetry and music to the people.

MF: *Actually, some of the best jazz being recorded by state-of-the-art American musicians who live in New York and Chicago comes out of Milan—Black Saint and Soul Note Records, you know—poets, musicians who work in Italy to pay their rent in New York or Chicago—not just Italy, but the rest of Europe and Japan, too.*

AG: In Rotterdam, at the Rotterdam Museum, there's a poetry festival every two years, and London had a festival every couple of years that was an outgrowth of our Albert Hall concert in '67. In Italy the major cities—Genoa, Rome, Milan—have festivals. They have them in Germany. But there's no place to invite the Europeans here. There isn't one single, official, international poetry festival throughout the United States.

MF: *Is America ripe for it now? Any city in America?*

AG: Oh, *yes!* If somebody *does* it, then it is ripe. If nobody does anything, then it's not ripe. See, the whole point is, the first city in America that holds a big international poetry festival will get this giant bath of publicity. They invite Borges, they invite Octavio Paz, Gunter Grass, and Yevtushenko and others from Russia. Invite a bunch of the American poets, invite the French poets, invite African poets, invite Nicaraguan

poets ... It's never been done in America, because of American chau-
vinistic blindness to the fact that it's happening all over the world. The
American poets are going there and being influential all over, but we
never return the hospitality. So the first city that does it is going to have
this great wave of publicity about it.

MF: *I think there's a basic difference between the Reagan administration and its plans for the National Endowment for the Arts and the sort
of support for the arts that there is in some European countries, and that's
something we have to live with.*

AG: But the Europeans do it on a municipal basis. It's not a big state
thing; it's the municipality of Rome, commune of Rome, commune of
Naples does it. Their budget is not very high, maybe about a hundred
grand, a hundred twenty grand.

MF: *Have you ever applied for grants from the NEA? Do you have
trouble getting them, for political reasons?*

AG: I got an NEA grant. The Rockefeller people like me and have
asked me to apply for ninety-thousand-dollar grants, and I haven't.

MF: *Why?*

AG: I just didn't want to get that involved. But they've given me several ten-thousand-dollar grants. We're not applying for a big grant for
the Kerouac Festival. But I really am not a good grants person. I hate it,
and I've avoided learning it. Until this year. But I have a lot of weight in
terms of prestige in the grant places. They assume I'm one of the cultural
institution ... what do you call it? Those national ... the national treasure type person. So if I go ask for something, they listen, and they'll give
something. But I'm not comfortable in that area, and I avoid it.

MF: *What do you live on in New York?*

AG: My apartment costs me two hundred dollars a month. Then I
make money from readings, all I want—as much as I can work, 'cause I
get fifteen-hundred or two grand for a reading, or three grand if I go to
Italy, for each reading. From books I get ten grand, twelve, seven, nine—
depending. But I have a secretary, and I pay my musicians. I paid Tom two
hundred to get here, and I'll pay him a couple of hundred. I produce my
own records. The stuff I did with Dylan cost me fifteen thousand dollars
in 1970—full-scale, Record Plant, studio recordings.

MF: *How many records do you expect to sell?*

AG: I don't have any idea. But I got a very good deal, 'cause they didn't give me an advance, 'cause John Hammond didn't have any money. So I'll get two dollars a record. That's very good royalties.

MF: *When did your first record come out?*

AG: In 1968, from MGM, with "Songs of Innocence and Experience by William Blake, Tuned by Allen Ginsberg," with Jon Sholle—he's my main, old guitarist—and then Don Cherry and Elvin Jones.

MF: *Oh, really? It's out of print, right?*

AG: Mike Curb took over the corporation with Las Vegas money and immediately denounced all the people who were interested in dope and legalizing dope, and sort of undercut all their records. So within a month after mine came out and it was sort of like . . .

MR: *Cut out.*

AG: Then they reprinted it. I have prepared a beautiful cover with Blake illustrations. They reprinted the thing on Archive, or Archetype Series—they had a Billie Holiday thing—with a horrible cover looking like a gangster from Chicago—for a Blake record.

MF: *Can you tell me the name of the lyricist for the Clash that you were recently working with?*

AG: The singer, Joe Strummer. Peter Poetry is Mick Jones.

MF: *Is there a title for this album yet?*

AG: It's their album. I did a little tiny bit. I tinkered with their lyrics.

MF: *You helped tighten them up, or something?*

AG: No, no. They're never tight *[laughter]*. Strummer writes them out in his notebook and he hands me a Xerox, and I go over the Xerox and change a phrase or two and make suggestions. And he gets on and he sings, and maybe an hour later I have another idea of how to change a phrase, make it more pronounceable. And go into the studio and say, "Why don't we try it this way?" And he does that, and if it works, it works; if it doesn't, it doesn't. I've worked on about three or four numbers. Whenever I had to come in, I'd stay all night and work. I can't do it every night.

MF: *Rhythm is obviously very important in poetry writing and read-*

ing, and in music, too. Would you like to talk about any differences or similarities or problems?

AG: The thing I've been finding in working with my own recordings, and also with the Clash, is that the sense of time—the ear that one develops as a poet for pronunciation and rhythm—fits right in with the whole rock 'n' roll shot. To know where to take a phrase and reduce it to something that's pronounceable and singable . . . Instead of saying, "When my mother come home," you can say, "Mother come home." You don't have to say, "When my . . ." In the lyrics I was singing last night on "Do the Meditation," some of the words, syllables, could be cut out without loss of data and make it more singable. Or you could shift a syllable from one side of the caesura to another. You have to have the judgment to see on which side the caesura belongs, or whether you need it.

MF: *Which lyricists do you like?*

AG: Shakespeare. Kerouac. I like Leadbelly, and the classic line, "where the yellow dog meets the southern cross"—which is, I guess, Ma Rainey, or Bessie Smith. But Shakespeare wrote some of the most beautiful songs in his plays. So did Kerouac. I like Lennon. Lennon has great lyrics. I had a big anthology that I was making up of international twentieth-century poetry, and I put in "I am the Walrus" and "A Day in the Life," 'cause I thought they were great surrealist poems, like in the tradition of Apollinaire and others. Dylan, yeah. And Donovan had a couple of good ones. But actually it's the great black blues lyrics that are the golden treasure of American poetry not yet recognized by the Academy. There's a great book called *The Blues Line,* put out by Macmillan, for which I wrote the blurb in the paperback, pointing out that when anthologists come in a hundred years to collect American twentieth-century poetry, there will be this huge section of anonymous or named lyrics that come from blues and boogies and from the black tradition, that is as good, or better than, most of the white lyrics.

MF: *Same with jazz or, say, improvisational instrumental music versus classical.*

AG: But it's hard to say that to the Academy.

MF: *Where'd you get your harmonium?*

AG: Peter bought it in Benares in 1963. And I used it for a number of years. And then I went there in 1970 and bought my own, but I lost it on the subway a year ago, so I borrowed Peter's back. You've seen that Folkways record. It uses the Benares harmonium.

MF: *You mentioned that you were the cantor at Sue Graham and Charles Mingus's wedding.*

AG: Mingus asked me to come and do mantra chanting, so I sang for about half an hour.

MF: *How long have you been a Buddhist?*

AG: Formally speaking, taking vows, since 1973, I would say—'72, '73. But I've done Buddhist practice, sitting or parallel form, since '70 and I made a Buddhist pilgrimage with Gary Snyder to all the Buddhist holy places in India in 1963. And I spent time sitting and learning a little about Zen in Japan with Gary Snyder in July '63, for six weeks.

WAITRESS: Would you sign this menu, please?

AG: Yes.

From *Red Hand Book III*, edited by Tom Patterson and Steve Allgood (Atlanta, Ga.: Pynyon Press, 1982), 76–85. Reprinted by permission of Mitchell Feldman.

William Burroughs, Norman Mailer, Allen Ginsberg

How to Notice What You Notice, How to Write a
Bestseller, How to Not Solve Crime in America

ALLEN GINSBERG, 1985

WHEN ALLEN GINSBERG AND ANNE WALDMAN cofounded the Jack
Kerouac School of Disembodied Poetics at the Naropa Institute
(now Naropa College) in Boulder, Colorado, the idea was to offer an innovative creative writing program grounded in a strong Buddhist environment. Over the years, nearly every Beat Generation writer or poet spent
time at the school as a visiting teacher or lecturer. Ginsberg was a strong
presence on the campus or in its planning of curriculum; students lined
up to attend his summer classes. At Naropa, anything could—and often
did—happen.

The following began as a Ginsberg lecture, only to turn into a round-
robin discussion when William S. Burroughs and Norman Mailer dropped
by. Ginsberg happily deferred to the two novelists, becoming an interviewer in his own classroom.

In Boulder's *Daily Camera,* the encounter was described this way: "Norman Mailer, the aging macho mastodon of American letters, comes
head to head with author William Burroughs, decadent dark son of the
American Nightmare." Although Mailer and Burroughs could both be
described as "psycho-realists" of American prose, they come from entirely distinct literary universes. For years it had been Allen Ginsberg's
dream to bring the two together, and it was to his great satisfaction that

the 1984 summer writing program was able to include Mailer and Burroughs in its hefty lineup of guests [other notables were Amiri Baraka, Robert Creeley, Diane di Prima, and Anne Waldman].

Mailer and Burroughs crossed literary paths in ancient Egypt. Mailer's extensively researched *Ancient Evenings* documented the travels of the Egyptian soul through the afterlife. Burroughs, who was concurrently delving into the same realm, picked up *Ancient Evenings* as a resource for his own writings. The two were first able to discuss and compare their reflections at Naropa Institute. A well-publicized discussion on "The American Soul," moderated by Allen Ginsberg, was presented as a first forum. However, many left with the feeling that the topic never quite got off the ground, that it was too vague and over-staged. Meanwhile, Mailer asked Ginsberg if he could drop in on his writing class. He said he wanted to see him teach . . .

ALLEN GINSBERG: Just to fill you in on what went on this afternoon, Mailer and Burroughs got into a big discussion on souls. Mailer had done a vast amount of research on Egypt for his book, *Ancient Evenings*, and apparently the Egyptian conception was that there are seven souls, or seven different parts of the soul, which separate out at death and go their separate ways. Burroughs has been taking off from Mailer imaginatively in his own writing, and this was the first time they actually talked about it. It turned out they had totally different ideas of the significance of the seven souls. Then they went off to supper together. Mailer said they were coming to this class later, which surprised me. He said he wanted to hear me teach, which puts me in an odd position. So the problem is how to get *them* to teach, or get them engaged. So what I'll do is just continue from where I was until they turn up.

The theme we were on last class was Flaubert's *The ordinary is the extraordinary*. In other words, the way to point to the existence of the universe is to see one thing directly and clearly and describe it. Gertrude Stein had a phrase: *A rose is a rose is a rose*. Rather than, "a rose is a symbol of the great yellow rose of paradise." Other ways of saying it are Blake's *Labor well the minute particulars*; Kerouac's *Details are the life of prose* and *Don't stop to think of the words but to see the picture better*; Pound's *The natural object is always the adequate symbol* and *Direct treatment of the thing*; Williams's *No ideas but in things* and *Clamp the mind down on objects*; and Trungpa's *Things are symbols of themselves*. If you have an unobstructed perception of a thing, then it stands in eternity with its own characteristics and is an eternal object (if you want to use that kind of vocabulary). If you see something as a symbol of something else, then you don't experience the object itself, but you're always referring it to something else in your mind. It's like making out with one person and thinking about another. So along the same lines, I'd like to refer you to some poems by Charles Reznikoff, who is one of the erudite, lesser-known writers of the early part of this century. He lived in New York and was a friend of William Carlos Williams and Ezra Pound, and was one of the original imagist-objectivist poets of 1918–1925. He printed up his own books in editions of two hundred, so he's not generally well-known. I occasionally ran across him in Bryant Park and he read at St. Mark's Poetry Project in New York a few times. These are from a series, "Sunday Walks in the Suburbs":

A bitch, backbone and ribs showing in the sinuous back, sniffed for food, her swollen udder nearly rubbing along the pavement.

Once a toothless woman opened her door, chewing a slice of bacon that hung from her mouth like a tongue.

This is one of the most vivid pictures I've read, or seen. Thinking about this quality of Reznikoff's writing, I came to the conclusion that vividness is self-selecting. In other words, you know something's vivid because you remember it. You saw some detail or some scene and it was clear, or it stood out from the background because it was so sharp or strange or curious or you were in a mood to look. Asking "How do you select vivid things?" is like saying, "How do you notice what you notice?" And as far as I'm concerned, that's the big technical problem. How *do* you notice what you notice? Wordsworth's phrase is, "poetry is emotion recollected in tranquility." Recollecting your mind or recollecting an image that you saw. So Reznikoff recollected, "Once a toothless woman opened her door, chewing a slice of bacon that hung from her mouth like a tongue." Which is one of the most interesting, ugly, horrible pictures I've ever seen, and yet it sticks in my mind and finally becomes pure beauty because he saw it clearly and wrote it down so simply. And it makes me wonder, where did he get the compassion to actually recognize that event as beautiful? He didn't shut it off and say, "I don't want to write about *that* one; that's too disgusting to lay on people . . . or even myself. I don't want to go down as the poet that wrote about that toothless woman! I didn't even get to write a great love poem! That's what people will put on my tomb!" So I guess he wasn't afraid of that sight, because it was vivid.

There is another particular image which I've always liked because it's the most vividly microscopic detail that I know in all of Reznikoff or anywhere.

He crammed all into the stove and lit a match. The fire ran over the surface and died out. He tore the letters into bits and lit match after match, until nothing was left but brown pieces with black, crumbled edges.

As the papers twisted and opened, tormented by fire, Darling *had stood out in the writing against the flames for a moment before the ink was grey on black ash that fell apart.*

Has everybody *seen* that? As the paper burns, the ink turns into a thin grey mark just before the burnt ash disintegrates. I always wondered, how did he notice that? How did he notice that he had noticed that?

So the question I have is, why do we get off on details like these—the bacon hanging from her mouth, or the tracery of the word "darling"? My theory is that it's the *quality* of his attention when Reznikoff noticed the grey ink. He was there one hundred percent with the thing—enough to notice things which other mind-perceiver poets might have passed up. Or, had they noticed it they forgot it, or pushed it into the backs of their minds, didn't value it, or didn't notice that they noticed it. But he not only noticed that he noticed it—but in his original noticing he was one with the universe, there in that moment, with maybe no other thought in his mind. And so actually it's an example of epiphany, of unified consciousness. An epiphany I would say is when the attention is right there where it is. All of a sudden you're actually seeing, instead of "making out with one person and thinking about another." So because of the quality of Reznikoff's attention, the artifact he's brought out of that absorption, when presented to other people, reminds them of the possibility of absorption in existence. It reminds them of their own epiphanies, i.e., their own instances of absorption.

Now what I'm talking about is one hundred percent ordinary, in the sense of ordinary mind, rather than super-conscious mind, romantic mind, or symbolic mind. That's why I'm putting so much emphasis on the literality, because in this sense what is ordinary and literal leads to epiphany, to complete absorption in the cosmos, or to "cosmic consciousness," if we want to use the phrasing. Cosmic consciousness is just really being there in the cosmos where you are. In a sense, that's the most finely absorbed, the most dramatically tragic, state of being. As with Charles Reznikoff's line, "'Come in,' he said, his face lashed with wrinkles." I've wept over that one, because it's absolute.

Ultimately I think that's the basic function of poetry: to touch on that level of consciousness and awaken other people, by making little models of epiphanous moments which will then catalyze their awareness, cut through their daydreaming, and wake them up, concentrate other people's microscopic attention on that little, small spot. Blake says, pay attention to "*minute* particulars." Take care of the little ones and the big deal with take care of itself. Just see what you see. Certainly that's the function of meditation. And Burroughs sees it as the function of his writing. Rimbaud was interested in that. And really, how many poets have *not* been interested in visionary consciousness? I suppose some people did it [writing] for money [*laughter*]. And then some people did it because they adored beauty or something like that, but then when you ask them their particular definition of beauty it finally comes down to Blake's "labor well the minute particulars." Can anyone suggest another equally interesting reason for writing?

Oh . . . Come on in. [*Enter: Norman Mailer and William Burroughs. Applause.*]

So, Norman and Bill, I was just talking about Charles Reznikoff. I try to teach his writing here each year because he has these great little novels in twenty lines or so—prose narratives that can be considered poetry as well. And I was discussing vividness and minute particulars. I'll just read these two poems again, to give you some flavor. [*Reads.*]

NORMAN MAILER: I think there's something extraordinary in Reznikoff's particular sort of vividness, because he's leaving presences in your consciousness that you can't forget. The superb one is, of course, "Darling." But the bacon is also unforgettable. Any time you are that vivid and you create such a presence, you suggest that there's more meaning there than meets the eye. So his absolute vividness keeps his poems from being depressing and full of self-pity. What makes self-pity so bad for a poet is that it's never vivid and specific; it's always general emotion.

GINSBERG: Norman, before you came in I was saying that, as far as I'm concerned, that kind of vividness, which catalyzes a certain consciousness in people, is the function of art. It's what I'm interested in. Do you have some ideas about what you do that might be comparable? What's your angle?

MAILER: Oh, I don't know if I can formulate it, really. I never trust myself when I'm talking about what I'm up to.

GINSBERG: It's the trouble with teaching: when you teach you start talking a lot.

MAILER: Well, I don't talk, and so I've always been afraid to teach. I had a feeling I might start fooling with my underpinnings. I only talk about writing in the most mechanical fashion: good habits, bad habits, how to know when you're working right, how to know when you're working wrong. I almost never like to think about the aim. I assume the aim just comes out of the deepest part of your consciousness, if you're serious about the job. There are purposes you can state, but it could be misleading to talk about them, because there are other deeper purposes that you can't state.

WILLIAM BURROUGHS: Absolutely. I agree with that.

GINSBERG: I remember you saying before that a novelist is like an athlete.

MAILER: The inner daily life of a novelist is probably closer to that of a professional athlete—not an amateur, but a professional athlete—than that of a poet. Because what a professional athlete is thinking about is keeping up a certain level of performance every day. Let's say a basketball player is playing three or four games a week. No matter what is happening in his personal life, his public life in the media, his economics, his habits . . . he can't let any of that get into the performance. And what generally makes a good novelist is that he or she is reasonably good day after day, week after week, season after season. And then, at the end of a year or two, you have a novel.

GINSBERG: Do you write every day?

MAILER: Well, it varies greatly, depending on what the book is demanding. There are some books where you just have to stop every few days and learn some more about your subject. There are other books where you get on a roll and you're afraid to stop because you know if you do, you'll have trouble getting going again. And of course ego is involved when you're writing a novel. You have to keep up your notion of yourself, which is very difficult. A poet doesn't have that problem of ego. They have other problems . . .

GINSBERG: You don't have ego problems if you're a poet?

MAILER: Well, in the sense that, if you can write it down in an hour or even in a week, it's not hard to believe that you're truly doing something important. If you can at least get a first draft finished in a short period, then you can contemplate it and go through many moods about it later. But as a novelist you have to keep your idea going even when you know that you're not writing your best—you can sense it, you can feel that something flat has gotten into the work. You have to keep it moving; you have to keep fighting to support it. It's very much like an athlete in a slump. So stories make demands on you. And they change your life. I know I'm making a large generalization, but I'd say that almost all novelists would write novels without stories if they could get away with it. Characters are much more interesting than stories. But if you get two interesting characters, it's almost obligatory that they start doing something together. *[Laughter.]*

GINSBERG: I think Bill has abandoned the story line.

BURROUGHS: I haven't abandoned the story line at all! My last two books have had very definite, elaborate story lines.

GINSBERG: But you're coming to it late. Because now you're trying to write a bestseller.

BURROUGHS: I am not trying to write a bestseller! *[Laughter.]* Allen, don't you realize that someone cannot just sit down and write a bestseller? Bestsellers are written up to the limit of a man's ability. The public may be stupid, but they will immediately see the insincerity of a book that was written to be a bestseller.

GINSBERG: Well, you did teach a course here on the subject.

BURROUGHS: Of course I did! *[Laughter.]* I gave the two main formulas for a bestseller. One is that you write about a thing people know something about, and want to know more about, such as the mafia, the inside of Hollywood, or Madison Avenue. The other is the "menace"— the problem posed by the menace and the resolution of the problem. It may be *Jaws,* it may be an epidemic, or any number of things. But thousands of books are written on these formulas. In fact, the majority of books on the market can be broken down into these two categories. It doesn't mean any of them will be a bestseller.

MAILER: Bestsellers are like successful assassinations: only the badly conceived ones ever work. If you conceive a novel too well, you're going to be out of fashion, because the fashion must have been already hanging around long enough in one place for you to have conceived it that well. And a perfectly planned assassination will always fail because the odds are just too great that one step somewhere will go wrong. But if you were off somewhere—maybe you calculated ten degrees to the left or the right of the target—then there's a chance you'll hit it right on. And the same thing happens with bestsellers. Maybe a novel gets the wrong editor, so it becomes a bestseller. *[Laughter.]* If it had the right editor, they would have worked on it too hard and you would have missed the starting gate. You can't "write a bestseller" because that implies more control of the immediate literary universe than anyone has.

GINSBERG: You have written bestsellers.

MAILER: Yes. My real bestseller was the first one, *The Naked and the Dead.* That was an absolute accident. That is, no one thought it was going to be a bestseller at all. But it just happened that the public was waiting for a war novel, so I was lucky. If it had come out a year later it would have sold maybe a third as many copies.

GINSBERG: What I've been wondering is, what are all these airport package books—the ones with the shiny, silver embossed covers?

MAILER: Why do you assume I know more about those books that you do?

GINSBERG: Well, Burroughs might know about them, because he's been reading them.

BURROUGHS: Yes, I read a lot of popular junk. They have interesting things like, "He laughed a dry laugh like a snake shedding its skin. . . ." I say, well, that's good enough to *steal*. I'll grab that. Why not steal everything in sight?

MAILER: You know, I have advice for someone who wants to write a bestseller.

GINSBERG: What?

MAILER: The mark of good prose writing is that you never use an adjective without backing it with your personal irony. Burroughs, for instance, uses the corniest adjectives, and they're superb. You feel his personal irony every time—"He laughed a dry laugh . . ."

GINSBERG: One thing that's always interested me about Bill's writing is that he sees, visually, what he's writing.

BURROUGHS: It's a film. I'm seeing a movie as I write. If I don't see anything, I can't write.

GINSBERG: Years ago in Tangier, in '57, I remember watching Bill sitting, hovering over the typewriter and staring at the wall. I was on the bed watching him write and wondering how he was doing it. He was poised with his fingers above the typewriter, and I said, "What are you thinking about, Bill?" He said, "Hands in the darkness pulling in nets from the sea." And I thought that was some great cosmic vision and I wondered, gee, where did that come from?

BURROUGHS: It came from down on the beach! *[Laughter.]*

GINSBERG: Right. Down on the beach. It was the fishermen of the Tangier beach pulling in the nets in the morning. But it was quite literally a picture movie running through his mind at that moment. So he apparently thinks visually more than most people, or more than I do, certainly.

MAILER: And more than I do.

GINSBERG: My mind is more like the *New York Times*—just a bunch of editorials. Norman, most of your writing comes from research, as I understand. Are there any examples of straight descriptive writing in any of your books, based on observation, that you particularly dig?

MAILER: There's a description in *The Executioner's Song* that's about a page and a half of just straight descriptive detail. The scene takes place about an hour after Gary Gilmore has committed his first murder. We don't know what he was thinking; all we have is the physical evidence of where he went. He ends up in a motel room. I became fascinated with this room, so I went and slept a night there. I had quite an experience just sitting in that room and looking at it. I took tremendously long notes. I had always disliked motel rooms, but I never really looked at them that hard before. I had a notion that some of the violence of America comes out of the super-coiffured surface of so much transient life. In Gilmore's case it was particularly pathetic because this was his idea of how to live. Earlier he says, "I wanna sleep in a good place tonight. Let's go to the Holiday Inn." And I felt that it's part of the *pathétique* of American life, that when you finally get to that place where you want to be, to that fancy lawn party in the suburbs, the drinks are served in a goddamn plastic glass—which takes off everyone's pleasure. And then you leave and you wonder, why was that party a bummer? Something was wrong. It wasn't as good as it should have been. So I just thought, I want to really get this, once and for all. I want to get what it is that I truly detest about this stuff. Instead of fulminating, I'm gong to observe. Because my vice is to fulminate rather than to look carefully. There were times when I was tempted to have gone for five pages rather than one and a half, because it truly would have given people cancer to read those five pages.

GINSBERG: Do you still have the original sketch?

MAILER: Somewhere.

GINSBERG: Why don't you publish that as a little prose poem?

MAILER: I'd have to spend ten pages explaining why I was publishing those five boring pages.

GINSBERG: No, no! You see, if you call it a poem, then people have to use their heads. That's the advantage of it—with a poem you can get away with anything. *[Laughs.]* Any questions out there?

QUESTION: *Mr. Mailer, does writing from research material create certain kinds of problems? It seems like a very different approach to what Allen was describing earlier.*

MAILER: Well, it's a lot more dry, but it's also easier on the nervous system, up to a point. Because when you're doing research you're not writing that day. When you're writing, even when you have a good day, it's tough on the nervous system. So, in a way, research can be dangerous because you can fall into it. I've often spent three months doing research when I would have been wiser to have spent one month, because finally the stuff was not useable; I got into too much detail. But maybe I'm not addressing the brunt of your question. It seems to me that there are no real problems when you've been writing as long as Mr. Burroughs or myself. You don't think about it that way. We're like dentists who go in on any given day, and sometimes they might find a mouth full of cavities and they think, "My, I'm going to have to work a little harder today." *[Laughter.]* So maybe we think, "Oh boy, today there's going to be a shoot-out and three people will get killed. I'm going to have to work a little harder today." After you've been writing for some time, most often you're dealing with stuff that you sense you can do: you probably can do it; you should be able to do it. The question is, can you do it so it's a little newer and a little better than you've done it before? That does create tension, but I wouldn't see it as a problem, exactly. So let's say, it's nice to be able to do research, then you can fall into the pit. Writing is nothing but pitfalls. If I was seventeen and going to do it over again, I think I'd start off by walking tightropes.

QUESTION: *What strategies have any of you worked out for writing about sex?*

BURROUGHS: As far as I'm concerned, it's the same movie. *[Laughter.]* If I don't see a movie I can't write about it. As I get older I lose interest in sex, so there's less and less sex on the film. That's all. As for strategies, although sex scenes might seem to be the easiest, they are the hardest to write. Sex scenes and descriptions. Narrative is usually a cinch. But describing a sex scene, or just describing a landscape is always very difficult.

MAILER: When you get to sex, some of your readers are going to be more sophisticated than you are, and some are going to be much more innocent. All of one's personal embarrassments, as well as one's hard-earned liberties, are somewhat on the line. It's just hellish to write sexual scenes. At the same time, it's exciting because there's so much perception there. But it's very, very difficult to ever write about sex successfully. I think the writers who do are either geniuses like D. H. Lawrence, who commit themselves absolutely to it, and for whom writing about sex is virtually a religious act, or else people who treat it comically. Kingsley Amis is the sort of writer who can write a good sex scene.

GINSBERG: In my own experience, I take sex states of mind as sacramental. There's a Buddhist notion that there are certain moments which naturally open your mind or create more space in your mind, such as on the death bed, during orgasm, and at the moment of shock or surprise, such as when breaking a leg or hearing that someone has died. At those times you suddenly see the space where you're at. So I was always interested in developing a kind of writing that would simultaneously be an experience of vast awareness and at the same time be a notation of the minute particulars observed during that epiphany. So a few times Peter Orlovsky and I have tried a sex experiment which, while making sex, writing was going on. Then a number of the best things I've written on sex are literally masturbation fantasies, either recollected or, in a few cases, deliberately simultaneous with the writing, using a tape recorder. Samples of that are the poem "Please Master," and there's another one that begins, "Come on, Jack, spank me and hit me . . ." *[Laughter.]* And then there's a whole other category of poems which I've written rising from a bed of love and going into the can or into the kitchen and writing as fast as possible in Skeltonic rhyme or doggerel. There's a series of poems in the last two books, *Mind Breaths* and *Plutonian Ode*, which were written right before or after love-making. Spontaneous notation.

QUESTION: *I'd like to ask Mr. Mailer how he'd suggest dealing with the problem of crime in this country in a meaningful way.*

MAILER: Crime is not a problem; it's a phenomenon. It's deep, human activity that contains extraordinary variations. And just when criminal activity seems to get very interesting, it can also become extraordinarily boring. If criminals uniformly lived more interesting lives than we did, then everybody sooner or later would become a criminal. So the great balance of the universe is present there, too. In terms of how I relate to it in my writing, each time I do it, I do it differently. I go at it from another angle. And I never try to solve the problem. The worst thing you can ever do as a writer is try to solve problems. My notion is that, if you don't know quite what you're doing, but you just feel in rather a good state when it's over, chances are you've written something fairly good. Solving problems is beyond your scope as a writer entirely. It has to be. Otherwise you're writing a polemic, which is a low form of literature. In that case, you're just trying to drive people through a gate, so that rather than thinking of *this* enclosure, they'll be thinking of *that* enclosure.

BURROUGHS: Norman, I have a solution for the whole crime problem in America: everyone from the ages of eighteen to ninety, after a period of training, gets out and patrols the streets of America. We'd wipe the muggers and rapists right off the streets!

MAILER: Wouldn't work.

BURROUGHS: What do you mean it wouldn't work?

MAILER: It sounds marvelous but it goes deeper than that.

BURROUGHS: It sounds very sensible to me. The Guardian Angels have already shown us the way. They're getting out and stopping crime when it happens. And it used to work in the frontier days.

MAILER: That's right, you have vigilantes and after a while they start shooting the wrong people, and shooting each other, and then you have another round of feuds. There's no answer to it. You could kill every criminal there is, or lock them up forever and explode them, but then the people who were doing it would be the criminals. This stuff goes deeper than solutions.

QUESTION: *Don't you think that writing about crime inspires crime?*

BURROUGHS: I would say that there is one type of writing that certainly does inspire people to commit crime and that is the writing you read every day in the newspapers. Something like sky-jacking becomes an epidemic when it's played out by the media. But people as a rule are not inspired to crime through fiction because they know it's make-believe. They are much more so by television because it's a mixture.

QUESTION: *Sometimes I feel shocked by the images that seem to spontaneously come up when I'm writing—either sexual or violent. Do you think there's any value in writing these down?*

BURROUGHS: What did Poe do about his horrible nightmares of being buried alive? He wrote about them.

MAILER: I think you finally have to assume, if you are essentially optimistic about yourself, that there's some purpose to writing such scenes. If they're good, then they belong; they should be written. What's bad about crime in the newspapers—and I do agree with Bill Burroughs on this completely—is that it does not capture the nature of the reality. And when you get facts without reality, you are breeding all sorts of tensions. If you have people who are violently inclined and you give them more tension, that'll end up as a crime of violence. If you write about violence very well, or with a perception that wasn't brought to it before, then presumably you are increasing human consciousness. And I think one notion we can always hold is that the more consciousness we contain in any given moment, the less likely we are to be violent. Violence comes from a failure of consciousness.

BURROUGHS: Oh, absolutely. The thing about criminals is that they don't seem to have any buffer between thought and action. Most people are held back from criminal action not by morality but by simple truths—like you don't step in front of a moving car. But that buffer seems to not operate in criminals. They don't consider what's going to happen. That's a failure of consciousness.

QUESTION: *Mr. Mailer, do you think it's important for every novelist to do the kind and extent of research you do?*

MAILER: Well, I think it varies from writer to writer. But I think that to the degree you go out and consciously seek information in order to write your next chapter, you're in trouble. In a pinch, if it's bad enough, you just have to go out and look for the material. That happens once in a while. Sometimes you get trapped in the logic of your own work and you've got a story that's going along and suddenly you've got a middle class family that's upset and they want to go and look for a private detective. If you know nothing about private detectives you've got to go out and learn something about them. You can start by reading *Cities of the*

Red Night. There's a very good private detective in there. In general, the more you know the better off you are when it comes to the next sentence.

GINSBERG: On that note, I think we should end this class. Thank you for coming, Mr. Mailer and Mr. Burroughs. *[Applause.]*

From *Naropa Magazine* 2 (Spring 1985): 16–19. Reprinted by permission.

Dreams, Reconciliations, and "Spots of Time"
An Interview with Allen Ginsberg

MICHAEL SCHUMACHER, 1986

THIS PREVIOUSLY UNPUBLISHED INTERVIEW was conducted as part of the research for *Dharma Lion,* my biography of Allen Ginsberg. His volume of poetry, *White Shroud,* had just been published, and Ginsberg was in Chicago, promoting the book. The questioning began with a discussion of some of the poems in the new volume, but it wound up going in an unexpected direction: a look at Ginsberg's dream poetry. Ginsberg, Kerouac, Burroughs, and others of the Beat Generation kept detailed journal notations of their dreams, largely as a method of recording another level of consciousness. Ginsberg's dreams occasionally found their way into his poetry, but rarely as strongly and personally as in "White Shroud" and "Black Shroud," which again found him contemplating his relationship with his mother.

MS: *I wanted to ask you about the work in* White Shroud. *One of the themes that comes through in a lot of the poems in this book is concern over illness, sickness, old age, death, and so forth.*

AG: Well, I'm getting older. It's obvious. When you get older, old age, sickness and death are more obvious, though it always was part of the poetic apparatus. It's built in "Howl" and "Kaddish" and "Don't Grow Old" and "Plutonium Ode" and a lot of other things. Old age, sickness, and death are part of the Buddhist view of eventual human condition, so I'm just sticking with that, with an old theme.

MS: *I also saw complementary themes in the poems, in the respect of your working in cycles. When I talked to Antler about his* Last Words, *he talked about he called "mirror poems." You start here and end up here* [gesturing], *and, in a way, they seem to be flashing off each other. With your poetry, you have the obvious "Kaddish"/"Black Shroud"/"White Shroud" cycle, but there are also some interesting examples in the new book: "Thoughts Sitting Breathing II," which is the continuation of the original "Thoughts Sitting Breathing," and "I'm a Prisoner of Allen Ginsberg," which seems to resonate from "I'm a Prisoner of the Telephone."*

AG: Yeah. I never thought of the last two, but that's a good idea.

MS: *"221 Syllables at Rocky Mountain Dharma Center" reminds me of "Ayers Rock"—*

AG: Yeah. That's a similar format.

MS: *And, of course, there's "Empire Air"/"Capitol Air"/"Industrial Waves." Was this a conscious recycling of recurrent themes?*

AG: It's not that conscious. I didn't think of the correlation between "Empire Air" and "Capitol Air," or "Ayers Rock" and the one-line haikus in "Rocky Mountain Dharma Center." It never occurred to me. It's just the same mind, thinking in cycles like, I guess, anyone else. I think in a certain pattern. The thing I'm gambling on, aesthetically, for long-range structure, is that, by simply recording diverse appearance of phenomena as and when appearances rise, following that phrase of Thomas Hardy that I quoted in *Empty Mirror,* presumably the whole thing will make sense. *[Laughs.]* That the whole sequence is, you know, like a tapeworm, one year after another, will make some cumulative sense, as poems and thoughts and events relate to each other. But I don't know that anybody's ever tried to make the actual events of their lives the subject of a whole cycle of their life poetry, as directly. It might have been, maybe, but I don't know if you can apply that Whitman personalism directly to personal matter. So it's an interesting experiment. I don't know if it can go on to the deathbed, though, because there are certain things that intervene, like interferences with other people's lives or invasion of other people's privacy. If you have a human relation and then things go odd, do you want to tell . . . you can't be kissing and telling, so to speak. You can't really write about them autobiographically, unless you have their permission, and as I grow older, that's a little more difficult.

I mean, I never thought of that when I first started, because I started out just doing it for myself. I didn't realize that it all was going to be famous and published. "Howl" wasn't written with the idea of publishing it. I didn't think anybody would read the poem except poets or some cognoscenti or something. In *Annotated Howl,* Carl [Solomon] gets the chance to respond to the use of his name, and give some history of the difficulties the poem caused him, but I didn't think about that at all when I started. So I got myself sort of like painted into a corner, and the only way of not getting painted in a corner is to make sure there are a number of poems that can be published after I'm dead and others are dead, poems that will actually cover these areas that would be inconvenient for them.

MS: *Something like "Many Loves."*

AG: "Many Loves" is like that, but I have others, a lot of others—enough to fill out areas that I can't publicly deal with now. It poses a problem because the original thing was: how can you break down the distinction between the public and the private?

MS: *I see what you mean. You've described your poetry as being a graph of your mind, but it can cause a problem when you have to be sensitive to other living sensibilities.*

AG: It's much harder in Russia or other countries, because there you get put in jail for what you're thinking or saying. See? There, everybody has to write for the future—and not just a few poems for the future, what they call "poems for the desk." All the great poetry of Russia is for the desk drawer because they can't publish it now, or half of it now. I'm fortunate because I only have to put in the desk drawer those things that are personally offensive to others, or are an invasion.

MS: *All this is coming around to something you hinted at, the idea that you've written your whole life—*

AG: It as just a casual comment in *Collected Poems,* and I didn't mean it to be taken that literally, heavily. There was just an element of autobiography that might be noticed. It isn't that I'm trying to write an autobiography.

MS: *It gets close at times, very close.*

AG: Yeah, but it's not ... it isn't ... Okay, have it your way. *[Laughter.]* As far as *I'm* concerned, as far as *my* perspective is concerned, there's an *element* of autobiography, but it's not *real* autobiography because major things are not there. I just didn't write poems about them. So it's like *spots,* spots of time that you flash on with a flashlight, and it's very accidental whether it's something that's really important or not. A lot of "important" things happened that I just never wrote poems about. The first time I met Dylan, I just didn't write a poem about it, and yet for *me,* autobiographically, subjectively, that was an important event. So it's not *real* autobiography, though it's chronological.

MS: *I've always been fond of your travel poems, the work you've done when you were on the road and observing new things. I was especially affected by the poetry [in* White Shroud*] that you wrote while you were in China.*

AG: Almost everybody seems to like those, because they're clear and they're grounded. There's a certain common humane element that isn't involved in asserting anything, or proposing anything Buddhist, or proposing anything sexual or political. It's just a sort of record of being sick and reading and thinking in bed. In fact, there is that whole part [in "Reading Bau Juyi"] saying, "a noble ambition, but that of a pathetic dreamer." And that is kind of an interesting poem, I thought, because that gives away all my ambitions and, at the same time, is a kind of resignation against them, or a confession of total failure. There's also a commentary there of my own meditation practice which is pretty sloppy. So at least it's honest and accurate.

MS: *"Why I Meditate" is an interesting poem when you put it up against Anne Waldman's poem of the same title. It's sort of a mirror-poem.*

AG: Yeah. Anne also likes to teach. There's a poem by Mayakovsky, "A Conversation with the Sun," and a poem by Frank O'Hara, which is a mirror of that. Actually, I'm embarrassed to be talking about myself so much. *[Laughter.]*

MS: *There's a line in "White Shroud" that I found reflective of the major themes in the book: "How older than our shouts and banners, we explored brick avenues we lived in to find new residences"—*

AG: Yeah, well, the theme is that you're getting tired of running around, and want to settle down and enjoy a peaceful old age. But it also is related to a consistent dream that goes all through the journals, that Gordon Ball pointed out, which is like an archetypal dream that a lot of people have had, like the archetypal dream of being chased by the boogeyman, or being found downtown with your pants down or pants off, or being late to school or late to work, or going back to your house and finding it not there, or finding it there but finding your room . . . I don't know. Have you ever had any?

MS: *Room dreams?*

AG: Room dreams, yeah. Have you ever had that?

MS: *Yeah.*

AG: It seems to be archetypal, and I've kept track of them all these years. A long time ago, I suspected the room was actually the body—you know, trying to get settled in one place—and the dream of not having a room was a foretaste of what it will feel like after you're dead, not being able to locate exactly where your place is and where you belong, feeling lost and not being able to grasp the actual street or building of your life. The nearest I ever came to that in actual life—waking life—was 1975, passing through Paris for a couple of days, maybe a whole week, visiting Gregory Corso, who was married and had a baby there. I had no business in Paris except to see him, so my mind was not occupied with anything, and there was not really enough time to go sightseeing. And I had lived there, you know. I remember riding in a taxi in Paris and seeing all these familiar buildings and feeling that it was all ungraspable, that I couldn't settle down and live there and do what I used to do, go shopping every day, go see friends, sit around at the rue, just sit in a café and do nothing, be immersed in the presence of Paris and my own settled-down home there. It was like everything had turned to water. Or Paris—all the solid buildings of Paris—was still there, but *I* had turned to water. *[Laughs.]* There's a line by [Robert] Creeley, "You can't step into the same river twice," and "Everything is water if you look long enough." But, anyway, it's the nearest I had, awake, to a situation that was just like that dream, of a feeling of not being able to grasp onto my body, so to speak, or your house, or the place where you belong.

Toward the end of his life, my father had a bunch of dreams that actually turned me on to the fact that these might be premonitory dreams about rehearsing the feeling you'll get slightly after your death, just after you're dead: not being sure where you are, being disoriented, not being able to put the key in the lock, not finding the key. Or, you know, thinking you've got the key in your hand and then looking at it again in the dream and finding it isn't there. My father dreamt that he had driven his car into Newark, as he was used to, to teach his class, which he did after he retired from teaching high school—he taught a class at Rutgers in Newark—and when he got out of his class, he came out and he was lost. He didn't know where he was and he couldn't find his car. And there was nobody in any of the houses in the suburban streets. There was an old phone booth, but he didn't have any money with him to call home. He just needed one dime. Or he went in the phone booth and found the whole phone molded. He put in his dime and he heard a buzz, and then the thing went dead. So he couldn't communicate and he was lost there. It reminds me of my own dream because it was a recurrent dream. That dream recurred to him as he approached his death. The sensation or feeling, familiar to anybody who's cramped at all, of the ungraspability of the situation, or being disoriented with no reference point.

MS: *That happened in your poem "Black Shroud."*

AG: Yeah. It's common. There are a number of dreams that I've had, of visiting the dead. I had a dream of meeting Kerouac and, for the first time in a dream or life, [he gave] total approval for a speech I'd made at the writers' conference in Peking. I'd improvised something and he liked that. In the dream that night, I saw Kerouac and he said, "Well, you finally did a speech that's right." *[Laughter.]* Just like dreaming that I reconciled with my mother. I had a dream of reconciliation with my father, also. I wrote it out in poetry form, but it was more diverse and I couldn't shape it, and I didn't want to change it. It was a really interesting dream with my father and Neal Cassady and Gregory—all in the same dream. It was a very good one. In this case, I was with Neal and a group of other people, maybe Kerouac, and I suddenly realized that I was spending a long time with them but I hadn't seen my father recently. In fact, I'd neglected him for a long time. And so I went to see him in his apartment with my friends, and he offered us a place to stay overnight, and I wondered why I had ignored him so long. It was really awful. You know, I hadn't seen or visited or phoned my own father in many years. I finally did get back to his apartment, and he gave me a pallet to sleep on and I awoke in the middle of the night, a little cold, and I realized my father was sleeping on the floor: he'd given me his only bed. Everybody else had little cots, but my father was on the cold floor. So I told him he should take the pallet. When I woke, I suddenly realized the reason I hadn't visited my father was that he was dead.

It was like the "White Shroud" thing: an emotional visit, reconciliation. And then there was another dream, relating to Williams, with Williams giving me advice. It's something, I guess, that's coming in old age, in older age, of understanding more and reconnecting with archetypal conditioners, people who had conditioned me, and regulating things with them, rearranging or re-rapports. Or finding that their lessons or teachings had borne fruit, and now coming back for their approval or understanding.

MS: *Do you feel good after one of these dreams?*

AG: If I get to write them down, I feel that some enormous gift has been given to me and I was adequately receiving it. I couldn't have written a poem like "White Shroud" on willpower. It involved my whole nature, both the dream consciousness and waking consciousness. In a sense, neither of those is under our control. You can *will* yourself to sit down, but you can't will yourself inspiration—or even will yourself a moment's gift in phrasing. So if I have a dream which has a kind of visionary element, like Shelley's last great poem, "The Triumph of Life," which has the same structure ... Shelley's out in the country, and he's lying under a tree, reading, and he falls asleep and dreams. And then there's this vision of the world, which is like a coherent Dantean vision, and his opening is he's just a guy out there and he goes under the tree and takes a nap. So if there's a dream in which I have an element, like my mother being a shopping-bag lady, which hooks into the present ground and, at the same time, relates to other poems and reconciles and reveals my own feelings ... if it happens with a beginning, a middle, and an end, and I can remember enough of it to transcribe it, or invent enough in character that it sounds genuine and still has a shifting mystery—if you get into it without knowing what it is, and then it reveals itself as a dream and you wake up—that's pretty rare. Or to remember Williams talking and be able to get something that sounds right and wise, beyond my own intelligence, or my own conscious intelligence . . . it's, you know, a miracle.

MS: *Your mother was so real in the middle of "White Shroud"; you're describing her almost the way Williams would have described her, with the pots and pans and so on.*

AG: That was conscious application of the objectivist, naturalist, William Carlos Williams imagist, no-ideas-but-in-things, minute particular detail method of composition, to the evanescence matter of dream. In that sense, I felt that something had come to a natural conclusion in my poetry. I had been preparing myself for that all along: to transcribe an unusual state of consciousness by making use of ordinary, direct treatment of things, ordinary mind, instead of getting excited and blowing your mind and batting your head against the wall, trying to describe an abstraction; to actually get down with grounded details in a situation where the mind was in an elevated state, either in actual illumination, in waking, or a dream of extraordinary coherence. So, when the moment came up, my ax was ready. I had prepared, practiced enough poetry that I could actually take it down without getting distracted, and without getting off into abstraction, but staying with the facts. To the very end, actually: "And when the ink ran out of my pen . . . / I went downstairs to the shady living room, where Peter Orlovsky / sat with long hair lit by television glow to watch/the sunrise weather news . . ." I got all the information in.

Previously unpublished. Conducted November 1986. Printed by permission of Michael Schumacher.

No More Bagels

An Interview with Allen Ginsberg

STEVE SILBERMAN, 1987

ALLEN GINSBERG WAS SIXTY-ONE when this interview was conducted. Not surprisingly, he was in a reflective mood when talking about his career and how he had changed over the years. In his advancing age, he was concerned with his health, energy, and the subjects of his poetry.

MY PARENTS WERE YOUNG NEW LEFTISTS during the sixties, and Allen Ginsberg's name was a household word. In muslin *shmatte* and finger cymbals, he personified the spiritual aspect of the vision of a new society. The public affection between Ginsberg and Peter Orlovsky presented a model of gay relationship unfettered by the trivializing roles set aside for homosexual men.

I saw Ginsberg give two poetry readings on the anniversary of Neal Cassady's death in 1977, and that summer I became one of his apprentices at Naropa Institute. I was nineteen and too shy to show my hero but one poem, so my "apprenticeship" consisted of typing his journals. There was a small army of people like me.

This past January, I interviewed Ginsberg in his apartment on the Lower East Side. The walls had been freshly painted white, with crates and stacks of books everywhere, unanswered correspondence, and hundreds of manuscripts sent by poets seeking a blurb or advice. The electronic telephone burbled constantly. There was a portrait of Whitman in the kitchen, a Sunday-school upright piano in a room to the side, and a little shrine with an orange meditation cushion below the bedroom window.

Ginsberg's right eye and cheek were paralyzed slightly—a vestige of Bell's palsy. But he was hardly frail. I told Ginsberg how important "Howl" had been to me as an adolescent, when I saw in its sincerity and spiritual hunger and homosexual fearlessness a reflection of my own inner life. It was too bad, he said, I hadn't stumbled on Gide or Genet.

STEVE SILBERMAN: *Walt Whitman said he wished to be remembered as "the tenderest lover." He is remembered as a great heart, but also as one of the most significant formal innovators in 19th-century poetry. How do you wish to be remembered?*

ALLEN GINSBERG: What a question! I don't really want to interfere with my karma. A question like this has a feedback in that it directs people's attention, and just at this moment I'm more interested in what other people respond to than what I respond to—finding that out. Trying to check my subjectivity against the imagined world of others.

It would be nice to be remembered as an ecstatic poet, or a poet whose work could inspire or elevate others' minds; or a poet who spread some sense of expansion of awareness, or expansive consciousness. It would be nice to be remembered for generous energy—patience and generosity in energetic thought. But that's sort of like a neurotic self-idealization. I'm really at this point less interested in my own projection than curious about what it really is on the outside of my head. So maybe I'd like to be remembered as somebody who was curious about what it was like outside of his head!

SS: *Your career was established outside of the Establishment, printing in small presses and not teaching in the academy; not being taught in the academy until later. How does it feel to be teaching at Brooklyn College and to have Harper and Row as your publisher?*

AG: It seems like a ripening—that the culture has changed sufficiently that it will take me more or less on my own terms. Although some of my edges are smoothed down now. I don't insult people inadvertently or advertently—I try and treat them with a kind of Buddhist gentility, gentleness, even if I feel that they're neurotic or incompetent. I try not to pin them wriggling to the wall, but try and help 'em get out of that space, or make their situation workable rather than challenging them. Trying to enrich them rather than challenge them.

I have twelve years' experience at Naropa helping run the poetics department so I'm really an old-dog teacher now, and Naropa—inasmuch as it's accredited—is in a sense institutional too. So we actually built a new institution inside the shell of the old, successfully. That's one of the signal community commune meditation-oriented projects of the ethos of the sixties that survived through the eighties and is flourishing. So I feel kind of proud that I was part of that—something real, in that sense, socially.

Brooklyn College in a way is anticlimactic. Courses in literary history of the Beat Generation that I developed at Naropa I'll be teaching at Brooklyn College. The students are less spiritual than at Naropa, so there's a question of now having to give them a spiritual infusion in the secular Brooklyn community scene.

ss: *How large are your classes?*

AG: Small—so small that I asked for an undergraduate larger class to get at younger meat, maybe meet someone I could sleep with or relate to emotionally. 'Cause the MFA students are all jelled already—fixated and solidified into their corsets and neuroses.

ss: *Why do you think Naropa had the stability to maintain its integrity into the eighties?*

AG: First of all they had a central organizing motor which was meditation. So they had a workable central thesis that was not based on the ego of the leader. Secondly, they didn't have a democratic baloney grounding—they were in practice democratic, but in theory totally autocratic under the guru. If you have a sort of selfless guru who's not on a power trip—or who's on a Vajrayana power trip rather than on a personal power trip—you have a worthwhile basis for a community, based on devotion and meditation and actual awareness practice; rather than theory of getting high, or ecstatic, or … And the Buddhists after all have several thousand years' experience in organizing nontheistic intentional communities.

The Buddhist thing is bohemian, by its very nature. Or admits more bohemia. It's nonjudgmental, let us say—its practice is awareness rather than rule of law and judgment like Hebrew or Christian sharper aesthetically, like the artist's mind which is the same as the meditative mind: no matter what thought you have, you're interested in it, rather than rejecting it.

President Trungpa would come up with really interesting ideas, like methods of teaching poetry, methods of holding classes, methods of having assemblies—school assemblies to meditate rather than listen to a lot of yak. Methods of relating to but avoiding political animosity; relating to politics but not getting into the aggression of it.

They just knew how to solve a lot of problems that, say, Western hippie communes wouldn't conceive would arise—like how to raise money. The traditional Buddhist thing is you ask a patron for money, and he doesn't give, you ask him again, he doesn't give, you ask him a third time. If, after the third time, he gives or doesn't give, you don't ask a fourth time. You just ask three times—that's good manners! It communicates but it's not aggressive. You're inviting him, but not strong-arming him. Whereas a Western commune might hit somebody up for money too many times, not knowing the middle path.

ss: *You came as close as any poet has since Frost to national celebrity.*

AG: International, now. It's amazing.

ss: *How has that helped or hindered your poetic practice?*

AG: "Uneasy lies the head that wears the crown." This year I got a Golden Wreath from the International Poetry Evenings in Struga, Yugoslavia. A real wreath of gold—24 carat! "Howl" is now translated into Mainland Chinese, and a book of my poems has come out in Russia—

ss: *Unexpurgated in China?*

AG: No—they translated "cocksuckers" as "suckers of corks," so something to do with alcohol probably.

ss: *A million Chinese Ph.D. students will be—*

AG: Examining this translation for centuries to come, 'til they finally liberalize and get back to "cocksuckers," and have pederasts as their alcoholics. So ... it leaves it kinda wide open to do what I want and say what I want and this year, for the first time, the American academic community and the media are treating me like an elder statesman rather than a young upstart or a media creep. There was a Modern Language Association symposium on "Howl" and they invited me to read—so I gave a reading of "Howl" on the thirtieth anniversary for an assemblage of something like 500 English professors from all over the country. That really is hitting a nerve center—and it was a good reading, with Steven Taylor playing music.

So we actually presented the material in a way that people doing scholarly studies had not related to—hearing the authentic sound of it, out loud with the right voice. I was all dressed up properly, for their point of view, so clothing wasn't interfering ... my haircut was short, so they just had the voice and the words, no distractions to bother them. That probably puts the nail in the coffin as far as respectability and acceptance.

So the question is what, how does it feel? A feeling of what's it all for, and if I'm famous, gee the world must be in a terrible place. If I gotta serve for being the most famous and prestigious poet, then the world is really bad off. *[Laughing.]*

Now that I'm in the position of being a loudspeaker I don't know what to say. I don't have any aggressive intention, as I did when I was younger to some extent. It's more just trying to save my own skin—straighten out my own karma. Relate to the alterations of my relations with Peter Orlovsky and growing old, and real subject: death of my family, father and mother and aunts and uncles.

I didn't get too angry and outrageous out front on the whole Reagan era—thinking that aggression was not appropriate any longer. My own aggression. And in a way I'm glad because Reagan and his whole White House macho self-contradiction is auto-destructing, like the traditional Buddhist image of the snake of conceptualization uncoiling in mid-air. I'm glad I didn't go off half-cocked in an angry rage, tilting at their windmill, but simply observed what was going on and let it happen and didn't feel obliged to become a Don Quixote. And waste a lot of time writing about ephemera, as I did to some extent in the sixties.

ss: *You have spent the last decade and a half publicly identified as "Buddhist student Allen Ginsberg," but you were once regarded as one of the most articulate exponents of psychedelics as a means of personal, if not global, transformation. How do you view the Reagan administration's attempts to police consciousness via urine tests and sobriety checkpoints?*

AG: All scientific research on LSD has been stopped, except for very few projects done under the military, and that's a major catastrophe for human mind engineering and scientific advancement and psychology. The heroin problem stands as it always was: a conspiracy by heroin police, narcotics bureaus, their bureaucracies and budgets—with their working relation with Cosa Nostra and organized crime in maintaining a black market and high prices and sales under the desk—as well as regular organized crime dope laundry money, and that whole network extends from the White House to the Vatican. Contras-White House-Vatican. So the whole public approach by Reagan is just complete hypocrisy.

I've changed my mind about the relationship between acid and neurosis. It seems to me that acid can lead to some kind of breakdowns, maybe. So that people should be prepared with meditation, before they take acid. There should be an educational program to cultivate meditative practice and techniques, so that when people get high on acid and get into bum trips they can switch their minds, easily—and there are ways of doing it, very simple. But nobody is doing mass training in that, and it might be interesting for high school kids. It's like . . . give junkies needles, give kids condoms if they're gonna screw so they don't get AIDS. If they're gonna try acid—which is probably good for an intelligent kid—they should also be prepared with some techniques in meditation, so that they can switch their attention from bum trips back to their breath, and to the current space around them.

So I think in the sixties I wasn't prepared to deal with acid casualties from the point of view of a reliable technique for avoiding those casualties.

SS: *AIDS is not mentioned in "White Shroud."*

AG: No. I've had a couple of tests for myself for AIDS, and apparently have come out negative. Maybe been saved by my preference for straight kids. And I haven't met too many people that've had direct AIDS horror show—haven't avoided it exactly, it's just that I move in funny circles and I don't live in the Castro. But it's affected my sex life a lot.

I use condoms now and do safe sex, and I'm very hesitant to blow somebody and take their sperm unless I know them real well and know their history, and they've been tested. And even then ... even friends that I think are safe, I don't think I would fuck them without a condom or be screwed without a condom—at the moment.

I've somewhat exhausted my aggressive grasping for constantly getting laid. I seem to lay off—relax a little bit more, want a quiet night at home working, more than running around urgent. It's added another element of ... let's say discouragement of the idea of going out and trying to find new meat. Or more hesitant to try and put the make on students, simply because it's another barrier to go through ... to explain to them that I've been tested and I know how to do safe sex ... or, you know? Certainly there are a few people who I wanted to make out with who were worried about AIDS, who otherwise, maybe in another generation, might've been willing to swing to see what it was like.

I imagine in the next year I'd want to get into more contact with the actual AIDS clinics and people involved. At the moment I'm having hypertension from stress of doing too many things at once. So it's like taking on another activity. I'm sort of waiting for it to happen naturally. I've raised money for them but haven't had any real direct contact with people suffering.

ss: *What is the state of your health currently?*

AG: I have reactive hypoglycemia and arrhythmia of the heart, mainly due to overwork. Like I was up 'til seven this morning, eight-nine o'clock the night before trying to finish little projects. So, I've gotta change my life! Stop doing so many things. 'Cause right now I'm involved in poetry, photography, and music. And I've got this full-time job as a professor.

I've cut down on traveling and reading, and been hyperactive in publishing books: from *Collected Poems* to new *White Shroud* poems to "Howl" book, all in three years. It's actually broken my health a bit, and I have to start meditating more and do more t'ai chi. And control my diet. I have just this little office and one secretary—too many things going on, too much paper going over my desk.

Now we've located all my old journals. They've been typed and they're going to be edited. Following that, Bob Rosenthal is editing selected essays. Then Barry Miles is doing a biography of me, and will then be editing selected correspondence, and there's another book of selected interviews. In a way it's kind of . . . dismaying . . . because I'm trapped with things I've already done. My time is taken up framing things. If I were really free, I'd have a much happier time. It's kind of a drag to be so well known, because it's work.

The thing I enjoy most at the moment, aside from writing poems, just poems, is photography; and I always like to sing. Now for the first time I have complete opportunity to do all of them. Somebody will fund records, somebody will put out for the photography books, a good publisher to put out big books, journals and anything I want to print. But the more opportunity there is, the more things I can think of to do, and it gets really hyperactive, workaholic. So I'm coming up against my own karma that way . . . what is the limit of what I want to do . . . what do I most want to do before I kick the bucket.

About a month ago, one doctor told me I had heart trouble and should carry nitroglycerine around. Turned out he was wrong, but it was a good opportunity to review the time I have left, to figure out what is it I find most essential. And the thing I found most essential was doing nothing. Waiting for the Muse. Maybe with a camera. With a Leica.

ss: *How do you feel about death?*

AG: Well, I don't know anything about it. I never died before that I can remember. The deepest feeling I have is of the poignancy of having to say goodbye to everything—that I like so much. But I seem to be doing that inch-by-inch. I told you about the slight loosening of anxiety about sex, in addition to which I'm taking high blood pressure pills which cuts down sexual activity. Now, I've had to give up . . . for hypoglycemia . . . I have to say, bid farewell forever to matzo balls! To—

ss: *Knishes?*

AG: Challah! To knishes . . . potato knishes, to potatoes boiled, mashed, fried . . . borscht I can't take because I have gout and kidney stones, and borscht has calcium oxalate. I can't eat pasta, and I can't eat good old black bread, rye bread or toast much, or English muffins, Danish pastry, pies, cakes—

ss: *Onion rolls?*

AG: Onion rolls, bagels, farewell! As well as I can't eat red meat any more so rare that I can sink my teeth into a big juicy pastrami sandwich or corned beef or roast beef . . . I'm slowly gravitating towards celery and cucumbers and endives and lettuce and olive oil and lemon juice and maybe a lil' kasha, which has less starch and complex carbohydrates. No more candy, no more soda, no more cranberry juice, no more orange juice hardly, just oranges themselves. So, I'm already having all these little deaths.

But then you begin to explore the texture of what you eat—the texture of your environment. For instance, for forty years I always had salt with my soft-boiled eggs, and then I was told no more salt for high blood pressure; and I really developed a taste for soft-boiled eggs without salt. Then, for five years, since a Tibetan doctor told me to drink a glass of lemon juice with hot water every morning, I've had that with honey. I had to give up honey a month ago, and I suddenly discovered the lemon juice is sweet in itself! Funny explorations that I've been making . . . is death so bad? Is saying goodbye to matzo balls, is that so bad? Or bagels—or sucking semen directly into my gut—

Today I got up and—WHAT CAN I EAT? So what I did was I made a giant salad for breakfast. Crunching big juicy lettuce. So. What else we got?

ss: *One of the revelations of the annotated* Howl, *for me, was the amount of material that was eventually rejected. It is contrary to the public image of you as not revising, to realize that "Howl" was the product of a rigorous selection process. Did you use such a process in subsequent compositions, or change habits or strategy?*

AG: "Howl" was a special case, of a structure that was so good it needed perfection. It looks like a lot of revision and a lot of revision it is, of little details and some addition and all that . . . nonetheless, the main structure of "Howl" is right there in the first draft, and the most interesting phrasing. Like, I think "hydrogen jukebox" is there to begin with, and "Moloch whose name is the Mind"—maybe it came in somewhere early—"smokestacks and antennae crown the cities."

So, it's just a question of cleaning it up and pushing it into shape. The reason I kept insisting that "Howl" was spontaneous—though it's not at all—is that the original impulse of the original writing was a spontaneous momentary burst. And I think that has to be respected. Though I perhaps over-emphasized the nonrevised aspect of it—lied about it outright and bald-faced to John Ciardi when he called me up in Paterson in 1958 and said did I revise it and I said, "No, not at all." It certainly was cleaned up a lot.

The most interesting composition is the four pages of improvisation in the Moloch thing. That's actually pretty good and funny. You know, like jamming—

ss: *"Moloch whose cock is the Washington Monument."*

AG: Yes. Now, "Moloch whose cock is the Washington Monument" as an image is not so good . . . as a sound there's a very good DA dat da Dat da da DA-DA-DA, DA-DA-DA! It's got good syncopation. The reason I kept that through many drafts was it was just . . . good sound. And also, maybe the possibility of a kind of national image. But it's too garish. It's too obvious a trip. Also, why insult the Washington Monument?

But that section of improvisations really would be good study for a young poet to see how BAD you can get, but how loose you can get, and how GOOD it is to get bad and loose and genius-like. You could get something out of it.

I think I just needed to allow any thought to come through—any embarrassing thing—and not worry about writing down things that were stupid. Allow that, because you can never tell what's gonna be stupid later on. I couldn't satisfy Kerouac's very strict freestyle non-revision. And he's given a great example—of his prose and "Mexico City Blues"—of doing it.

ss: *Not stepping backwards.*

AG: Yeah—not changing anything. The mind got accustomed to his work, right away. It was perfect—as is. I didn't think mine was perfect as is.

It's a how-to book. How to write "Howl." Or how to go about this style of poetry. I always wanted to explain that, and never had the chance. 'Cause a lot of people are interested in the poem and a lot of people write in that style or learn something from it . . . so this is a chance to really, really explain in a way that other people can make use of the methods that I inherited and developed.

ss: *That wouldn't necessarily result in a Ginsbergian—*

AG: No, it would result in a genre of poetry that's common 20th-century heroic international style from Whitman, Apollinaire, and others. But it would be applied individually. The method is simply liberation of the imagination, and a certain intelligence and choice of what you want to include.

I guess the best lesson is seeing the quality of the things that I included and the vulgarity of the things that I excluded .. ?cause a lot of people write vulgar "Howls." There's not enough refinement. Thinking that the freedom is the whole point and not the refinement part, also.

ss: *You have said all along that the personal, if expressed with particularity, is archetypal. However, in many other poets' work, the personal remains personal and does not become archetypal.*

AG: I think you'll find that it isn't personal, it's generic, that people do generalizations and don't get down to specific observation of detail which would then make it interesting. Anything that somebody really sees, is able to notate precisely, of course it's interesting.

It's when they don't see something, but just make a general curse à la Bukowski, or what they think I'm doing . . . you know, "Fled from the demands of the middle class down the alleyways of high-cost supermarkets . . ." That's not interesting. What are the ways of the middle class you're talking about? Can you particularize and specify what it is you're referring to . . . then somebody else can find it. Offer me a glimpse of somebody else's life.

From *Whole Earth Review,* no. 56 (Fall 1987): 20–25. Reprinted by permission of Steve Silberman.

Ginsberg Accuses Neo-Conservatives of Political Correctness

KATHLEEN O'TOOLE, 1995

GINSBERG'S BATTLES against censorship had been a lifelong endeavor. "Howl" had emerged victorious in a landmark 1957 obscenity trial in San Francisco, but in Ginsberg's view, there was still much work to be done. There was censorship in the other arts, and over the ensuing four decades, he became involved in countless skirmishes on the state, local, and national levels. Neo-conservatism, a powerful presence on the American political landscape since the election of Ronald Reagan in 1980, only strengthened his resolve.

STANFORD—Under the rubric of "getting government off our backs," neo-conservatives have been recycling the ideas of Stalin, Hitler, and Mao in their wars against art, Beat poet Allen Ginsberg told a Stanford audience at Cubberley Auditorium on Friday, February 10.

Ginsberg made his critique of neo-conservative politics during a panel discussion on "Writing Out of Bounds," part of a series of events on the subject of formal and informal means of censorship sponsored by the Stanford Humanities Center. His visit to campus, which included a poetry reading later that evening, was sponsored by Elliott Levinthal, professor emeritus of mechanical engineering, and his wife, Rhoda. Other participants on the panel, all from the Bay Area, were poets Carl Rakosi and Ronald Silliman and writer Leslie Scalapino, who also runs a small press that publishes poetry. Stanford English professor Marjorie Perloff served as moderator.

Stalin attacked art as "elitist individualism," Ginsberg said. Mao Ze-dong called it "spiritual corruption," and Hitler used the phrase "de-generate art"—descriptions that Ginsberg said have been picked up by neo-conservative commentators and politicians in the past decade to de-scribe art they don't like. In recent U.S. history, Ginsberg asserted, "The original speech-code puritanism came from the Heritage Foundation and Dinesh D'Souza, who founded the *Stanford Review,* which is con-stantly attacking speech codes. I emphasize them rather than left-wing political correctness because somehow the right wing has propagandized what was originally a joke in the left wing—self-criticism for the most part, an ironic accusation on the part of the left wing . . . that was then taken very seriously as a literal thing and reversed as an attack on the left, while the neo-conservatives and right-wing politicians were enacting law to prevent certain words from being said."

The law to which Ginsberg referred is the 1988 law introduced by Senator Jesse Helms, adopted by Congress, and signed by President Reagan, banning "indecent" language on radio and television, language deemed unsuitable for children age twelve or under. The ban meant, in effect, that high school students who can read Ginsberg's "Sunflower Sutra" in their school anthologies could not hear it on the radio, he said. Occasional news articles suggest that some conservatives would like to expand the ban to electronic mail, he said.

Ginsberg joined in a lawsuit that got the ban reduced to part-time: from the hours of 6 a.m. to 8 p.m. The Federal Communications Com-mission appealed, and an appeals court in Washington, D.C., currently is considering whether to extend the ban to midnight, he said.

Defends Archive

Ginsberg also attacked the conservative publication *Accuracy in Aca-demia* for distorting the description of the archive he sold to Stanford University Libraries last fall. Reading first a detailed description of the archive from the September 7 *San Jose Mercury News,* Ginsberg next read the shorter description in *Accuracy in Academia.* The latter mentioned his tennis shoes, beard clippings, and old utility bills, but not his four hundred notebook journals or four thousand letters, including correspondence with Timothy Leary, Abbie Hoffman, William S. Burroughs, and Robert F. Kennedy. "So the reductionism and the vulgarity of this so-called accuracy turns out to be this con of distortion and omission—the sin of omission parading as accuracy," he said.

According to Ginsberg, the archive was his attempt since the late 1940s to "keep track of this spiritual war for the liberation of speech and spirits in America, to keep an archive that would record all these battles back and forth, which involved not only LSD but literature, film, radio, and television." Ginsberg said that during the 1950s and 1960s there were steady victories for free speech through court decisions, including the famous battle over publication of his poem "Howl."

The tide began turning in the 1980s, he said, when the first attacks were made against government funding of art. That was also the time, he said, when neo-conservatives began setting up local campus newspapers, borrowing the techniques of social critique used by an earlier generation of leftist students. "The impertinence of the left newspaper, the critique, the chutzpah, was not just simply taken over by the right wing but funded very wildly," he said.

"The first blow in this counterculture war that ended in real censorship," Ginsberg claimed, was leveled by D'Souza when he wrote articles for the Heritage Foundation *Policy Review* in 1982 denouncing grants to poets who used certain words in books of poetry funded in part by the National Endowment for the Arts. "He had gone through all the books that had received grants from 1978 and then went back further . . . looking for what amounted to, in his mind, politically incorrect phrasing," Ginsberg said of D'Souza.

Asked later in the discussion to critique a call for censorship from the left—Andrea Dworkin's stand on pornography—Ginsberg noted that Dworkin's own book was seized by Canadian customs when that nation implemented a law based on her ideas for restrictions. At a bar mitzvah recently, he said, he told Dworkin, "'I had some intergenerational friendships with younger men—17, 18, 19—legal and all that . . . what are you going to do—put me in jail?' and she said, 'You ought to be shot.' Her anger has gotten the best of her, and I don't think any literary program based just on anger can be helpful to anybody."

Popularity of Poetry

Current efforts in Washington to cut back or eliminate grants by the National Endowment for the Arts and the National Endowment for the Humanities were the focus of many remarks by other poets on the panel. They agreed that censorship, rather than budget cutting per se, was the motive behind proposed cuts, but whether those cuts would ultimately hurt art or cause an artistic renaissance was a subject of debate.

Silliman and Scalapino said they were most concerned about the loss of small grants to publishers and distributors of innovative work rather than to artists themselves. Nonagenerian Rakosi, one of the objectivist poets of the '20s and '30s who were ignored by publishers until much later, said he was more concerned that true innovators today will get lost in what may be a flood of poetry. An estimated one thousand poetry books were published in the past year, he said, including one by former President Jimmy Carter, and the Internet makes it possible for almost anyone to distribute a book instantly.

Ginsberg speculated that repression will bring a renaissance. "You are going to see in the immediate future on the platforms of poetry houses, slam clubs, and coffee houses an enormous renaissance of poetry, once the poets are liberated from the idea that somehow they need to be subsidized."

Good American poetry has not shrunk in popularity, he said, citing the success of American blues throughout the world. "There has always been growth in interest in language, rhyme, poetry, rhythm, social critique, encapsulated, condensed speech." Some people may see current rap as "overly vulgar," he said, but, like poet Robert Duncan, Ginsberg believes that popular interest in poetry that poets themselves wouldn't read is "the compost pile out of which a poetry culture arises."

February 14, 1995, news release [edited for this volume]. Copyright 1995 Stanford University. All rights reserved. Stanford News Service, Press Courtyard, Stanford, California 94305–2245. Reprinted by permission.

A Conversation with Allen Ginsberg

THE FOLLOWING INTERVIEW, an expanded version of the published piece, is an example of Ginsberg's later career-assessment conversations. Although he had no way of knowing that he had two years left to live, Ginsberg was now taking a more reflective approach in many of his interviews. He could still be combative or impatient in his responses to questions, such as his defense of the North American Man/Boy Love Association (NAMBLA) or condemnations of censorship, but at the same time, he seemed more measured in his answers to questions.

SINCE ENVISIONING THE FEVERISH, APOCALYPTIC LINES of "Howl" in 1956, poet Allen Ginsberg has documented our country's evolution for almost 40 years. Along with Jack Kerouac, William S. Burroughs, and Neal Cassady, Ginsberg created a new aesthetic of "spontaneous bop prosody," an approach to writing that not only liberated the minds of countless emerging young writers and artists in the Sixties, but rippled its way throughout the American psyche in a multitude of unexpected ways. You can see it in everything from Bob Dylan's innovative approach to songwriting in the Sixties, to our country's blossoming interests in the environment, Buddhism, gay rights, and free speech.

And, of course, there is the writing itself. A practitioner of the "open form" of poetry, Ginsberg is a direct literary descendent of mavericks like Walt Whitman and William Carlos Williams, who believed in using the unique rhythms of American speech rather than the more formal, prosaic approach to language that had dominated the literary scene for most of the century prior to the Beats' emergence.

His most recent collection of poetry, *Cosmopolitan Greetings*, was published last year, as was Rhino Records' monumental four-CD retrospective of his spoken word and musical career, *Holy Soul Jelly Roll*. Ginsberg and I chatted for nearly two hours inside fellow poet Lawrence Ferlinghetti's studio at City Lights Bookstore in San Francisco's North Beach district, not too far from where his legendary first public performance of "Howl" took place (available for the first time on the box set). We then concluded our conversation a few weeks later over the phone after he had returned home to New York.

In person, Ginsberg is a charismatic and articulate presence, someone who possesses a tremendous sense of humor, but someone who also is deadly serious about being understood. As he approaches his seventh decade, Ginsberg continues to tirelessly reflect where America has been and where it is going, with an energy and enthusiasm that truly is amazing to behold.

TM: *I wanted to talk to you about the importance of dreams and visions in your development as a poet. First, you had the "Blake vision" after reading Blake's poem, "The Sick Rose." You later said it was "the deepest spiritual experience I had in my life" and "determined [your] karma as a poet." Then, a few years later, you had a dream about Joan Burroughs [the deceased wife of writer William S. Burroughs, who accidentally shot her to death] that gave you the idea of "jump cutting from one visual image to another." Do you think these kinds of dreams or visions come from somewhere outside ourselves?*

AG: No, I think it's from us. It's just from a larger aspect of our own awareness. It's not just the linear rational filtered mind but the whole mind and the whole body. I don't think it comes from the outside, no. It's just straight out of our own heart centers.

The dream of Joan was a dream of her tolerance to her ex-husband, William Burroughs, who committed manslaughter, and her thing was not at all reproof or recrimination. It was, "AH! I feel really good now." It was such a tolerant, funny attitude. I realized it was completely human.

But the point is, in this dream, I was gratified that Joan and I had this common feeling of total interest, devotion, and curiosity about Burroughs transcending the tragedy. "So what's Burroughs doing now?" she says. I had cooked that up out of my own imagination. It was my projection. I don't think I saw a real Joan Burroughs from outer space coming to see me. I saw my Joan Burroughs imaged in my own mind, in my own heart.

I once had a dream of having breakfast with poor Richard Nixon at this breakfast nook in his house.

TM: *A recurring nightmare! [Laughter.]*

AG: No! Don't mock it. Seriously, it was this poor Richard Nixon, who was completely fallible and vulnerable, not knowing what he was doing, wanting my approval. It was poignant. No, it wasn't a nightmare. That's the whole point. It was the opposite.

TM: *I wanted to ask you a few questions related to "Kaddish." One slogan that you often use is, "Candor ends paranoia." Has growing up with a mother who was mentally ill caused you to be more open about your own anxieties and fears?*

AG: I think so. In a reverse way, she had all these fears of secret assailants and conspiracies. And so I really got allergic to secret conspiracies. If I thought there was a secret conspiracy, I would be talking about it immediately. Also, if I got in such a way that I thought that I was the center of a conspiracy, I would check it out, ask other people to see if I was on firm ground or just spinning off a fantasy. Also, it inured me or got me inoculated against long-winded crazy people; I developed a lot of patience. Maybe it de-sensitized me to other people's tragedies, because I felt I had to get an extra thick skin so I could sit through people fixing me with a hypnotic eye and telling me about the Martians coming to get them, or get me.

TM: *Has this chaos in your early life affected your ability to be a good friend, sympathetic listener?*

AG: Yes and no. On the surface, yes. Really, I'm untouched, maybe de-sensitized. The nerve has been cut so that it doesn't affect me as much. I'll think, "Oh well, they're nuts. What can I do? How can I reassure them, fill in the gap here?"

TM: *So you're trying to be helpful, even though—*

AG: Well, for my own safety! My own peace of mind and safety that I don't have to listen to this forever. *[Laughter.]* You know, how to deal with the situation practically. Not resenting it or yelling at them, but thinking how to resolve the situation. Getting rid of the uprightness. Sometimes by being very blunt and saying, "You should see a psychiatrist. You have a systematic thinking disorder. You may not be aware of it, but it looks that way to me. Or if you want my advice, what you're saying is not making very much sense so . . . I've had enough of it. My mother gave me enough of that, and I recognize it now. Please, don't be like my mother." Or something like that, where you actually mirror it back to them.

TM: *Do you think if she had been more candid it would have helped her?*

AG: I don't think it would have made any difference. She had a definite chemical, metabolic problem. Of course, her problem came from a whole social circumstance, too. My father's family was dominant and her mother-in-law was a threatening figure to her. She wasn't quite accepted by the family, so she always felt a little weaker or hesitant with them. Then, finally, she began to project evil intentions on her mother-in-law. No amount of straight-forward talk would've gotten her grounded there.

Also, there was some neurological problem, because I remember at one point she had hyperaesthesia. Every touch for her was like pain. She had to lie in a dark room, the light hurt her eyes, that painful stab of light. Even movement against a rough blanket grated. The doctor said she had this neurological illness where the nerves were apparently exposed. The volume was turned up completely, and she was in continuous physiological pain. Other times she complained about three big sticks forced down her back. Apparently, there were three streaks of stiffness . . . she didn't know what it was. But it was obviously a physical thing that she interpreted as sticks that had come into her back and were sticking her, which were connected with seething electrodes. I never understood what it was, but it was so recurrent for many years that I reckon it must have been some physiological component that she was talking about. She was living in a different physiological world than I was.

If you read Oliver Sacks, you [gain] some insight into some of those neurological reversals. You can't really judge what people are going through. When a junky is going through withdrawals, how can you know the physical pain he's going through? Cramps, nausea, instability, vomiting, diarrhea—all of that at once. I have night cramps from taking a diuretic, and so I take some Quinine for it. If I didn't have that, all the muscles in my body would be constricting like worms. It would be horrifying.

TM: *What facilitated your own mental breakdown back in the late 1940s?*

AG: I had had that Blake visitation, so to speak. I didn't have the language or the social or cultural background to be able to integrate it into some sort of practice. It seemed like a break in nature, like seeing God or something, and I kept using Western religious terminology saying, "I'm seeing God." People thought I was nuts—and I was, to use that kind of language. And I was too insistent on my vision being understood by everybody ... sort of like an LSD person who tries to explain his trip to everybody and gets to be an old bore. Or to take LSD and take off your clothes and jump in front of the cars and say, "Stop the machines, the world's coming to an end!" I was confused about different levels of reality, and I also thought I had to reproduce that visionary state any way I could, and I began thinking maybe I had to die to reproduce it. So I was quite confused.

But basically, I got into trouble with Herbert Huncke and a group of junky friends who were using my place as a drop for their stolen goods, and we all got busted. I had a choice between going to a jail or going to a bughouse like a nice young middle-class student. I chose to go to a very polite mental hospital. When I left eight months later, they said, "You were never psychotic. You were just an average neurotic." But it was like an apartment hotel. I could get out every evening from four to eight, and get out Fridays to Sunday nights. It was really a shelter where I had food and occupational therapy and free psychotherapy. It was pretty good. In fact, I stayed there longer than they wanted me to, waiting for my parents to get settled in a house.

TM: *As I read other people's accounts of your involvement in their lives, it seems that you often adopt the role of "The Fool" to diffuse tension, paranoia. Do you see that quality in yourself?*

AG: Yep, the old coyote. Also, I *am* a fool. I feel sort of naturally stupid. I don't tend to be wise or anything like that. To the extent that I'm wise is that I know that I'm dumb. So it leaves room for other people to talk and me to listen.

TM: *There's an interesting story in Marianne Faithfull's autobiography that describes the first meeting between Bob Dylan and the Beatles. She said you were in the room, and the two camps were hovering around each other but not talking, until you sacrificed yourself by swaggering over to Dylan's chair and putting your arm around him and—*

AG: No. She wasn't there in the room. Dylan sent for me to come into the room, [and] I walked in and there was total silence. They were frozen, paranoid. I don't know why ... maybe they were wondering who was on top. So I sat down on the arm rest of the big sofa Dylan was sitting on and Lennon sneered, "Why don't you sit a little closer?" And I thought it was so funny that he would be such a kid in such august company that I fell over laughing on his lap. And I looked up and I said, "You ever read William Blake?" And he says, "Never read him!" His wife says, "Oh John, stop lying." And then, the ice was broken.

No, I wasn't swaggering into the room. I was quite modest. I was kind of awed to be in the room with Dylan and the Beatles. There was a whole suite of people dying to get in there to see what was going on. So I had a very nice role. I wasn't a rock star. I didn't have anything to win or lose. I was a poet. I'd won anyway, no matter what happened, because I was the one person there whose work was immortal. They were popular, but I'd be immortal. Maybe now Dylan and certain lyrics of Lennon will be immortal. But I felt quite empowered to be myself and not worry about status. I was willing to be "The Fool." That was a funny scene.

A couple weeks later, I had a birthday party and got drunk and got into my birthday suit, naked, and Lennon and George Harrison came.

They were shocked that I was naked. Within a couple years, [Lennon] and Yoko Ono were posing naked for magazine and record covers. But at the time, they were relatively innocent. They thought I was a vulgar American or something. So I think they thought of me as a fool, but pretty soon they were doing the same thing.

TM: *I wanted you to comment on one of your lines from your poem, "Cosmopolitan Greetings": "If we don't show anyone, we're free to write anything." When you first started out writing, did you write your poems with the intention of reading them aloud publicly?*

AG: "Howl" was written under that circumstance. It was not intended to be published. It was private for the desk. So I could say, "I got fucked in the ass by handsome sailors and screamed with joy." I didn't want my father to see it. The reason "Howl" is so good was that it was never intended to be read by anyone else except Kerouac.

TM: *Did becoming a public figure affect your ability to remain uninhibited in your writing?*

AG: Apparently not, if you judge by "Please Master," which is an S&M poem. *[Laughter.]* It's so clear, it's almost embarrassing. That was written twelve to thirteen years later.

TM: *Here's another line from "Cosmopolitan Greetings": "Mind is outer space."*

AG: When you open your eyes, you can see the vast night sky and stars to the end of the sky, as much as can be seen. When you close your eyes, it's the same sky. It's that same vastness. Gregory Corso has an excellent poem proving that: "A star / is as far / as the eye / can see / and / as near / as my eye / is to me." It's an Einsteinian paradox.

TM: *You've said that inspiration can be taught. How does one go about teaching inspiration?*

AG: I think Dylan has taught inspiration by demonstrating physical inspiration . . . inspiration of unobstructed breath. I think people hearing the first reading of "Howl" or "Kaddish" or some other poems like "Father Death Blues" will recognize that depth of feeling in themselves, that ecstasy and rapture and transport and realize that it . . . stretches, and that they can do it too.

TM: *Ideally, what would you like the afterlife to be like, if there is one?*

AG: God, I don't know. The Buddhists say you go to the "Pure Land" and learn from the Buddhas and then go back and see what you can do to help other people in the real world without getting reborn. It's probably the same as this. Maybe worse. Once you're trained to deal with trouble, maybe they send you some place worse to help out.

TM: *Describe the context of "Wales Visitation."*

AG: Fifth hour of an acid trip in mist streams ... narrow green green valley of Wales where cultivation was grass to the very doorstep. The waves ... almost like undersea currents of mists ebbing through the valley, and my own breath identified with that ebbing and flowing. So it was a kind of nature unity poem. I was thinking of Wordsworth's "Ode to Intimations On Immortality" and "Tintern Abbey."

TM: *Are you familiar with Terence McKenna?*

AG: Yes, I've heard of him. I have not met him, I haven't read anything of his. But I know friends [of his] and he has quite an interesting reputation as a psychedelic, New Age, Gaia apotheosis pioneer.

TM: *He believes our civilization is going to end in the year 2012. Have you had any dreams or visions of our planet's future?*

AG: I don't see how our civilization will end so soon. How does he feel this can be so abrupt?

TM: *He's developed a computer model of civilizations, which he calls "Timewave Zero." He believes that civilizations are exponentially moving toward this final moment in history. He doesn't say that the world necessarily will blow up, but just that civilization, as we know it, will end, and that humans will transform into a different realm of being altogether.*

AG: It sounds a bit hyperbolic. I would say that it would take a couple hundred years, and the situation will be more like a gridlock. As Eliot said, "Not with a bang, but a whimper." I was discussing [the world] coming to an end with Gelek Rinpoche, a Tibetan lama who is my teacher, and Philip Glass, and he didn't think it would end with any explosions, or anything like that. He thought it would be more like slow karmic gridlock, population expansion and cars not being able to move more than an inch an hour, or whatever.

Another interesting aspect is that we're not going to lose the planet. The planet can take us, it can take asteroids bumping into it, explosions, reversal of the poles, Ice Ages. It's done that thousands of times, but we might lose *our* own footing on it.

TM: *We might be replaced by insect consciousness, or something like that.*

AG: Well, it just would just be a different thing, not replaced. Something else would develop. In any case, we might lose our own footing, our own nourishment. I don't think the species would die out, but it would be much reduced. Who knows? But to me 2012 seems to be a little too mechanical an idea. Who the hell would know all the variables?

TM: *In what ways has the Beat culture survived to the present day?*

AG: The basic themes, as I understood them in 1945 from a conversation I had with Kerouac and Burroughs, was some sense of a spiritual change. The terms we were using back then were a "New Vision" or "New Consciousness." For all we know, it might have been referring to the old, more natural consciousness [being] recovered. Like Kerouac said, "The Earth is an Indian thing."

So it was like a spiritual revolution that was interested in various forms of literature and poetry and drugs and exploration of the underworld, and underground, counterculture, marginal cultures, etc. Burroughs had studied anthropology and archeology at Harvard, so he introduced that aspect. Kerouac had the minority Canuck culture, and I had the old Jewish intellectual culture. But those were all sort of marginal cultures. Burroughs and I were gay. So, for one thing, there was a beginning of marginality, looking at the culture from the outside. We were reading Spengler's *The Decline of the West*, which Burroughs had given us, about the rise and fall of empires. It impressed Kerouac, both for its prose in translation and for its notion of cycles.

At the time, the American culture was being advertised by the C.I.A. or *Time* magazine as being the "American Century." The image of an upper class gentleman-type was called, "The Man of Distinction," which was an English looking gentleman in tweeds in a library raising a glass of some kind of scotch whiskey for an advertisement. So there we were, hanging around Times Square with Huncke and being interviewed by

Kinsey for *The Account of Sexual Activity of The Human Male*. He was on Times Square at that time interviewing a sort of floating population. So our orientation was quite the opposite of the middle class.

Our basic themes were some kind of "new consciousness," sexual cancor, and tolerance. It was a sexual coming out of the closet between myself and Burroughs. Kerouac was straight, but nonetheless he was friendly with us. I even wound up sleeping with him a few times, but there was no sense of real fear, at least on our part once I came out of the closet. So there was this gay liberation aspect. It wasn't called that then. It was just ordinary life. *[Laughs.]*

Then, there was an interest in psychedelic drugs. Drugs from the point of view of a change of consciousness and a "new consciousness." Then in 1948, a new element was introduced, which was some sort of natural visionary experience or break in the ordinary modality of consciousness. I experienced it, I think Jack did, probably Burroughs had already, and Gary Snyder also did, unbeknownst to us, in '48 at Reed College. With myself, it was the occasion of thinking I had heard Blake's voice or some hallucination of Blake's voice. So there was this natural, un-drug psychedelic experience, and then two to three years later, we experimented with psychedelics: Kerouac, Neal Cassady, and I tried peyote, and our explorations into that area were reconfirmations of what had occurred [to us] naturally. Then, there was marijuana around. Burroughs began experimenting with heroin, as I did, but I saw he got a habit so I was much more careful than he.

There was a realization that the whole drug law situation was fraudulent. Marijuana was a more or less benevolent narcotic. No big deal. But the official government party line was completely hyped: "It drives you crazy, into madhouses with frothing teeth, or something." That began a questioning of the cover story or official party line, as distinct from [our own] direct personal experiences, and then our realization of the whole hype of the drug wars of those days, that it was somehow tied up with the complete corruption by the cops who were selling it themselves. The local narcs. We knew that by direct experience, through Herbert Huncke and others who were junkies.

Then there was a concern for ecology, reinforced by '55 with Gary

Snyder who was a woodsman, mountain climber, and dharma bum. He, Michael McClure, and Philip Whalen were into Northwest ecology, American Indians, and the realization that the woods were being cut down in the Northwest for lumber. They wrote very early poems about deforestation. That developed a great deal in Burroughs, Kerouac, and Gary Snyder.

Then there was an anti-war peaceableness, which bore fruition in activities by Snyder, Whalen, myself, and others during the Viet Nam war. A pacifism or Buddhist anarchism.

Then there was a whole introduction of Eastern thought and meditation, which has grown from the small seed of *The Dharma Bums* in 1957, or Gary Snyder's meditation and translations of Chinese poetry in 1955, to a full-scale acceptance of Buddhism as almost a chic thing here today, as an acceptable clear path. Previous to that, [Buddhism] was considered some 5&10 cent store eccentricity; now there is a great deal of respect. There are a lot of growing Buddhist institutions that have affected medicine: holistic medicine that's affected diets, that's affected meditation practice, that's led to the institution of the Naropa Institute as a long-range thing and several other Eastern-oriented colleges.

So the basic introduction of Eastern thought and the mixture of Eastern and Western mind, corresponding with a geographic shrinking because of airplanes and easy access. Whereas women in the 19th century could talk about *A Passage to India* as an imaginary passage, or the transcendentalists could read the *Hindu Vedas* or *Shastra* or some other Buddhist text but didn't really have a chance to get over there until the beginning of the 20th century. It all reached a crescendo in the 1960s, with thousands of Europeans and Americans going to Asia and studying the teachers and becoming translators for Tibetan and Hindu.

I think the gay liberation, sexual revolution led, to some extent, to igniting women's lib and black lib. Kerouac was interested in be-bop and blues, and he introduced the spoken cadences of black culture into his own writing. He imitated the talking back and forth of the wind and reed instruments in Harlem in the late '30s–early '40s that he'd heard directly. The musicians imitated street talk and street cadences, and Jack imitated them in his writing, bringing that back to the streets. What I was interested in was the cadences of the African spoken rhythms taken into the wind instruments and then restored back by Kerouac to spoken word. So there was an interest in Eastern and African American cultures and an absorption of that into the literary world.

Then, most importantly, there was the opening up of verse and prose forms to new experiments: open form poetry rather than the Eliotic–Robert Lowell closed form, the whole explosion of energy coming from splitting the atom of the verse line.

TM: *By "Eliotic," you mean T. S. Eliot?*

AG: Yes. He was the dominating sensibility of the '30s and '40s, and imposed a sort of English blank verse line that dominated the academic poetry world. But there is another lineage of open form, an experimental free-verse that's an American measure of cadence. Ezra Pound, William Carlos Williams, and Charles Reznikoff, and many other poets led the way as modernists, and we followed them and had personal relations with Pound, Williams, and others. So there was this explosion into a *spoken* poetry, which Kerouac excelled at, and that ignited interest in Bob Dylan, who said that Kerouac's *Mexico City Blues* was the first American poetry book that really spoke to him. So, between myself and Kerouac and a few others who influenced Dylan, this caused the whole explosion of popular song.

TM: *And the way popular songs could be written.*

AG: Yeah, that they could be real poetry and they could be quixotic poetry that people could study the lyrics aside from the music, too.

TM: *As great a songwriter as John Lennon became, I don't think he would have written them in quite the same way if Dylan hadn't established the foundation.*

AG: Yes, but after all, they were called *Beat*les. They brought elements of the Beat Generation into the English scene. "A Day in the Life," for instance, is a really excellent free-verse poem.

But let's summarize. The open form of spoken poetry that people could understand, as distinct from the poetry that was a rehash of older poetry styles, led to living tongue of poetry, and living thoughts, and living emotions, and that's led to this big explosion of poetry going on now with the poetry coffee houses and magazines. It made a whole cultural change, and a lot of that change has been absorbed from ecology, from sexual revolution, through disillusionment with the government party lines on drugs, wars, etc. Plus, finally, individuals began to express themselves outside the constrictions and censorship of the mass media.

Because you know there is censorship. There is official legal censorship from 6:00 A.M. to 8:00 P.M. on the main marketplace of ideas, radio and television supervised by the FCC.

TM: *"Howl," for instance, can't be played during those hours.*

AG: They're not supposed to, according to this new law introduced in 1988—by Senator Jesse Helms, no less.

TM: *He certainly is* not *a friend.*

AG: *[Irritated.]* What I'm trying to say is something very specific. In October of '88, he introduced a law imposing censorship on radio and television, specifically that the F.C.C should prohibit all so-called "indecent" language twenty-four hours a day. We got together a consortium of lawyers with the PEN (Poets, Essayists, Novelists) Club, an international organization with an American chapter of several thousand writers, the American Civil Liberties Union, the Emergency Civil Liberties Committee, and the Rabinowitz and Boudin law firm, which is the best constitutional law firm in New York. We fought the Jesse Helms law up to the point where we got it reduced so that now there is what is called "A Safe Harbor" for something like "Howl" or anything else that contains so-called indecent language between 8:00 P.M. and 6:00 A.M. We're still fighting in court over the 6:00 A.M. to 8:00 P.M. prohibition. So it isn't just that "Jesse Helms isn't a friend." It's much more than that. He has literally, with the help of the beer and tobacco interests, and the Fundamentalists, imposed censorship on all mass media. So that affects my box set. Many of those poems, like "Howl," "Kaddish," "Sunflower Sutra," "Please Master," "America," and some of the songs cannot be played during daytime hours, when students are studying them. And that's quite a specific thing. It's not just some ironic comment that "he's not a friend." It's a real nail in the heart.

TM: *I didn't mean to be flippant about that. It's just that I know Jesse Helms also was the person behind dividing the gay community over the NAMBLA issue.*

AG: Yes, yes. Do you know how he did that? He put a resolution, which a lot of senators in Congress signed, that said that no money could go to the U.N. if they had as a consultative group any gay group which had relations with NAMBLA. So the regular gay advisory groups had to break with NAMBLA in order to have a voice in the U.N. So these things are very specific. It's not some general, vague thing. That's why I'm defending NAMBLA from attacks by people like Jesse Helms, who are accomplices to mass murder with D'Aubisson, the head of the death squads in Salvador, and Jonas Savimbi, that guy in Angola who's been conducting civil wars that are costing thousands of lives, as well as imposing censorship attacks on poetry, the National Endowment for the Arts, as well as the odd fact that he is a representative of the tobacco industry. [Helms is] a big windbag actually, and the papers have let him get away with it. His position paper and his law on censorship on radio and television from '88 were formulated for him by the Heritage Foundation in Washington, a right-wing think tank, which was funded originally by Coors Beer. So it's alcohol and tobacco against literature and open-heartedness. He's gotten away with being considered some sort of arbiter of ethics, but that's the fault of the media for not calling his cards.

TM: *The media says NAMBLA is an organization filled with child molesters.*

AG: NAMBLA has nothing to do with that. NAMBLA is just a talking organization of people who like young boys. That's all. It is not a sex club. They're like a self-empowerment group. In 1984, I read an article in *Time* magazine that said NAMBLA was a group of predatory authoritarians who preyed on unsuspecting, less powerful individuals. It sounded like a perfect description of *Time* magazine. So I joined NAMBLA as a civil liberties matter because the F.B.I. had set out to entrap them. I get a lot of flack for it, but they have the right to talk about what they're interested in. I think [J. Edgar] Hoover may have been preoccupied with them.

TM: *Why do you think he was so interested in NAMBLA?*

AG: Well, because he was gay and a transvestite and a closet queen. There was a big scandal about it last year. There was an article in *Vanity Fair* and a whole biography about him that covered it quite clearly.

TM: *I remember there also was a biography about [Hoover's assistant] Roy Cohn a few years earlier that talked about Hoover's secret life.*

AG: The one about Roy Cohn by Nick von Hoffmann also took up the fact that the late Cardinal Spellman was gay. They used to have orgies on Roy Cohn's yacht.

TM: *That's pretty amazing.*

AG: Nah. Standard. Standard for repression and closet queens.

TM: *Is it true that some of the Stanford alumni are pressuring the University to withdraw its million-dollar offer to buy your personal effects because of your relationship with NAMBLA?*

AG: Yes. Of all the dumb ideas on their part. I'll have to make sure I have complete copies of my "NAMBLA Bulletin" when I send everything out there! *[Laughter.]* The "NAMBLA Bulletin," by the way, is a regular discussion magazine about laws and about psychology.

Also, something I forgot to mention earlier [about the Beats' role in social change] was the battle to end censorship in books and movies, which was successful from 1957 with the "Howl" trial up to 1961 or 1962 with Grove Press winning the *Naked Lunch* case. In between, there were battles over D. H. Lawrence's *Lady Chatterley's Lover,* Henry Miller's *Tropic of Cancer,* and all those other cases that Grove Press won. That liberated literature, including classics like *The Satyricon* by Petronius Arbiter. You may not know it but in the old Modern Library editions of Petronius Arbiter the sexy passages were written in Latin. So even classics were censored. So those fights began in '57 and continued until '62. That led to a series of fights over movies led by a filmmakers' co-op, featuring films by Andy Warhol and others, with naked people in them. And that led to the end of censorship in movies. So now Pat Buchanan, Helms, the American Family Institute, and Pat Robertson are leading an attempt to reimpose censorship.

TM: *Where is "Moloch" now? [a god that Ginsberg refers to in Part 2 of "Howl"]*

AG: Well, Moloch is a god to which you sacrifice children in the Bible. It's a false god that was worshipped by the Hebrews when Moses came down from the mountain and found people worshipping the golden calf and false gods, and all of that. And I think he broke the tablets of the Law. Moloch is a horned creature of brass with seven brass furnaces in the belly. Somewhere in the Bible it says, "Thou shalt not suffer thy seed to pass through the fire to Moloch." It's a god to which parents sacrifice their children. So it's the commercial, mechanical heartless god that's described as "Moloch whose breast is a cannibal dynamo / whose ear is a smoking tomb / whose eyes are a thousand blind windows." So it's the god of hyper-technological megalopolis civilization that devours its children in the heart of cities . . . and maybe finally devours the planet itself with an ecological disaster. It is the hyper-technological machine industry that Blake called "Satanic Mills," meaning the satanic mills of the mind as well as the external factories that smoked up the air and stank up the heavens, [and now] punch a hole in the ozone layer. So it's the robot mechanical civilization that begins devouring its creator.

TM: *How do you think human civilization can escape "Moloch"?*

AG: I'm not sure at this point that it's reversible.

TM: *One thing I notice among people of my generation, especially those like myself who live in an urban environment, is that people don't seem to be interacting that much with each other in public, especially on the streets. It's common courtesy now to not acknowledge each other. I came from a more rural area, and when I first moved to San Francisco I still had the habit of saying "hello" to someone when I made eye contact with them . . .*

AG: Kerouac noticed that years ago in his book, *The Lonesome Traveler*, that people were furtive on the street. [*Laughs.*] If you made eye contact, you'd be accused of being gay. Just think of the pressure and paranoia that African Americans must feel walking down the street.

TM: *I don't know what the solution is. Sometimes I feel that when I'm in an exuberant mood I can somehow transcend that paranoiac atmosphere and create something that's good.*

AG: You know I've been thinking quite a bit about how this box set would relate to what you were just talking about, this new generation's pre-millennial alienation, and I wrote a few speculations. Do you want to hear it?

TM: *Sure.*

AG: Here's a couple of paragraphs with commentary:

"I was told these poems already had some radical effect on U.S. poetry, American popular song from Dylan, rock-n-roll, The Clash, punk, Sonic Youth. Now this collection of highlights of recordings and performances amassed over forty-five years heard together for the first time in the whole intensity and range might help renew invention and performance of poetry and music all over again. First, there's the emotional power of some classic works: the first complete reading of 'Howl,' the epic 'Kaddish,' the electric oratory of 'Wichita Vortex Sutra,' the heart tones of 'Father Death Blues.' So in that you have some kind of self-empowerment, some prophecy, erotic rhapsody, world proclamation, ecstasy, serious devotion, tears, joy. But open feelings, which might be medicine to generations of emotional uncertainty: the ironic voidoid punk grunge X blank slacker century-end alienation, mainly in 'imperial world weariness,' as in Spengler.

"Then, the other thing is that there's a whole rainbow range of forms that's audible: 'Lower limit speech, upper limit song.' There's archaic verse stanzas, a short line free-verse, long line anaphora (that's like a litany where you go back to the same word). There's list poems, there's imitation sutra which is a Buddhist form, there's mixed short and long line surrealist anthology pieces like 'America' or 'Sunflower Sutra,' there's the Hebrew biblical rhythms of 'Kaddish,' there's modernist free-verse, there's regular old 12-bar blues, and punk rock with The Clash, and set percussion sound poems with Elvin Jones, which is like a rhymed rap duet. There's 'Om Ah Hum Vajra Guru Padma Siddhi Hum' mantra, there's Blake hymns and the sing-alongs like 'All the hills echo'd' ('Nurse's Song'), and old-fashioned tunes like your mother sang like 'Green Valentine,' there's modern poetry jazz from 'The Lion for Real.' There's LSD notations, there's a little 'CIA Dope Calypso,' and church spirituals like 'Gospel Noble Truths,' and the serenity of 'Father Death Blues,' and a capella voice.

"It's a range of forms that are comparatively rare in any collection of poetry or songs. So I hope it will amuse several generations of lyric pop rock/ blues sensitive genius poets, maybe turn them onto new ways of experiment and new ways of self-expression and invoke more liberty of form and emotion, wild performance, good text. I'm hoping that any kid who listens to all 4 CDs might get opened up a little, energetic, serious, some glimpse of sacred eyeball world, wild skin-and-bones word magic."

What I'm noticing is that there seems to be a big emotional gap. The ecstatic rhapsody of grief or enthusiasm would be helpful now. That's what I like about this CD set; it's full of feelings.

TM: *I know this is a highly speculative question . . . but if you hadn't become such a successful poet, what occupation do you think you would have taken up to make a living?*

AG: I might have been a market researcher. That's what I did before. Or a sailor. Or a good dishwasher. I did all of those things. Or I might have become a lawyer. I started pre-law actually, but then I got distracted meeting Burroughs and Kerouac, and I realized that poetry was a full-time sacred vocation.

TM: *How would you like to be remembered?*

AG: Through the poetry and the music. If people can remember, "O mother / with a long black beard around the vagina / with your belly of strikes and smokestacks." That line [from "Kaddish"] I like a lot. It's sort of like a cinematic montage for an old Russian Eisenstein movie.

TM: *Are you a movie buff?*

AG: I used to be, but I don't go now. Looking out the window is as big a movie as anything.

TM: *The last poem in* Holy Soul Jelly Roll *is a poem called "After Lalon." At the end you say, "I had my chance and lost it . . . Allen Ginsberg warns you don't follow my path to extinction." What lost chance are you referring to?*

AG: Salvation. Liberation. Nirvana. It's a double-edged sword. The "Pleasure Parajnaparamita Sutra [Highest Perfect Wisdom]" says, "No nirvana. No path. No wisdom. No attainment because no non-attainment." Liberation lies in realizing that there is no special attainment, no special consciousness, and that ordinary mind is where it's all at. So if I had my chance and lost it, it means I am also resigning the ambition to be liberated too, as well as remembering the fact that I'm not liberated. So you can take it either way. As far as "Don't follow my path to extinction," is there anybody who's going to avoid the path to extinction?

So I'm kidding, but at the same time I'm serious. I've made my mistakes, probably should've paid more attention to teachers and gone on a three-year Tibetan Buddhist retreat and finished all of my prostration preliminaries, and all that. But I didn't, and I lost it. So it's both. That's the characteristic of Baul [Indian] poetry. It's a trickster poem in which I'm asking, "Am I Allen Ginsberg or am I not or maybe I'm somebody else or maybe I'm dead and don't even know it. How should I know?" And those are common thoughts that everybody's had.

TM: *Would you describe the feeling that comes over you when you've finished writing a poem?*

AG: Just ordinary, saying what I think. But then later on, I chuckle, realizing, well, that's kind of curious or this will outrage people. Like the NAMBLA thing. The last poem I wrote and read in San Francisco [at the Cowell Theatre] was, "Come on Pigs of Western Civilization Eat More Grease," followed by another one called, "Excrement." So I thought, Jeez, how will people take this? Is this too far-out? I thought it was funny, but some people won't think so.

TM: *One thing that's easily discernible after listening to* Holy Soul Jelly Roll *is that over the years your performance style has become more expressive, more self-assured. Was this just a natural evolution or did someone help you develop it?*

AG: Some . . . Robert Duncan once pointed out to me in '65 that I used more of my body in my voice when chanting mantras than when I was reading my poems. And that determined me to sing more and also to get more OOOMPH!, more variety of tone, pitch in my poetry reading.

What's interesting is the progression from the monotone or duo-tone of "The Green Automobile" and other poems from that time—late 1940s—and finally by the end there's a whole variety of tones, different pitches of the voice.

TM: *I sometimes wonder . . . I know that Dylan has said that your writing profoundly influenced his own writing when he was growing up in the 1950s, especially those powerfully compressed Imagist poems like "Howl" and "Sunflower Sutra"—*

AG: "Kaddish," he said, particularly. And a recording of "Kaddish." But he also learned from Burroughs and Kerouac. Dylan once told me that *Mexico City Blues* was the book that hooked him to poetry. I asked him why and he said, "It's the only book of poetry I ever read that spoke in my own language: American. American rhythms and diction." This was a conversation we had at Kerouac's grave in Lowell [Massachusetts].

TM: *What kind of advice did Dylan give you when you first started writing your own songs?*

AG: His encouragement was: 1. You ought to learn an instrument; 2. He showed me the three-chord blues pattern. Nobody had ever shown me before, and at the age of 45, or whatever, I didn't know the difference between one chord and another; 3. He said, "If you need a back-up band anytime, just call on me, and I'll play back-up for you if you need a guitar player." Of course, he couldn't do that. But he did on several different occasions . . . deign to come down to Earth and record with me on my songs, playing back-up and chorus.

TM: *Do you have any interest in working with rap artists or exploring any other music forms?*

AG: Well, there is that one rap thing with Elvin Jones, that Sandinista thing ["The Little Fish Devours the Big Fish"], and I've written one or two rap songs . . . I'm pretty good at quick rhyme and improvisational blues, which doesn't need such quick rhyming. But if I met some young rap artist who liked me enough to take me by the hand and show me what to do, I'd love to . . . or who'd go to bed with me, for that matter. *[Laughs.]*

In a way, "Birdbrain" is a strange kind of extended rap. It does not rhyme but, on the other hand, it has the discipline of being able to fit a long line or a short line into a sixteen-bar space, and there was enough musicianship on my part to know how to stretch it out or slow it down so that it fits appropriately into sixteen bars between the chorus "Birdbrain" and the next line.

TM: *I remember hearing that song about ten years ago when I worked as a disc jockey for a community radio station. Then, I tried finding my own copy but never did, until this boxed set was released.*

AG: It sold three thousand copies actually before the matrix wore out, and when we went to look for the actual tape it was gone. So we had to take it from one of the 45s.

TM: *Do you write every day or do you wait for inspiration?*

AG: No, I didn't write much at all when I was in San Francisco, and then yesterday morning I woke up and I wrote about twenty pages of account of everything that went on over the last two weeks. It's irregular. Whenever I think of something and I have the time, I just write it down. But I don't schedule anything.

TM: *You've said many times, "First thought/best thought." How much editing do you actually do?*

AG: Bits. But it requires the first structure, first glimpse, first visual picture and keeping your eye on that picture, filling in the details. If your attention there lapses and you lose it, you may have to go back and refill it in from the mind picture, not the mind thought, [but] the visual aspect.

TM: *That's where I get short-circuited with my own writing. The initial inspiration might help me with seventy to eighty percent of what I construct but then afterwards, I have a hard time regaining that mind picture.*

AG: Don't. Leave it there. That's the whole point of "First thought/best thought." Your first draft is it. Then, you can touch it up a bit but don't try and add. If anything, take out where your attention lapsed and you go into generalization. But keep the picture parts.

TM: *I feel like I'll be writing something with a really strong, radiant energy, but then suddenly there will be a sentence or two that's weak—*

AG: Cut 'em out.

TM: *And I cut it out, but then I'll try to insert something in there and it doesn't work.*

AG: No, no, no. Cut it out . . . unless it's an abstraction that can be filled in with a particular fact like, "I started down the freeway in my old Ford, rattling, and I then I ran into trouble, but then I got home." Then, [you could change] "then I ran into trouble" to "then I had a flat tire outside Candlestick Park, banged into the car in front of me, nicking the fender and got a . . . ticket from the police." *[Laughs.]* So if you generalize, abstract, and space out, you can always go back and fill in the particular detail like you're filling in a blank in a bureaucratic form. But unless you have the eye to realize where you're departing from—if you can't tell the difference between fact and a generalization like "I ran into trouble"— then it's hopeless. But if you can tell the difference, it's workable.

TM: *What for you defines good poetry vs. bad poetry, in your writing or in others?*

AG: Musicality that's competent melodious, variable with different pitch, and word wit. Or as Ezra Pound said: "Phanopoeia, melopoeia, and logopoeia." Phanopoeia—casting an image on the mind's eye. Melopoeia—having a musical cadence. Logopoeia—the play of intellect among the words. Or as Pound's student, Lou Zukofsky, translated it, "aspects of sight, sound, and intellect."

TM: *You certainly can hear that in Dylan's song lyrics, especially during the 1965–1966 period of* Highway 61 Revisited *and* Blonde on Blonde. *It's not only in the lyrics themselves but in the way his voice "savors the vowels and appreciates the consonants," as you would say.*

AG: That I noticed in Dylan. When he draws his lips back and shows his teeth, he's actually enunciating. It isn't that he's sneering. He's actually being precise about ... "Sweet Marieeee."

TM: *With a lot of the formal distinctions falling away between poetry and prose writing, what are some of the qualities for you that distinguishes one from the other?*

AG: It's an artificial boundary. Is the Bible prose or poetry? Is Homer prose or poetry? Is Ecclesiastes prose or poetry? Is Whitman prose or poetry? Is Blake or Williams prose or poetry? Maybe in the old days you might say poetry had a different kind of form and rhyme, but they don't necessarily have that in the Bible or *Gilgamesh.* There might be some more measurement of the cadence in poetry.

But I would say poetry is maximum information, minimum number of syllables. Condensed. A rhythmic articulation of feeling. But you also have that in Kerouac, Joyce, Melville, and Thomas Wolfe with prose. So that's an artificial distinction. Is Rimbaud's "Season in Hell" prose or poetry? It's the highest poetry *and* it's the highest prose.

TM: *You've said that you thought that Dylan and John Lennon would be two of the most remembered poets of our time. Do you think they are the* best *poets, or is it because popular songs have the potential to survive longer in pop culture?*

AG: Well, it's because they are memorable, and that's one of the criteria of genius poetry. But I think there are some very brilliant lines that will always be remembered. Like Oscar Wilde said, "Each man kills the thing he loves." So now Dylan says, "To live outside the law you must be honest." Everybody's going to remember that. Not too many people remember too many verses of Wilde, but they remember certain ones. And that's also true of Poe, Keats, and Shelley. I don't know if you can say they're the best poets, but when you consider the range of Dylan and the colossal productivity ... the prolific expansiveness, the abundance and exuberance of his work, you really have to take into account that he may be the great bard of this half of the century.

TM: *I think "It's Alright, Ma, (I'm Only Bleeding)" is one of the greatest combinations of melody and lyrics ever created. "Visions of Johanna" is one of my favorites, too.*

AG: I think [they're] generally more in the genre of surrealism, but from about 1968–1969 he began trying to be less redundant and actually make it more like Emily Dickinson: paradoxical but clear.

TM: *You mean around his* John Wesley Harding/Nashville Skyline *period?*

AG: From then on. He told me around that time that he was trying to take out the excess verbiage and make each line significant following the other. And I think he was beginning to read a lot of Emily Dickinson and Blake, and things like that.

TM: *What do you think about Lennon's importance?*

AG: There was something very charismatic and brilliant about him. Experienced and wise. He got interested in my work late, actually. I had known him since '65, but about ten years later, he said to me he had been listening in bed to WBAI [a New York radio station] with some earphones, and he heard this voice reciting this big long poem and he thought it was Dylan. But at the end he found out it was me reciting "Howl." He said he was amazed because he always knew of me being around, but he never knew exactly what I did! *[Laughter.]* He explained that he didn't get much from reading. He got everything from the ear.

A little earlier, he recommended I try an "Eleanor Rigby"–style string quartet with "Jessore Road." Ten years later, we actually did have the chance to do that with a string quartet, which is at the beginning and the end of the Dylan version of "September on Jessore Road" that we have on the box set.

TM: *Would you describe what the atmosphere was like in the North Beach cafés when you and your friends first started reading your poetry in public?*

AG: It was a small intimate group of people who knew each other and went to the same place, called "The Place," down at the end of Grant Street, before you go up the hill.

TM: *Were there a lot of people who were part of the scene back then?*

AG: No, just thirty to forty people. But they all knew each other so that seemed like a lot. They were all poets. Robert Duncan would come out and give a reading, and whenever there was a reading afterward everybody would go to the same place. "The Place." That's back in the mid-50's. There was a kind of camaraderie, and then later, around 1958–59, there were a lot of music poetry places . . . jazz poetry places. But originally it was just straight poetry. San Francisco Street had the Poetry Center run by Ruth Witt-Diamant who invited Dylan Thomas, Randall Jarrell, Louise Bogan, and others, and so we got to meet all these Eastern poets coming through. Rexroth was an elder, and Kenneth Patchen lived on Telegraph Hill. I remember him reading at City Lights, and later he took me up to his place and loaned me a copy of Blaise Cendrars's "Trans-Siberian Voyage" poem, translated by John Dos Passos and published by the Black Sun Press. It was a rare expensive book in those days, and even more so now. He just gave it to me to read and bring back to him. Gary Snyder was living in Berkeley. Michael McClure was in town as a young pretty boy. Jack Spicer and [Robert] Duncan were living up on Portrero Hill near me. I once knocked on their door to borrow a cup of sugar. *[Laughs.]* Ferlinghetti had City Lights Bookstore. Neal Cassady was in and out of town as a brakeman on the Southern Pacific Railroad. So every other day he was in town visiting friends, distributing marijuana. *[Laughs.]* Kerouac came in. Robert Creeley came from Mallorca and Black Mountain College, and a whole group of poets from there showed up. Some of them are still living out in Bolinas. Everybody was really well-educated. Peter Orlovsky was there, too, and a bunch of painters.

So it was a comradely group, but the main common element was we were all interested in reading William Carlos Williams. And Gertrude Stein. Spontaneous writing and open form, rather than closed stanza.

TM: *It's really interesting when you compare that atmosphere with the atmosphere of most cafés today. Now a lot of people go to cafés to put quarters into Internet machines so that they can correspond with someone else across town who also is using the Internet.*

AG: Really? They have machines in cafés now? That's kind of unusual.

TM: *What I notice is that people are more closed off, not really interacting with anyone except their own friends. And it's not just in the cafés. It's become an urban courtesy for people not to acknowledge each other. Especially in the evenings. Do you have any prescriptions for helping people overcome this kind of urban alienation?*

AG: I know I'm out for love myself, and if you're out for love you better not get hooked to a television screen, you better get hooked to flesh. So when I go out I'm hoping to meet somebody, get picked up, or at least have a conversation with some twenty-two-year-old angel who likes my poetry and is willing to talk to me and give me a kiss when we say goodbye.

From *Magical Blend*, no. 47 [May 10, 1995]. This is an expanded and edited version of the published interview, with additional material provided from transcript. Reprinted by permission of Tom McIntyre.

The Beats and the Boom

A Conversation with Allen Ginsberg

SETH GODDARD, 1995

UNLIKE MANY LITERARY FIGURES content with satisfying their audiences of decades earlier, or settling on their past achievements, Allen Ginsberg was always looking for ways to connect with younger readers. He wasn't resting on his literary laurels. He loved his association with punk and new wave artists and fans, and he enjoyed attending poetry slams. He could naysay any interest in his literary legacy, as he did in an interview earlier in this volume, but he clearly wanted a new generation of readers to read and appreciate the works of the Beat Generation. As in his earliest days as a spokesman for the Beats, he continued to reassess and teach the group's literary merits.

ALLEN GINSBERG'S INFLUENCE on literary culture and countercultures of America may continue forever. In 1943, while the baby boomers were still three years from conception, Ginsberg, William Burroughs, and Jack Kerouac planted the seeds of the Beat Generation in New York City. Eleven years later, Ginsberg relocated to San Francisco and joined the Bay Area's burgeoning literary scene, producing such classic poems as "Howl" and "America." He proclaimed in the former: "I saw the best minds of my generation destroyed by madness, starving / hysterical naked." He asked in the latter: "America when will you be angelic?" During the '60s, Ginsberg participated in Ken Kesey's Acid Tests, joined fellow Beat poets Gary Snyder and Michael McClure to lead the crowd in chanting "OM" at the 1967 San Francisco Be-In, and was a key figure in the anti-war movement. In 1994, Ginsberg sold his letters, journals, photographs, old tennis shoes, and snippets of his beard to Stanford University for one million dollars.

SG: *Were the philosophies of the Beat Generation picked up or left behind by the baby boom generation?*

AG: We didn't have what you could call a philosophy. I would say that there was an ethos, that there were ideas, and there were themes, and there were preoccupations. I would say the primary thing was a move towards spiritual liberation, not merely from Bourgeois, '50s quietism, or Silent Generation, but from the last centuries of mechanization and homogenization of cultures, the mechanical assault on human nature and all nature culminating in the bomb. So it was then either a revival of an old consciousness or the search for a new consciousness.... I don't think we [Ginsberg and Kerouac] had it clearly defined, but we were looking for something, as was Burroughs, as a kind of breakthrough from the sort-of hyper-rationalistic, hyper-scientific, hyper-rationalizing of the post-war era.

Now it was not an assault on reason. That's been much misinterpreted. It was an assault on hyper-rationalizations, you know, this fake science, fake cover-up, quasi-logical reasoning. The best example might be the inadequate science of the nuclear era. Although, like the sorcerer's apprentice, [scientists] were able to conjure up the power of the bomb, they weren't able to take care of the detritus and the waste products of the bomb. They still have not been able to. It's a half-assed science. It's not a real science . . .

The sciences that we were interested in, or arts, particularly from the mid-'40s, were some breakthroughs of consciousness or new consciousness—let's say a spiritual revolution that took form in changes in the literary method, bringing up the old literary forms and the release of a new energy: the long verse line or the spontaneous prose of Kerouac, or Burroughs's investigation into dreams, hypnosis and drugs, and the prose that arose from that—and then the verging on the illegal, the expressions of sexuality which were forbidden and censored in those days.

All of our work was really done with the idea that it would never be published—that is "Howl," *Naked Lunch, On the Road.* When I wrote it ["Howl"], I had no intention of publishing it. First of all I didn't think I would want my family to see my personal sex life. So I was writing it for my own fun . . . I'm giving you the roots in the '40s and the '50s. I'm giving the conditions of spiritual liberation leading to literary liberation—not revolution, but liberation—leading to liberation of the word. That was from '58 to '62, in a series of legal trials which opened up these books to be published because otherwise they wouldn't have been legal. . . . At that point, the private liberation of the artists was spread out into the public properly with the actual artifacts that were written words or books. At that point, it begins to have a strong social effect on the next generation, that would be your baby boomers. Just about the time they got into adolescence, if they were born in '45, by 1960 they'd be 15 and 16, and they'd now be ready to be handed copies of "Howl," *On the Road,* and finally *Naked Lunch*—particularly *Naked Lunch,* which had an enormous influence up til now, actually, on rock and roll and everything.

[Bob] Dylan himself said that Kerouac's *Mexico City Blues* was the book given him in 1959 that opened him up to poetry and inspired and made him want to be a poet . . . We were standing over Kerouac's grave in Lowell, [Massachusetts], filming his *Renaldo and Clara.* He pulled *Mexico City Blues* from my hand and started reading it and I said, "What do you know about that?" He said, "Somebody handed it to me in '59 in St. Paul and it blew my mind." So I said "Why?" He said, "It was the first poetry that spoke to me in my own language." So those chains of flashing images you get in Dylan, like "the motorcycle black Madonna two-wheeled gypsy queen and her silver studded phantom lover," they're influenced by Kerouac's chains of flashing images and spontaneous writing, and that spreads out into the people. From '64 on, people are beginning to look carefully at the texts of the Beatles and Dylan and beginning to develop another literacy. People began turning the text inside out looking for hints.

SG: *Did you think then, or have you thought since, what type of effect this liberation might have on a culture of adolescents?*

AG: In 1959, when *LIFE* [November 30] magazine came around, I said, "If they think that we got something going, they must be scraping the bottom of their own barrel and they must be in a pretty deprived place *[laughter]*." Actually, after I talked to [*LIFE* writer, Paul O'Neil], I lay in bed trembling, realizing that we had an enormous responsibility. If the mainstream culture was so vulnerable—'cause he was, he didn't know what he was doing—and so ignorant and so curious about what we were doing, then they must be pretty empty like a paper tiger, and we would have to supply some kind of real culture in America, or real inspiration. That was back in '59. So from then on there was what Pat Buchanan now calls a spiritual war for the soul of America. And in '59 I did write an essay saying exactly that. By 1962 or '63, Cardinal Francis Spellman and J. Edgar Hoover were denouncing the Beatniks, along with the eggheads, communists, and others, as the greatest threats to America.

SG: *Did you take any pride in being considered such a threat to America?*

AG: No. It was a dismay that they were so mean-spirited and lacking in humor and enthusiasm in old American values. What would they do with Walt Whitman? What would they do with Thoreau if they were going to do that with us? They were out of sync with basic American values—Emerson, Thoreau and all that. I thought they were sort of un-American.

Kerouac was all-American if anything. Neal Cassady was an all-American kid, foot warts and all. But it really was Americana and Americanist, something in an older literary tradition that runs through Whitman and William Carlos Williams and Sherwood Anderson. There was that old Americanist tradition of recognition of the land and the people and the gawky awkward beauty of the individual eccentric citizen. Or as Kerouac said, "the old-time honesty of gamblers and straw hats." His 1959 [*Playboy*, June] article on "The Origins of the Beat Generation," that's his statement on what he intended, a kind of yea-saying Americana which was interpreted as some kind of negative complaining by the middle class who were themselves complaining. So yes, we were, or I was quite aware of the [cultural] impact. But so was Kerouac, in "Origins of the Beat Generation" and in *The Dharma Bums*. He predicts a generation of long-haired kids with rucksacks. He predicts and asks for it.

SG: *So, as you watched this younger, boomer generation in the 1960s, what was your response?*

AG: I thought that the spiritual liberation aspect and the artistic purity was being somewhat degraded by the Marxist, SDS, Weatherman strain of politicalization on the basis of rising up angry. Anger was not the answer. . . .

SG: *There were a lot of young people calling themselves Beatniks in San Francisco, but who did not follow a literary tradition.*

AG: I think they were Frankenstein replicas created by the press. Remember, the very word *Beatnik* is a press invention.

SG: San Francisco Chronicle *columnist Herb Caen.*

AG: He invented it as a denigration. The origin was the time of Sputnik, so it was like, ah, these guys, these Beats are disloyal. Beatnik, that was his intention. He's proud of it, I'm sure, but it really actually added a slightly demeaning element. Also there was a problem that the police were quite malevolent, not only towards the false Beatniks, but also some real poets. . . .

SG: *Is America adjusting well to the themes that the Beat Generation brought forth?*

AG: The sexual revolution seems to have been accomplished in some way despite AIDS, and despite the reaction of Buchanan and his spiritual war trying to stem the flow of history, and despite the Moral Majority. Literature has been liberated considerably. The poetic form has been changed to inaugurate a new poetic form, an American form working in the tradition of Whitman, Pound, William Carlos Williams, as a continuity, as a lineage, as an Americanist lineage. I think that's established. . . . Poetry is more popular and more read than anywhere, not only spoken poetry but sung poetry of a high order, from the inspiration of Dylan and the Beatles on to Beck today. You know Beck? He's quite good, actually, good words man. The ecological preoccupation that both Kerouac and Snyder introduced is now like mainstream thinking, though the government has not yet reacted to it appropriately. It's still now ingrained in poetry. Before, my father used to kid me, saying, "Chicken Little, you think the sky is falling," until a hole opened up in the ozone layer.

SG: *You have told* New York *magazine that you were trying to "save and heal the spirit of America." Is it sicker than it was in the '50s?*

AG: Oh, well, in some ways. In the '50s, there was some sense of generosity and hope, generosity in America and generosity among the poets. There was hope that once the problems were clearly announced—like say clean energy, the diminished fossil fuel, less dependence on Middle Eastern oil, more dependence on clean energy sources—that we might be able to solve some of these problems. But once Nixon and others got in the White House, especially Reagan, they bankrupted the country, put it in hock so that there's no money for these major efforts. Let's say mass transit, or clean energy, or large-scale medical treatment for addicts or even alcoholics, or to solve the problems that were created by the wars, by the disdaining, the neglect of the infrastructure of the cities, and the neglect of the clean-up of the poison wastes everywhere left by industrial sites and even the neglect of the final disposal of nuclear waste. Science needs toilet-training and it never got that. It would be expensive. Nuclear science needs toilet-training, certainly.

Among other problems, when they emptied out the mental hospitals, the rationale was to build inner-city places for housing the mentally ill so they wouldn't be rotting vegetables in the back wards, but would have some interaction in the society. That money was never appropriated; those places were never built. So you have this gigantic homeless problem because of the interference and neglect of the government, because of the wars and the military expenditures, and the deliberate bankruptcy of the country, and Reagan putting it deliberately in hock to do that! So that by now, many of the problems we saw in the fifties have become almost impossible to deal with.

That's why you have all this apathy among the younger generation, or so-called apathy or slacker. I don't think that it's real apathy. I think that the press and the government and the corporations have blockaded the amelioration of the situation that might still take place. I think that this right-wing temporary wave that seems to be already deflated was sort of the last-ditch denial that there was a problem.

I think Clinton means well. He started out on an even keel trying to integrate gays into the military. Then you had old jerks like Sam Nunn in his own Democratic Party betraying him. You've got to give him credit for trying. I don't think he's been given credit for trying. It's sort of like a bad mark that he tried to do something good. I don't think he got much support from the press on that. The press has had that same cynical attitude, especially in the eighties, especially on the drug issue. I keep coming back to the drug issue because politically everybody keeps saying that it's the second largest issue aside from jobs ... The drug issue is resolvable if anybody has the courage to finally do it. . . .

SG: *So a lot of the problems you saw in the '50s have—*

AG: Persisted. They just never were moved on. The clouds opened up a bit in the sixties—some people got a glimpse of the possibility of the future—and then closed down with the war and Nixon.

SG: *If you could have grabbed the proverbial shirt collars of the those in the sixties who glimpsed this opening, knowing now that it would fade away, what advice would you have offered?*

AG: I would have said that it would've been really important for the left to vote for Humphrey, as I did, rather than sit out the vote and let Nixon slip in. Nixon's secret plan to end the war actually was to nuke North Vietnam, according to [Daniel] Ellsberg, who was working for Kissinger. That would have torn the country apart, so he didn't do it, but he did prolong the war and escalated it to unimaginable proportions of cost and pain and ecological destruction. . . . So I would have said that the left should have followed more the old Beat mode of spiritual wrath and generosity, but not anger, and not to bring the war home. . . .

SG: *What about today, if you could grab the same shirt collars of the boomer generation?*

AG: Don't get intimidated, read great literature, learn to meditate in order to become conscious of their own minds, and purify their own aggression, realizing that any gesture you take in anger creates more anger. Any gesture you take in equanimity creates equanimity. Make peace with yourself and see what you can do to relieve the sufferings of others. That's the main compass.

SG: *Did they have that in the sixties?*

AG: Yeah. Well, actually they had that in 400 B.C.; that's the basis of Buddhism and Christianity. That's the really wild thing about the Moral Majority—they are claiming to be Christians and they want to persecute the poor. The Bible says you're supposed to take care of the poor. It's incredible.

SG: *Do you feel hopeful?*

AG: I don't think hope or fear are important. I think the main thing is a continuous generous activity, exuberant activity, no matter what's happening. Even if the ship is sinking, you can relieve suffering in any situation. Death is not—well okay, my meditation teacher, Chögyam Trungpa Rinpoche, visited William Burroughs's son when he was waiting for a liver transplant. He was not sure he'd survive and he said to the young man, "You will live or you will die, both are good." That's my attitude. Both are good. That attitude of a little non-attachment and, at the same time, compassion and affection are sufficient.

From *LIFE* magazine, online edition, July 5, 2001.

Allen Ginsberg
An Interview

GARY PACERNICK, 1997

THE FOLLOWING, an expansion of the published version, was one of the last lengthy interviews of Ginsberg's lifetime, appearing in print several months after his death. When the interview was conducted, Ginsberg had less than fourteen months to live. He had spent much of his life worrying, off and on, about dying and whatever lay beyond, and he would consult with his Buddhist teacher, Galek Rinpoche, on how to prepare for his death. He seems at peace with himself in this interview, even though there is an air of finality to it.

ON SATURDAY, FEBRUARY 10, 1996, I interviewed Allen Ginsberg by phone via telephone answering machine with tape recorder.

GARY PACERNICK: *The tape is on now; this is the beginning.*

ALLEN GINSBERG: "This is the forest primeval, the murmuring pines and the hemlocks, bearded with / moss . . ."

GP: *Allen, what have you found the hardest thing about being a poet?*

GINSBERG: Nothing particular. I mean, nothing particular. No hard part.

GP: *Okay.*

GINSBERG: Making a living at it. Making a living.

GP: *Well, what about inspiration? Has it always been easy?*

GINSBERG: Inspiration comes from the word *spiritus. Spiritus* means breathing. Inspiration means taking in breath. Expiration means letting breath go out. So inspiration is just a feeling of heightened breath or slightly exalted breath, when the body feels like a hollow reed in the wind of breath. Physical breath comes easily and thoughts come with it. Now that's a state of physical and mental heightening, but it's not absolutely necessary for great poetry. Though you find it's a kind of inspiration, a kind of breathing in Shelley's "Ode to the West Wind" or "Adonais" or Hart Crane's "Atlantis," or perhaps the Moloch section of "Howl." But for subject matter, which is what you mean, for ideas, ordinary mind and thoughts that occur every day are sufficient. It's a question of the quality of your attention to your own mind and your own thoughts.

GP: *Where does this breath come from that you find in the second part of "Howl," for example?*

GINSBERG: Well, it's a more excited breathing, longer breath, that you find in the examples that I cited which build sequentially as a series of breaths until finally there's a kind of conclusive utterance. "Moloch whose name is the Mind."

GP: *You talk in the* Paris Review *interview and other places about being inspired by Blake reciting "Sunflower."*

GINSBERG: An auditory hallucination, hearing it, but that's a different kind of breath, completely. That's a quieter breath from the heart area. Like my voice now rather than the stentorian breath of "Atlantis" or "Howl."

GP: *So you're not talking about what we usually talk about in terms of prophesy, in terms of some divine voice.*

GINSBERG: Now wait a minute. You're switching your words now. We were using the words inspiration and voice. Now what are you talking about? What's your question, really?

GP: *What is a breath unit?*

GINSBERG: A breath unit as a measure of the verse line? Why, a breath unit as a measure of the verse line is one breath, and then continuing with the sentence is another breath. Or saying "or" is another breath, and then you take another breath and continue. So you arrange the verse line on the page according to where you have your breath stop, and the number of words within one breath, whether it's long or short, as this long breath has just become.

GP: *Okay now, you're talking about great poetry—*

GINSBERG: No, no, I'm talking about how you arrange the verse lines on the page by the breath.

GP: *No, I understand, but when we were talking about inspiration you used the word breath again.*

GINSBERG: Because the word inspiration comes from the Latin word *spiritus*, which means breathing. So I was trying to nail down what the word inspiration means rather than have a vague term that we didn't know what we were talking about.

GP: *But to me—and obviously I could be totally off—it sounds like you're talking about poetry as a kind of series of breathing exercises.*

GINSBERG: Well it is, in a way, or the vocal part, the oral part, is related to the breath, yes.

GP: *What inspires the breath?*

GINSBERG: The breath is inspiration itself. Breath is itself, breath is breath. Where there is life, there is breath, remember? Breath is spirit, *spiritus*.

GP: *So every once in awhile this spirit breath visits you and other poets?*

GINSBERG: No, you're breathing all the time, it's just that you become aware of your breath. Every once in awhile you become aware that you're alive. Every once in awhile you become aware of your breathing. Or of the whole process of being alive, breathing in the universe, being awake, and so you could say that that's the inspiration or the key, that you become aware of what's already going on.

GP: *You probably didn't know this when you were sixteen, eighteen, twenty years old and first writing poetry.*

GINSBERG: Oh, well, pretty soon. A sort of latent understanding, yeah. That notion of awareness, conscious awareness.

GP: *Did Williams or Pound influence this?*

GINSBERG: Pound and Williams specialized in this. They broke the ground for this kind of thinking. Williams trying to write in vernacular speech and dividing it up into pieces, and dividing the verse line into pieces of vernacular speech, sometimes by counting syllables, sometimes by the breath stop, sometimes by running counter to the breath stop. Do you know what I mean by the breath stop?

GP: *You were in Dayton years ago and I was there with my wife and child, and I said to you, "What is a breath unit?" and you were sort of showing me with your hand as I spoke. Charles Olson talks about it. But Pound and Williams don't talk about breath, do they?*

GINSBERG: Well, it's implicit in what they were doing, because they were talking about actual talk.

GP: *I understand.*

GINSBERG: And measuring the measure—what Williams talks about was an American measure, a measure of actual speech.

GP: *Right.*

GINSBERG: And his disciples like Olson and [Robert] Creeley drew from that the notion of projective verse or verse by breath or measuring the verse line by where the breath stops.

GP: *But we both know that your breaths in "Kaddish" and "Howl" and your other inspired poems are—*

GINSBERG: Different from somebody else?

GP: *Not only different, but so long.*

GINSBERG: Everybody's is different. Everybody's breath is different. Everybody, like Creeley's is short and minimal, in a way.

GP: *Well, it's beyond short and minimal. It's like one one-hundredth of what yours is in some of your longer lines.*

GINSBERG: Well, sometimes. But on the other hand the poems that are like those, too, like Williams or Pound.

GP: *Does that mean, since your line is the longest, that you're the most inspired?*

GINSBERG: Well, the deepest inspiration, probably, yes, the deepest breath.

GP: *So you are, you're literally equating poetic inspiration with breath.*

GINSBERG: That aspect of it. There's two kinds I said. There is the deep breath, but there is also, in the more common use of the word inspiration, i.e., where do you get your ideas, is also just ordinary mind and ordinary breath, and short breath, too. Ordinary mind means what passes through your mind while you're sitting on the toilet.

GP: *But in your poem "Kaddish" you're doing more than that.*

GINSBERG: But I'm saying there are different kinds of poetry. In "Kaddish" what I'm doing is a longer breath, yes. Then, in other poems, like in "White Shroud" [or] the poem to William Carlos Williams, "Written in My Dream by W. C. Williams," it's a short breath.

GP: *Let's switch it a little bit, then maybe we can come back to that. In "Howl" you affirm the Beat lifestyle.*

GINSBERG: You know, one thing is, you're fixated on poems of thirty, forty years ago. I don't mind talking about them, but in context of a whole curve of poetry up to the present. But go on.

GP: *Okay, fine. You affirm the Beat lifestyle that often leads to madness and/or death.*

GINSBERG: I didn't use the word "lifestyle." That's a later sort of media term and I don't like you to use it. I think it's bullshit.

GP: *You said "Mad generation! down on the rocks of Time!" A lot of the people, most of the people have died.*

GINSBERG: Not so. Just the opposite, sir. Just the opposite. You've got it all wrong, inside out. Burroughs is alive at the age of eighty-three and just had a birthday. Huncke just had his birthday in February also, and he's eighty-one. Gary Snyder is in very good health in California and is a world-renowned influence in poetry. Philip Whalen is a Zen master now. I'm doing quite well at Naropa and Brooklyn College and writing poems. Michael McClure is touring with Ray Manzarek. So Kerouac died, Neal Cassady died, and Lou Welsh died. But on the other hand Gregory Corso is living across town. We're all in touch with each other. Anne Waldman has founded the Kerouac School of Poetics at Naropa and John Ashbery and everybody go there, and I go there between terms. So we have a better actuarial span than most insurance people. But you've got the stereotype I'm trying to get away from.

GP: *Let's go to "Howl" itself.*

GINSBERG: As I keep saying, you're fixated on images of that. Anyway, go on.

GP: *Well, those people are very unhappy, the people you portray in the poem.*

GINSBERG: Yes. They were young.

GP: *Okay. Let's just say you have survived.*

GINSBERG: And so have most of my friends.

GP: *Where do you draw your strength?*

GINSBERG: Oh, inspiration. I keep breathing. Also I never drank.

GP: *You never drank?*

GINSBERG: No. I never drank. And I was very moderate in my use of drugs. I was more interested in the politics than the drugs themselves.

GP: *But you have all those poems that are titled after drugs.*

GINSBERG: If you'll notice, it's about one percent of my poetry.

GP: *Okay. I'll go back and take a look.*

GINSBERG: You'll find a poem called "Nitrous Oxide" and another called "Aether," and another called "LSD," another called "Marijuana Notation," another called "Mescaline." And that's about it. And you have peyote for the central section of "Howl."

GP: *The religious visions.*

GINSBERG: And a couple other things, then you have some stuff from the "Yage" and that's it. Out of about eight hundred pages, you've got about fifty pages of drugs.

GP: *All right, that takes care of that.*

GINSBERG: You have the media stereotypes you're dealing with.

GP: *Well, I don't know you.*

GINSBERG: Well, you don't have to. Just look at the texts. I've named all the texts that are on drugs.

GP: *In "Kaddish," were you responding to the Hebrew prayer in any particular way, or were you responding in a more general way to your grief over Naomi's death?*

GINSBERG: Both. You know, I had never heard the formal rhythms of the Kaddish before, pronounced aloud, or never consciously heard them. They sounded familiar. But all of a sudden I realized it was some kind of interesting, moving, powerful cadence.

GP: *You must have been to a service.*

GINSBERG: Yes. But I never noticed or heard or consciously heard it, as I said.

GP: *But you have said it, though.*

GINSBERG: No, I've never said it. I don't read Hebrew. I wasn't Bar

Mitzvahed. And I was kicked out of Hebrew school for asking questions. I don't know.

GP: *Were you being sentimental when you named it "Kaddish"?*

GINSBERG: No, 'cause I used the basic rhythm of the Kaddish and I quoted the Kaddish.

GP: *But you said you didn't know it.*

GINSBERG: I heard it that morning. Someone read it to me that morning

GP: *The morning you wrote the poem?*

GINSBERG: Yeah, when I started writing it, or that evening. About 3 A.M. And I was impressed by the cadence and the rhythm and the depth of the sound, as it says in the very opening line, "reading the Kaddish aloud . . . the rhythm the rhythm—and your memory in my head three years after." It says exactly what it was. Mixed with "Ray Charles blues shout blind on the phonograph." With a similar rhythm, by the way. "I got a woman, yes indeed."

GP: *So . . .*

GINSBERG: A sort of repeated cadence that was right, like Ray Charles or the Kaddish.

GP: *So you're inspired by that prayer, you're inspired by music, by the rhythm of the music. What about the image, though?*

GINSBERG: What's the image? Which one?

GP: *Williams and the emphasis on—*

GINSBERG: Minute particular details. Now the phrase that I am thinking of is "minute particulars." Do you know that phrase? Do you know where that's from?

GP: *"Minute particulars."*

GINSBERG: Yes. "Labor well the minute particulars. Take care of the little ones." That's from William Blake's "Jerusalem." Little ones, the little details. And Kerouac says, "Details are the life of prose." And Pound says, "The natural object is the adequate symbol." And Trungpa says, "Things are symbols of themselves."

GP: *Well, let me ask you this—*

GINSBERG: So the image comes from, or the image is related to the following idea. If you want to give a mirror of your consciousness and you become aware of your consciousness, conscious awareness manifests itself sacramentally in the quality of the attention to clear-seeing focus on chance, minute, particular details that present themselves with charismatic vividness to author and to reader.

GP: *You do both that and hear music also? Simultaneously?*

GINSBERG: No. You have a picture in your mind, as Pound points out, in "Chinese Written Language as a Medium for Poetry," published by City Lights now. The Chinese is interesting as a poetic language because it consists in little pictographs. So you can't be vague and talk about beauty. You have to talk about something concrete and process. At the same time, the language has got a sonorous aspect, or sound or vocal sound, so you hear it in your head sometimes. Sometimes you make the language up out of the picture. Sometimes the language itself has its own melodic part that comes up by itself. Like the other day I got up off the toilet, and I said, "That was good, that was great, that was important!" And stood up to pull the chain. And I heard myself saying that, and I noticed I had said that, and I said, that's fairly interesting, that's like a haiku. How many syllables was that? "That was good, that was great, that was important!" That's eleven syllables.

GP: *Maybe twelve.*

GINSBERG: Ending on the twelfth. "That was good, that was great, that was important! " No, that's eleven. "Standing up to pull the chain" adds another six, so that's seventeen all together. So, okay, I noticed the situation, that there was the visual element, standing to pull the chain, the picture there, and there was what ran in my mind, so the picture gave the context for the interior utterance.

GP: *Okay, so the picture can sometimes inspire the music.*

GINSBERG: Not inspire! No, no, no! I hear you using that word over and over again, abusing it, using it out of its meaning. You're making it into oatmeal.

GP: *How would you say it? The picture induces?*

GINSBERG: The picture originates the poem or the origin or the flash. You flash on a picture, and you write it down. Or you flash on something you say to yourself, and you write it down.

GP: *And sometimes that can have music.*

GINSBERG: You can hear a tune. But the words "That was good, that was great, that was important!" have a rhythm. *[Demonstration of rhythm.]* That has its own cadence, you know what it's saying and the rhythm of the sounds are both the same.

GP: *It's not metrical, obviously.*

GINSBERG: It is metrical. *[Demonstration of rhythm.]* That's a meter. That's an old classic Greek meter.

GP: *Anapest? Short, short long?*

GINSBERG: It's an anapest. Ta ta ta ta-ta. One, two, three, four, five. There's a Greek rhythm that is a four-beat rhythm or a four-syllable rhythm. I don't know what its called, maybe dithyrambic or something.

GP: *Do you know Greek?*

GINSBERG: No, but I know some of the Greek rhythms.

GP: *You're the prototype, I guess it's a stereotype, of the free verse poet, but you're saying you hear meters.*

GINSBERG: Yes, sure I hear meters. My father was a poet, it's a family business, and I grew up with a facility for rhyme and stanza from when I was very young, without even trying. I know yards and yards of poetry, like Edgar Allen Poe's "Bells" or Vachel Lindsay's "Congo," poems by Edna St. Vincent Millay and Elinor Wylie.

GP: *But didn't you, I mean, you've said many times you had to go beyond that in order to write "Howl" and "Kaddish."*

GINSBERG: Well, naturally, you know, but the point is those forms are appropriate, they're called lyric poetry, or the shorter forms which have short stanzas, they're called lyric poetry. Now, what is the root of the word lyric?

GP: *Song, isn't it?*

Ginsberg. No, no. Think. What is the root, literally, of the word lyric? What instrument?

GP: *Lyre.*

GINSBERG: Right, right! And what was a lyre? It was a stringed instrument played by Homer or Sappho or the early poets, the Muse's lyre. So it's just like Bob Dylan or something, a stringed instrument, where you sing to stanza with rhyme and you have a melody that revolves around itself and has a recurrence, right? So because the melody has a recurrence, you therefore have a recurrence, a cadence for the stanza, and you use rhyme. When you stop using the stringed instrument and just write the form without the music, then it begins to degenerate and lose its muscularity and its variety and its syncopation. So when I came in, in 1950, people were trying to write those lyric stanzas, but without music. And that was the complaint that Pound and Williams had. And so historically—and also Whitman—so they moved away from a fake lyric, that is to say a half-assed lyric that did not have the musical accompaniment, but just spoken language, but arranged as if it were a song. They moved away to the use of living language, rather than a dead form, and began rewriting the idea of rhythm and measure. And so Williams had the idea of an American measure rather than the old English lyric, which was being imitated in the twenties by Edwin Arlington Robinson and Elinor Wylie and Sara Teasdale and Edna St. Vincent Millay and all the minor poets of that time. He moved out into trying to isolate the rhythms of actual speaking, and that led to my own generation of projective verse, writing in the living speech rather than in an imitation of an older English cadence. It didn't mean that there wasn't rhythm, it meant that the rhythms were the rhythms that you heard in speech, like "da dada da da dada dada." It didn't mean that there wasn't rhythm. That's a rhythm.

GP: *Frost supposedly hears a meter. There's meter in Frost as well as the rhythm. "Something there is that doesn't love a wall."*

GINSBERG: Okay, that's a metronomic meter, where it's recurrent. But you know, the classic meters of Greece were much more varied than the four or five, four usually, used in English. We have iamb, trochee, dactyl, and anapest.

GP: *Spondee.*

GINSBERG: And that's usually the range. Spondees are used less, but they come in. So now there are the two-syllable and three-syllable meters. We have mostly the iamb and the trochee, but then there's also molossos, the three-syllable meters. "Oh, good God!" Da da da. Or there is the bacchius meter, "Is God love? Believe me." Dada da, dada da. Then there are four-syllable meters, like, oh, insistently. Dadadada dadadada dadadada dadadada. Insistently, insistently, insistently. Or the ionic A minor, which is "in the twilight" dadadada dadadada dadadada. Or delightfully, delightfully, delightfully. That's the second ionic. Or the epitritus primus, "your sweet blue eyes," "I hate your guts." So then there's the epitritus secundus, "Bite the big nut," dadadada, or "Give her a dime" dadadada. And then there are the five-syllable ones. "I bit off his nose," da da da dada. Or the dulcimaic, which Hart Crane used, "Lo, lord, thou ridest!" Bom bom dadada. "Fall fruits and flowers." That's Ben Jonson. Dom dom dadada. Those were the ones we used as the climax of Greek plays, with the revelation of the moment. Bom bom dadada.

GP: *So there's a lot more, you're saying, than the simple two-syllable foot.*

GINSBERG: So, and they could use these different feet like a LEGO set and could build very various musicality, complex musical things, like Sappho. You know the Sapphic stanza?

GP: *No, I don't know much about it.*

GINSBERG: You know the rhythm of it.

GP: *No.*

GINSBERG: Trochee, trochee, dactyl, trochee, trochee. Trochee, trochee, dactyl, trochee, trochee. Trochee, trochee, dactyl, trochee, trochee. Dactyl, trochee. [*Demonstration of rhythm.*]

GP: *So the first line of "Howl"*—

GINSBERG: No, I wasn't thinking of that, but I was so trained and I had all those in my bones. But the one that pointed out to me, many years later—that the Moloch section [*demonstration of rhythm*], "Moloch whose eyes are a thousand blind windows"—was Ed Sanders, who's trained in classical prosody and versification. Then I got interested in what the names of these were.

GP: *Let me ask you something else.*

GINSBERG: Yes, well, that's what you're doing.

GP: *Have you ever considered yourself a Jewish poet?*

GINSBERG: Yeah, I am a Jewish poet. I'm Jewish.

GP: *You are? You surprise me.*

GINSBERG: I'm Jewish. My name is Ginsboig. I wrote a book called *Kaddish*.

GP: *No, that's great!*

GINSBERG: My last book has a long poem called "Why I'm Jewish."

GP: *I'll have to take a look. I've got it.*

GINSBERG: It's called "Yiddishe Kopf."

GP: Cosmopolitan Greetings?

GINSBERG: Yeah. "Yiddishe Kopf."

GP: *I'll have to look it up. So you're a Jewish poet.*

GINSBERG: I'm also a gay poet.

GP: *I know that.*

GINSBERG: I'm also a New Jersey poet.

GP: *You're a Buddhist poet.*

GINSBERG: And I'm a Buddhist poet. And also I'm an academic poet, and also I'm a beatnik poet, I'm an international poet.

GP: *What was the Jewish influence? Your mother, essentially?*

GINSBERG: No. My mother, my father, my grandparents, were all Jewish. My whole family is Jewish and that's just the whole thing in my bones.

GP: *What about the Bible? Did that influence you?*

GINSBERG: Yeah, I read a lot of the Bible, sure. I read it all through, a number of times. But you know, like I know, "Wherever the golden bow be broken and the silver cord be loosed wheel be broken at the cistern" and so forth.

GP: *Is there [a] cadence?*

GINSBERG: The cadences of Ecclesiastes and the psalms. "The Song of Songs."

GP: *And you probably get some inspiration from the parallelism of the Hebrew prophets.*

GINSBERG: Oh, of course. But also, you know, indirectly. One of my great models as a poet, or for me a great model, is Christopher Smart.

GP: *Right. "Jubilate Agno."*

GINSBERG: Right. And he was a fantastic translator of the Bible, of Hebrew.

GP: *Of psalms?*

GINSBERG: Of psalms and everything like that. And his "Jubilate Agno." I don't know if you've seen my annotated "Howl"?

GP: *I have, yeah.*

GINSBERG: Well, at the end you'll find a selection from Smart.

GP: *That's right. I remember that.*

GINSBERG: If you'll notice, it's done in the parallelisms of the Bible. And my own verse line in "Howl" and elsewhere is drawn from that. The Bible via Smart, as well as the Bible itself that I'm familiar with. You know, my father was a poet and so all this stuff, the "Song of Songs," was part of the family heritage.

GP: *Are being Jewish and being gay connected in any way? I mean, being oppressed?*

GINSBERG: I've known gay Jews. Who was it, David and Jonathan? I mean, that's an old business. What is it, Jesus and young John?

GP: *Here's a chance to talk about the present. Because I started out interviewing Stanley Kunitz and Carl Rakosi, who are in their nineties.*

GINSBERG: Yeah, marvelous people. Rakosi, I love. I love Rakosi.

GP: *Well, I was in Maine and I talked to him a lot. I was in Maine when he did that reading with you.*

GINSBERG: And I saw him last summer at Naropa.

GP: *And I interviewed him in December in San Francisco, and he's great.*

GINSBERG: I think he is our greatest poet, Jewish or non-Jewish.

GP: *He told me you like Reznikoff even more.*

GINSBERG: No, I like both.

GP: *It's good that you like him.*

GINSBERG: I think Rakosi—you know, his *Collected Poems* is a great volume.

GP: *Yeah, I have that. I got it in Maine. I really fell in love with it.*

GINSBERG: Did you think I liked Reznikoff more?

GP: *Well, Rakosi said that. He said that when I saw him in San Francisco.*

GINSBERG: I discovered him earlier.

GP: *But he hasn't gotten enough attention.*

GINSBERG: He got a lot from me.

GP: *Most of the attention has gone to the other Objectivists: Zukofsky and Oppen.*

GINSBERG: Well, fortunately, we pay a lot of attention to him at Naropa.

GP: *That's great.*

GINSBERG: And in Maine.

GP: *Are you going to go to Maine again?*

GINSBERG: I won't be able to this summer. It's there when I'm in Naropa.

GP: *I was there, I talked to you a lot. I'm going to England this time.*

GINSBERG: What's your business?

GP: *I teach creative writing and I write poetry and criticism.*

GINSBERG: Where?

GP: *At Wright State University in Dayton.*

GINSBERG: Where?

SP: *Wright State University in Dayton.*

GINSBERG: I think I've been there.

GP: *Yeah, well, you were at the University of Dayton. You were with a poet named Herb Martin.*

GINSBERG: Long ago.

GP: *A long time ago.*

GINSBERG: Where is he now?

GP: *He's still there. He's become famous for his reading of Paul Laurence Dunbar.*

GINSBERG: He's doing Dunbar's work.

GP: *Right, he's doing a lot of that. Well, let me ask you another line of questions. Let's go on. Does maturity give you any kind of new, fresh perspective?*

GINSBERG: Look at my new poems. *Cosmopolitan Greetings* is all about that. There's one particular poem, but you know there are lots of poems about being a senior citizen in there.

GP: *Yeah. That's right.*

GINSBERG: But there's one particular poem that begins, "At 66 just learning how to take care of my body." Do you know that?

GP: *I've got it right in front of me. I'll look at it.*

GINSBERG: Hold on. I'll get it.

GP: *The one I really like is the one where you've got the photograph.*

GINSBERG: "May Days."

GP: *And then you've got all the details about the apartment. There's great concentration of imagery, the minute particulars.*

GINSBERG: Yeah, that's a good one. That was translated, incidentally, into Hebrew by Natan Zach, a Hebrew poet.

GP: *Did you take the picture, "May Days 1988," with the* New York Times *on the windowsill?*

GINSBERG: The new book has similar stuff, a thing called "Charnel Ground," which is going out the window and looking around at the neighborhood. Anyway, there's a poem called "Autumn Leaves."

GP: *It's also in* Cosmopolitan Greetings?

GINSBERG: "Autumn Leaves."

GP: *All right. How does one face death? You've written poems about death.*

GINSBERG: Every poet does. Shelley did when he was twenty-seven. Keats did when he was twenty-four.

GP: *Does poetry help?*

GINSBERG: Yes. I think poetry helps because you imagine your death, and you begin to blueprint and plan and realize mortality and then after a while you become consciously aware of the fact that mortality is limited and then you begin to appreciate living more, as well as appreciate the great adventure of dying, and then realize that it is part of the vast process and an occasion for lamentation and rejoicing and everything. The whole thing comes together. It's the great subject. Because, you know, without death there's no life. Without life, there's no death.

GP: *So, sort of like "Death is the mother of beauty."*

GINSBERG: I think in "Kaddish" I said, "Death is the mother of the universe."

GP: *What about love?*

GINSBERG: Well, what about it?

GP: *That's not as big? Okay.*

GINSBERG: I think above death and above love, I would say, in a poem I did say, awareness encompasses love, death, and everything.

GP: *Awareness of mortality?*

GINSBERG: No. Awareness itself. Conscious awareness. It leads to, encompasses compassion, love, and awareness of death.

GP: *What has poetry taught you about language, words?*

GINSBERG: I don't know. What have words taught me about poetry? You could say that's the same thing.

GP: *Well, how about it?*

GINSBERG: It taught me not to bullshit. It taught me not to indulge in abstract language which is undefined, but to try and nail down any generalization with a "for-instance." You know, like "give me a for-instance." So it taught me that. "No ideas but in things," as Williams says. Or: "The natural object is always the adequate symbol," says Pound. And again I'll repeat, as Trungpa said: "Things are symbols of themselves."

GP: *Okay. I like that.*

GINSBERG: That's a great one.

GP: *I believe in all that. It's just that it's all being challenged today.*

GINSBERG: By whom?

GP: *The language poets.*

GINSBERG: Well, they're saying that language is language. A word is a word.

GP: *But it doesn't symbolize anything. It's just a nonsense sound.*

GINSBERG: No, they're saying that it actually—there are conditions. Their angle on symbolization is something different, that the conditioning, the social conditioning is built into the use of the word. That the social conditioning outweighs the visual or the auditory meaning.

GP: *Well, they deconstruct or break down all the syntax and the meaning and you end up with nothing but sound.*

GINSBERG: But the purpose of the deconstruction was to break down the social conditioning associated with the sounds.

GP: *Right. And then you end up breaking down poetry, I think, as well.*

GINSBERG: Ah, I wouldn't worry about poetry. Poetry can take it. And sometimes it's interesting, like Burroughs's cut-up aspect was very interesting. A deconditioning to conditioned language. A whole way of inventing new, interesting phrases like "wind hand caught in the door" which is a by-product of Burroughs's cut-ups. "Wind hand caught in the door."

GP: *Your poetry always makes sense to me. I mean, you don't seem to try to distort—*

GINSBERG: Well. I try, and you know, I'm out of Williams. I come from the Williams lineage and Kerouac. Kerouac wrote spontaneously and wrote nonsense, but there was always this basic theme. Burroughs cut up his stuff, but there was always this basic theme. No matter how you cut it up, it's still Burroughs talking about authoritarian hypnosis from the state.

GP: *And you can always see that?*

GINSBERG: Yeah. It comes through, no matter how you cut up his works.

GP: *Because when I read these language poets, it's more like Gertrude Stein. I don't know what they're talking about.*

GINSBERG: Stein is interesting in her own way, you know what I mean? Have you ever heard her record?

GP: *No.*

GINSBERG: There's a Caedmon record of Stein, and if you hear her once you really get the idea what she was after. Williams told me that she had one specific simple thing and it was really great and, you know, if you get that then you get something. An inimitable voice. Speaking voice. A Yiddish voice, too.

GP: *A Yiddish voice. Not Stein! What place do you most identify with? In other words, what physical location, like Jersey or—*

GINSBERG: Living Lower East Side, probably.

GP: *Have you lived there much of your life, even though you've traveled all over the world?*

GINSBERG: Well, I've had this one apartment, where I am now, for twenty-one years.

GP: *I didn't know that.*

GINSBERG: And then before that I had—see, my mother, when she came to America, moved to about a mile from here on Orchard and Rivington. That was her first place of residence. Then they moved to Newark. So Orchard-Rivington is about a mile from where I am now.

GP: *So it's really your roots.*

GINSBERG: So, I'm really back where my mother's family—my father's family came to New York and then Newark. But before I lived here, I moved here in '75, I lived for five years or so on East Tenth Street, a couple blocks away. And, before that, on East Second Street in the sixties. And in the fifties, where I took all those photographs, early photographs of Burroughs and Kerouac, that's East Seventh Street.

GP: *You wrote a powerful poem about being mugged. It must have been down in one of those neighborhoods.*

GINSBERG: That was in 1972 on Tenth Street, when I was living there. Two blocks from here.

GP: *And where are you now?*

GINSBERG: East 12th Street.

GP: *In the Village?*

GINSBERG: East Village. Lower East Side.

GP: *If you could do it again, what would you do differently, if anything?*

GINSBERG: There's a certain guy I was in love with when I was young, who invited me to bed and I was too shy, because I was in the closet. And I've always regretted it. And I wrote a poem about it. I wrote about it in Sapphic verse, In *Mind Breaths*, something like that. One of the books. It's in my *Collected Poems*—1978 or so.

GP: *Helen Vendler—sort of surprisingly, to me—wrote very warmly of you, I think, in her anthology.*

GINSBERG: Yeah, I was surprised.

GP: *Right, I was surprised.*

GINSBERG: She likes me and Snyder and she has no reaction at all to Creeley or Corso or Kerouac's poetry or anyone else.

GP: *Maybe it was another critic I was reading, and she talks about what must have been the great difficulty for you, especially as a young Jewish man being gay. I thought that was a sensitive remark.*

GINSBERG: I didn't think it was that difficult, you know? I was in the closet until I was about seventeen. But then I had such nice company, with Kerouac and Burroughs, who were themselves so far out and Burroughs was gay. Kerouac was very straight, but nonetheless—

GP: *He wasn't gay or bisexual?*

GINSBERG: I wouldn't say so.

GP: *What about Neal Cassady, whom you're always writing about?*

GINSBERG: Cassady was a lady's man, but he was sort of pan-sexual. I made out with him, but I was one of the few people he made out with. Maybe he hustled as a younger kid, as a young orphan.

GP: *In a sense, you always had a family.*

GINSBERG: Yeah. I had my regular family. I was pretty close. And also an alternative family.

GP: *I mean a family of brothers. Because I've thought over the years that poets like Roethke and Berryman and Lowell, they were alone, even though they were straight.*

GINSBERG: They did have that community. Berryman, Lowell, they were all part of that southern agrarian second generation, from Ransom and Robert Penn Warren and Allen Tate. But the people who were their elders were such puritanical, such mean people, like Allen Tate was an alcoholic, and he kept putting down Hart Crane for being gay, and drank himself to death. Or drank too much.

GP: *I think he smoked too much, too.*

GINSBERG: Or smoked. And then I remember when *Big Table* was going to have a post-Christian issue, they invited him and Burroughs and myself and others to contribute, and he said he wouldn't appear in a magazine with Burroughs. So what kind of model is that for those guys? No wonder they didn't have a sense of family. Sort of intolerant snobs.

GP: *Well, I think in certain ways maybe it worked for you to have those people you mentioned.*

GINSBERG: Yeah. The funny part was that I had also connections with that *Kenyon Review* crowd through Lionel Trilling.

GP: *Now, when you say* Kenyon Review *crowd, you don't mean Ransom and—*

GINSBERG: Yes, I knew Ransom later, but Trilling was one of the major icons of the *Partisan Review*.

GP: *Were you published in the* Kenyon Review?

GINSBERG: No. Yes, later on, yes. It's now under the hands of a lesbian editoress.

GP: *I don't think she is editor anymore. I know whom you mean, Marilyn Hacker?*

GINSBERG: Yeah. She's a nice girl. Nice woman.

GP: *What is the most amazing thing about life?*

GINSBERG: Oh, the fact that it's here at all, and that it disappears.

GP: *What's the most amazing thing about your life?*

GINSBERG: I'm pretty dumb, quite stupid in a way. Even backward. I don't know how I got where I am now, to be like a kind of great poet of some kind. And I don't understand how it happened.

GP: *Well, from what you told me at the beginning, it had to do with breath.*

GINSBERG: Breath, but also the other quality was because I ran into Kerouac and Burroughs when I was sixteen and seventeen. I suddenly realized how provincial and dumb I was, and I resolved, rather than asserting myself constantly and arguing and being argumentative, which would have been my normal nature, I should shut up and listen and learn something. So I always took a kind of back seat and listened to my elders. I always had teachers and gurus, you know, from the very beginning. So actually I learned a lot from other people and had the quality of attention, to listen to Burroughs and serve him, in a way. You know, like work with him and be his amanuensis or his agent or work with him and encourage him and listen to him and do what I could to make his life workable, and I learned a lot that way. And I have relations, had relations like that with Chogyam Trungpa, the Tibetan lama, and Gelek Rinpoche right now, since Trungpa died, a Tibetan lama. And so I've always had teachers and I've always listened to them. And I think that's really delivered me to some kind of workable, practical self-confidence.

GP: *But you wrote "Howl." No one else did. I think that's what made you famous.*

GINSBERG: Yeah, but, you know, I was trying to imitate Kerouac.

GP: *That's interesting.*

GINSBERG: I was a student of Kerouac's, Kerouac broke ground, and I moved in on that territory. And he said, "You guys," me and Gary Snyder, "you guys call yourselves poets. I'm a poet, too, except that my verse line is longer than yours. I write verses that are two pages long!" Like the opening sentences in *The Subterraneans*, which are beautiful, poetic sentences, you know.

GP: *He was the key influence, then.*

GINSBERG: Yeah. I would say him and Burroughs. He was the key vocal influence or verbal, and Burroughs the key intellectual.

GP: *And then, of course, as everyone's written about, also Blake and Pound and Whitman and Williams.*

GINSBERG: Well, I had a good education, I had a regular Columbia education, but I also had the advantage of an education through Kerouac and Burroughs and the books they suggested, but also through my father, who was very well cultivated in poetry.

GP: *And wrote in a very, very traditional lyric style.*

GINSBERG: Yeah, well, you know, he would stomp around the house, not stomp, walk around the house reciting Milton and Shakespeare and Poe, "The Bells," "The Raven," "Annabell Lee." I memorized those when I was a kid. When I was eight years old, I could recite a lot of "The Bells."

GP: *Your parents are in the poem "Kaddish," which to me is probably the most powerful one. Did Naomi actually speak about the key in the window?*

GINSBERG: Yes, she did speak. No. After she died, a day or so after I got a telegram saying she was dead, I got a letter from her that had been posted just before she died of a stroke. And I'm quoting that letter, yeah.

GP: *And then that wonderful talk in there, that Yiddish talk, where she's talking about soup. That's pretty much what she sounded like?*

GINSBERG: She likes lentil soup. That's literal. Now that I look back, I said, how come she said that? How come I didn't ask her what she meant? That I wasn't more persistent. It was so vivid but I was a little shy of pursuing the subject. For fear that she was completely nuts rather than discovering that she had a good sense of humor.

GP: *You put more of the personal into that poem than just about anyone I can think of. I mean of that kind of material. And your father comes off, to me, as a very sad man.*

GINSBERG: In that poem.

GP: *But he wasn't that sad?*

GINSBERG: Then, but a little later on he and I read a lot together and we got closer and closer. We went to Europe together, and he blessed me on his deathbed, and I blessed him.

GP: *He remarried, I gather, at some point.*

GINSBERG: He remarried a very nice woman who was a very good influence on him, and brought us together quite well, and just had her ninetieth birthday this week.

GP: *A Jewish woman?*

GINSBERG: Yeah, yeah, Edith Ginsberg. She just survived, at the age of eighty-nine, two valve transplants. A pig valve and a sheep valve, so she says, joking, she's no longer *kosher*.

GP: *Let me ask you one—*

GINSBERG: I don't know if you know this, about a little film, *The Life and Times of Allen Ginsberg?*

GP: *I saw it.*

GINSBERG: She's in there. Very nice.

GP: *I'd have to see it again. I saw it in Yellow Springs, Ohio. Have you ever been to Yellow Springs, Antioch College?*

GINSBERG: Yeah, sure. Long ago, though.

GP: *I saw it there. It was too short, almost.*

GINSBERG: Well, enough for me. But mainly family-oriented, in a way.

GP: *How do you see your place in American poetry?*

GINSBERG: Well, I have a poem called "Ego Confessions," which is sort of like a grandiose vision. Take a look at that. Because I want to be known as the most intelligent man in America. Worst case scenario of megalomania. But the whole point of poetry is not to be afraid of worst case neurosis, but to reveal it, go right into the wind rather than being afraid of admitting it.

GP: *Well, you certainly showed us that.*

GINSBERG: So I'd like to be remembered as someone who advanced, actually advanced the notion of compassion in open heart, open form poetry, continuing the tradition of Whitman and Williams. And part of the honorific aspect of the whole beat generation.

GP: *You seem to have accomplished a lot of that.*

GINSBERG: Well, not really, because you know my major poems that we're talking about are banned from the air, from radio and television now, with a law suggested by Jesse Helms. He directed the FCC to ban all so-called indecent language off the air, I think it's between 6 A.M. and 10

P.M. And the Supreme Court just affirmed that by refusing to hear our appeal. And that's just been extended to Internet. So it may be that the text of "Howl" or "Please Master" or "Kaddish" or "Sunflower Sutra" will be soon inadmissible on Internet because of foul language that might offend the ears of minors. So the right wing is reimposing the same kind of censorship on the electronic media that we overthrew in the written, printed media '58 to '62.

GP: *That was the famous Berkeley trial?*

GINSBERG: Yeah. Well that, and also the trials of Henry Miller, D. H. Lawrence, Jean Genet, up to *Naked Lunch* in 1962, which liberated literature.

GP: *So, we're back there.*

GINSBERG: No, on a more grand, international scale, we're back with censorship in the electronic world, but not in the written book world.

GP: *Are we at the end of the long journey of poetry, then?*

GINSBERG: What do you mean?

GP: *I mean—let's put it this way: What can a late-twentieth-century poet, given what you've just told me about Jesse Helms and all that, what can a late-twentieth-century poet hope to accomplish?*

GINSBERG: Oh, the poetry doesn't depend on electronic media. You could pull all those plugs and it wouldn't affect poetry. Or plug them all in. Poetry is an individual thing that gets around by word of mouth. It's an oral tradition, as well as a written, printed tradition, as well as a spoken tradition. So it'll get around. Anything really good will get around.

GP: *You have that faith.*

GINSBERG: Well, it's experience. I mean, when "Howl" was on trial, I didn't care one way or the other. Well, I mean, I cared, but I realized if I lose the trial, I'll be a big hero and everybody will want to read my book. If I win, I'll be a big hero and everybody will want to read my book. All the police did was do me a big favor by publicizing my poetry. They always do that. They're so dumb. Like, do you think Mapplethorpe would be so famous if it weren't for Jesse Helms trying to quash him or something. It's amazing!

GP: *Well, they made you famous.*

GINSBERG: They made Mapplethorpe famous. They're going to make Michelangelo famous when they start censoring his statues of Bacchus or the Slaves. They're already censoring his David.

GP: *Oh, you're kidding me.*

GINSBERG: Yeah, you can't put that on the Internet, because it's got a big dick that minors might see. Frontal nudity. *[Laughter.]* So they just make people more conscious of the censorship and of the restrictions and of the mentality and mindset and then they'll cause a counter-reaction.

GP: *One base we haven't touched: How has Buddhism helped you?*

GINSBERG: Oh, it's made me more aware of the fact that everything can be done 'twixt earnest and joke. Things are completely real and simultaneously and without any contradiction, they are also completely empty and unreal. Just like a dream.

GP: *Both?*

GINSBERG: Both at once. Without contradiction, i.e., a dream is real while you're dreaming, but when you wake up it vanishes. There's no inherent permanence. Life is real while you're alive, but then when you die, it vanishes. It has no inherent permanence. So it's like—so, it's real, but it also simultaneously has that aspect. One aspect is the reality; the other aspect is the transitoriness or mutability, as Shelley said.

GP: *And you see both?*

GINSBERG: Well, everybody sees both. So it's the ability to see both simultaneously that gives life its sort of charisma and glamour and workability. You're never stuck. There's no permanent Hell. There's no permanent Heaven.

GP: *So that liberates you.*

GINSBERG: Sure! It liberates you from the nightmare of thinking, "Oh, God, I'm stuck, I'm gonna die, blah, blah, blah."

GP: *You're not afraid?*

GINSBERG: What's there to be afraid of? It's like being in a dream and realizing it's a dream, so then you're not afraid anymore.

GP: *And where do you end up? In the dream, just an extension of the dream?*

GINSBERG: Well, you end up waking up somewhere else, I guess. Or maybe you don't wake up. Maybe you just go to sleep and that's the end of it.

GP: *Maybe that wouldn't be so bad.*

GINSBERG: Well, have you ever been in a dentist's chair with nitrous oxide?

GP: *Yeah.*

GINSBERG: Have you ever been put out? Okay, so what's the last thing you hear? Or what's the last sense that disappears? To me, it was sound. The music, the Muzak. So what if the last thing to go is the end of the symphony? Like, the pain is gone, physical feeling is gone, sight is gone, taste is gone, smell is gone, the only thing left is sound. The sound is the music, then you hear the last note of the symphony and—

GP: *Well, that's a nice one. But then there's all the folks during the Holocaust who were butchered every second by the Nazis.*

GINSBERG: Yeah, but on the other hand, the last thing they heard was the sound of a scream and then the scream ended. And there was nice, peaceful—

GP: *Let's hope.*

GINSBERG: Well, unless they were reborn. Do you think they went to hell or something?

GP: *I don't believe that.*

GINSBERG: They wouldn't have gone to hell. Do you think they went to heaven?

GP: *I don't think so.*

GINSBERG: I don't think there's a heaven. So therefore where did they go? They certainly went to a peaceful place.

GP: *I hope so.*

GINSBERG: Well, where else?

GP: *I think you're right!*

GINSBERG: Can you imagine anywhere else? Can you even imagine someplace that wasn't peaceful?

GP: *I'm Jewish. I'll have to go with that.*

GINSBERG: The Sheol, or maybe Sheol.

GP: *Sheol. Okay.*

GINSBERG: The Buddhists might give the worst case, that they get reborn to go through it all over again. Reborn as Nazis. Reborn in Israel and persecuting the Palestinians.

GP: *That would be hell.*

GINSBERG: Okay. I gotta stop.

From *American Poetry Review*, July–August 1997. Reprinted by permission of Gary Pacernick.

Chronology

1926

Irwin Allen Ginsberg is born in Newark, New Jersey, June 3, the son of Louis Ginsberg, a lyric poet and high school teacher, and Naomi (Levy) Ginsberg, a teacher. Naomi, tormented by paranoid schizophrenia, will spend much of her adult life institutionalized in mental health facilities.

1943

Ginsberg graduates from Paterson (New Jersey) East Side High School and enrolls at Columbia University, where he hopes to study to become a labor lawyer. He meets Lucien Carr, a fellow student, who introduces him to William S. Burroughs.

1944

Lucien introduces Ginsberg to his friend Jack Kerouac, a writer from Lowell, Massachusetts, and former Columbia student. Carr, Ginsberg, and Kerouac discuss a "New Vision" for American writing, focusing on making personal actions and innermost thoughts the grist for literature.

1945

Encouraged by professors Lionel Trilling and Mark Van Doren, Ginsberg makes his first attempts at writing serious poetry. His attendance at Columbia is cut short when he is expelled for scribbling "obscene" words and pictures into the grime of his dormitory windows.

1946

Ginsberg returns to Columbia for the fall semester and, a few months later, meets Neal Cassady, who will become the inspiration and central character in Kerouac's novel *On the Road*.

1947

Hoping but failing to kindle a love affair with Neal Cassady, Ginsberg moves to Denver, where Cassady is living. He spends much of the summer in the city, writing "A Bricklayer's Lunch Hour," his first successful poem. When the Cassady affair falls through, Ginsberg ships out to Dakar with the Merchant Marine. His poetry sequences "Denver Doldrums" and "Dakar Doldrums" are written in response to his failures with Cassady. Ginsberg signs legal papers authorizing the lobotomizing of his mother, an action that will trouble him for the rest of his life but will lead to such poems as "Kaddish," "White Shroud," and "Black Shroud."

1948

Ginsberg experiences a series of auditory hallucinations, commonly referred to as his "Blake Visions," in which he "hears" the voice of William Blake reciting his poetry. Ginsberg interprets this as a sign that he has been called to devote his life to poetry. He begins writing the rhymed poems that will eventually be published in *The Gates of Wrath*.

1949

After allowing a small group of petty thieves (including Herbert Huncke, a model for Beat Generation writings) to store stolen goods in his apartment, Ginsberg is arrested and, in lieu of a prison term, confined in the Columbia Psychiatric Institute, where he meets Carl Solomon, a brilliant but mentally troubled inmate to whom "Howl" will eventually be dedicated.

1950

Ginsberg meets poet William Carlos Williams, who acts as his mentor, and Gregory Corso, a young, aspiring poet who will become one of his closest lifelong friends. With encouragement from Williams, Ginsberg writes many of the poems eventually included in *Empty Mirror*.

1954

After spending the early part of the year in Mexico and writing "Siesta in Xbalba," Ginsberg returns to the United States. He eventually settles in San Francisco and meets Peter Orlovsky, his lifelong companion.

1955

In one of the most productive writing periods of his life, Ginsberg writes "Howl," "Sunflower Sutra," "America," and the other poems that will be included in *Howl and Other Poems*. On October 7, he reads "Howl" for the first time in public, at the Six Gallery in San Francisco.

1956

Howl and Other Poems is published. Naomi Ginsberg dies. Ginsberg visits Jack Kerouac in Mexico, beginning a prolonged period of travel during which Ginsberg will be out of the United States for much of the next six years.

1957

Ginsberg visits Burroughs in Morocco and helps him edit *Naked Lunch*. "Howl" is the subject of a highly publicized obscenity trial in San Francisco, the poem eventually declared not to be obscene. Ginsberg moves to Paris and continues a fertile writing period that includes his first attempts at writing "Kaddish." Kerouac's *On the Road* is published, setting off a public fixation on the Beat Generation.

1959

Ginsberg is introduced to LSD-25 while participating in a study at Stanford University.

1960

Ginsberg travels to South America, taking part in a literary conference in Chile and sampling the hallucinatory drug ayahuasca (or *yage*). Late in the year, he completes "Kaddish," meets Timothy Leary, and samples psilocybin for the first time.

1961

Kaddish and Other Poems is published. Ginsberg spends most of the year abroad, first in Paris and Tangier, then in Greece and Israel.

1962

Ginsberg travels to India, arriving in February and spending the next fifteen months in the country.

1965

Trips to Cuba and Iron Curtain countries (Czechoslovakia, the Soviet Union, Poland) end in disaster when Ginsberg is expelled, first from Cuba and then from Czechoslovakia. Later in the year, he participates in the first antiwar demonstrations in Berkeley.

1966

At Senate subcommittee hearings on LSD, Ginsberg testifies against making the drug illegal. He writes "Wichita Vortex Sutra," his highly acclaimed antiwar poem.

1967

Ginsberg attends the "Human Be-In" in San Francisco. He travels to Europe, attending the "Dialectics of Liberation" conference in London and meeting with Ezra Pound in Italy. He is arrested, along with Dr. Benjamin Spock, at an antidraft rally in New York City.

1968

The "Festival of Life" at the Democratic National Convention in Chicago turns into a mass confrontation with the police, finding Ginsberg chanting mantras to calm antagonized demonstrators. *Planet News*, Ginsberg's most politically charged collection of poems to date, is published.

1969

Pursuing a long-standing interest in music, Ginsberg records *Songs of Innocence and Experience, Tuned by Allen Ginsberg*. He testifies at the "Chicago 7" conspiracy trial.

1970

Ginsberg meets Chogyam Trungpa in a chance encounter. Trungpa becomes Ginsberg's Buddhist teacher.

1972

Fall of America is published to strong critical reviews. The book eventually wins the National Book Award.

1973

Ginsberg is elected to the National Institute of Arts and Letters.

1974

With Anne Waldman, Ginsberg cofounds the Jack Kerouac School of Disembodied Poetics at Chogyam Trungpa's Naropa Institute in Boulder, Colorado.

1978

Mind Breaths is published. Ginsberg begins his investigation into the disposal of nuclear waste at the Rocky Flats nuclear facility in Colorado. He writes "Plutonium Ode" and is arrested for sitting on the railroad tracks to the Rocky Flats facility.

1981

Plutonium Ode and Other Poems, the final volume in Ginsberg's longstanding association with City Lights Books, is published.

1982

First Blues, a two-album recording of Ginsberg's original songs, including collaborations with Bob Dylan, is released.

1983

Ginsberg accepts a teaching post at Brooklyn College, where he will teach for the next decade. *White Shroud,* a new collection of poems, and an annotated volume of *Howl,* complete with facsimile reproductions of the variant drafts of the poem, are published.

1985

Ginsberg signs his first book contract with a large publisher (Harper & Row), a six-book deal that includes forthcoming volumes of journals, collected correspondence, and interviews. The first major volume, *Collected Poems 1947–1980,* is published.

1990

A lifelong interest in photography culminates with Twelvetrees' publication of *Allen Ginsberg: Photographs.*

1994

Ginsberg sells his archives to Stanford University for one million dollars. He uses the earnings to purchase a loft in New York's East Village. A new volume of poems, *Cosmopolitan Greetings,* is published. *Holy Soul Jelly Roll,* an ambitious four-CD box set of his spoken and sung poetry, is released by Rhino Records.

1997

After a brief battle with liver cancer, Ginsberg dies in New York City on April 7, 1997.

1999

Death and Fame, a collection of Allen Ginsberg's final poems, is published.

Books by Allen Ginsberg

Howl and Other Poems. San Francisco: City Lights Books, 1956.

Empty Mirror. New York: Totem Press/Corinth Books, 1961.

Kaddish and Other Poems. San Francisco: City Lights Books, 1961.

Reality Sandwiches. San Francisco: City Lights Books, 1963.

The Yage Letters (with William Burroughs). San Francisco: City Lights Books, 1963.

T.V. Baby Poems. London: Cape Goliard Press, 1967.

Airplane Dreams: Compositions from Journals. Toronto: House of Anansi, 1968.

Angkor Wat. London: Fulcrum Press, 1968.

Planet News 1961–1967. San Francisco: City Lights Books, 1968.

Indian Journals. San Francisco: Dave Haselwood/City Lights Books, 1970.

Scenes along the Road (with Ann Charters). New York: Portents/Gotham Book Mart, 1970.

The Fall of America: Poems of These States, 1965–1971. San Francisco: City Lights Books, 1972.

The Gates of Wrath. Rhymed Poems 1948–1952. Bolinas, Calif.: Grey Fox Press, 1972.

Iron Horse. Toronto: Coach House Press, 1972.

Allen Verbatim: Lectures on Poetry, Politics, Consciousness. Edited by Gordon Ball. New York: McGraw-Hill, 1974.

Gay Sunshine Interview (with Allen Young). Bolinas, Calif.: Grey Fox Press, 1974.

The Visions of the Great Rememberer (with illustrations by Basil King and letters by Neal Cassady). Amherst, Mass.: Mulch Press, 1974.

Chicago Trial Testimony. San Francisco: City Lights Books, 1975.

First Blues: Rags, Ballads, and Harmonium Songs. New York: Full Court Press, 1975.

Sad Dust Glories. Berkeley: Workingmans Press, 1975.

To Eberhart from Ginsberg. Lincoln, Mass.: Penmaen Press, 1976.

As Ever: The Collected Correspondence of Allen Ginsberg and Neal Cassady. Edited by Barry Gifford. Berkeley: Creative Arts, 1977.

Journals Early Fifties Early Sixties. Edited by Gordon Ball. New York: Grove Press, 1977.

Mind Breaths: Poems 1972–1977. San Francisco: City Lights Books, 1978.

Poems All Over the Place, Mostly Seventies. New York: Cherry Valley Editions, 1978.

Composed on the Tongue. Edited by Don Allen. Bolinas, Calif.: Grey Fox Press, 1980.

Straight Hearts' Delight: Love Poems and Selected Letters 1947–1980 (with Peter Orlovsky). Edited by Winston Leyland. San Francisco: Gay Sunshine Press, 1980.

Plutonium Ode and Other Poems 1977–1980. San Francisco: City Lights Books, 1982.

Collected Poems 1947–1980. New York: Harper & Row, 1985.

Howl: Original Draft Facsimile, Fully Annotated. Edited by Barry Miles. New York: Harper & Row, 1986.

White Shroud Poems 1980–1985. New York: Harper & Row, 1986.

Allen Ginsberg: Photographs. Altadena, Calif.: Twelvetrees Press, 1990.

Snapshot Poetics. Edited by Michael Kohler. San Francisco: Chronicle Books, 1993.

Cosmopolitan Greetings: Poems 1986–1993. New York: HarperCollins, 1994.

Making It Up (with Kenneth Koch and Ron Padgett). New York: Catchword Papers, 1994.

Journals Mid-Fifties 1954–1958. Edited by Gordon Ball. New York: HarperCollins, 1995.

Illuminated Poems (with paintings and drawings by Eric Drooker). New York: Four Walls Eight Windows, 1996.

Selected Poems 1947–1995. New York: HarperCollins, 1996.

Luminous Dreams. Gran Canaria, Spain: Zasterle Press, 1997.

Death and Fame: Last Poems 1993–1997. Edited by Bob Rosenthal, Peter Hale, and Bill Morgan. New York: Harper Flamingo, 1999.

Deliberate Prose: Selected Essays 1959–1995. Edited by Bill Morgan. New York: HarperCollins, 2000.

Family Business: Selected Letters between a Father and Son. Edited by Michael Schumacher. New York: Bloomsbury, 2001.

Spontaneous Mind: Selected Interviews. Edited by David Carter. New York: HarperCollins, 2001.

The Book of Martyrdom and Artifice: First Journals and Poems 1937–1952. Edited by Juanita Lieberman-Plimpton and Bill Morgan. New York: Da Capo Press, 2006.

Collected Poems 1947–1997. New York: HarperCollins, 2006.

The Yage Letters Redux (with William Burroughs). Edited by Oliver Harris. San Francisco: City Lights Books, 2006.

The Letters of Allen Ginsberg. Edited by Bill Morgan. New York: Da Capo Press, 2008.

The Selected Letters of Allen Ginsberg and Gary Snyder (with Gary Snyder). Edited by Bill Morgan. Berkeley: Counterpoint, 2009.

Howl (animated by Eric Drooker). New York: Harper Perennial, 2010.

Jack Kerouac and Allen Ginsberg: The Letters. Edited by Bill Morgan and David Stanford. New York: Viking, 2010.

The Essential Ginsberg. Edited by Michael Schumacher. New York: HarperCollins, 2015.

I Greet You at the Beginning of a Great Career: The Selected Correspondence of Lawrence Ferlinghetti and Allen Ginsberg 1955–1997. Edited by Bill Morgan. San Francisco: City Lights Books, 2015.

Wait Till I'm Dead: Uncollected Poems. Edited by Bill Morgan. New York: Grove Press, 2016.

Michael Schumacher has written extensively about Allen Ginsberg and the Beat Generation. He is the author of *Dharma Lion: A Biography of Allen Ginsberg* (Minnesota, 2016) and the editor of *Family Business*, a collection of letters between Allen and Louis Ginsberg. He recently edited *The Essential Ginsberg,* a volume of Ginsberg's poems, essays, songs, letters, journal entries, interviews, and photographs.